Divided Sovereignty

D1432094

Divided Sovereignty

International Institutions and the Limits of State Authority

CARMEN E. PAVEL

OXFORD
UNIVERSITY PRESS

OXFORD
UNIVERSITY PRESS

Oxford University Press is a department of the University of Oxford.
It furthers the University's objective of excellence in research, scholarship,
and education by publishing worldwide.

Oxford   New York

Auckland   Cape Town   Dar es Salaam   Hong Kong   Karachi
Kuala Lumpur   Madrid   Melbourne   Mexico City   Nairobi
New Delhi   Shanghai   Taipei   Toronto

With offices in

Argentina   Austria   Brazil   Chile   Czech Republic   France   Greece
Guatemala   Hungary   Italy   Japan   Poland   Portugal   Singapore
South Korea   Switzerland   Thailand   Turkey   Ukraine   Vietnam

Oxford is a registered trademark of Oxford University Press
in the UK and certain other countries.

Published in the United States of America by
Oxford University Press
198 Madison Avenue, New York, NY 10016

© Oxford University Press 2015

First issued as an Oxford University Press paperback, 2017

All rights reserved. No part of this publication may be reproduced, stored in a
retrieval system, or transmitted, in any form or by any means, without the prior
permission in writing of Oxford University Press, or as expressly permitted by law,
by license, or under terms agreed with the appropriate reproduction rights organization.
Inquiries concerning reproduction outside the scope of the above should be sent to the
Rights Department, Oxford University Press, at the address above.

You must not circulate this work in any other form
and you must impose this same condition on any acquirer.

Library of Congress Cataloging-in-Publication Data
Pavel, Carmen E.
Divided sovereignty : international institutions and the limits of state authority / Carmen E. Pavel.
pages cm
ISBN 978–0–19–937634–6 (hardback : alk. paper); 978–0–19–069217–9 (paperback : alk. paper)
1. International agencies.   2. International cooperation.   3. Humanitarian
intervention.   4. Sovereignty.   I. Title.
JZ4850.P39 2014
341.2—dc23
2014008952

Contents

Acknowledgments

I HAVE MANY people to thank for their support and encouragement. John Tomasi is the kind of graduate school mentor who gives one room to grow and resources to succeed. He is the best example of an open-minded teacher and a disciplined, thoughtful, and engaging scholar. Together with Sharon Krause, Charles Larmore, and William Galston, John guided my dissertation with a critical and constructive eye. This book grew out of that dissertation, but it is today much different from it. In their unique ways, each of my dissertation advisers has shaped the way I think about political philosophy. Since taking my first class with Sharon Krause on theories of rights at Harvard, I have learned much about the history of political philosophy, and about how to be a professional academic. I thank her for doing philosophy with generosity, and for inspiring women in academia to reach high and do it with integrity. David Estlund and Corey Brettschneider have read versions of this project when it was in its infancy, and I am in their debt for helping to shape it early on.

Loren Lomasky gave me a home in the Politics, Philosophy, and Law program at the University of Virginia for almost three years. Loren gives one reasons to believe philosophy can be as entertaining as it is inspiring. As a postdoc there, I taught and learned from great undergraduate students and had the privilege to interact with world-class scholars. Colin Bird, Jennifer Rubestein, Lawrie Balfour, Stephen White, George Klosko are just some of those who, at Virginia, read the manuscript and helped to make it better.

I have presented parts of this manuscript to different groups. Audiences at the University of Virginia Political Science Department, American Political Science Association, the Canadian Congress of the Humanities and Social Sciences, and University of Arizona Department of Philosophy have provided thought-provoking challenges to the views I advance here.

My greatest debt in writing this book goes to David Schmidtz. Dave and his wife Cate Johnson have been wonderful friends, and I cannot thank them enough for making me feel so welcome in Tucson and at the University of Arizona. The Arizona philosophy department offers amazing opportunities in political philosophy and Dave has increased these opportunities manifold with the Center for the Philosophy of Freedom. I am grateful to work with and to learn from him.

Dave organized a workshop on my book manuscript and invited Allen Buchanan, Steve Wall, and James Bohman to serve as commentators. Their tough and fair-minded criticisms have prompted me to think deeply about the content and contours of the book. John Thrasher, Keith Hankins, Chad von Schoelandt, Justin Tosi, Kevin Vallier, Bill Oberdick, Michael Bukoski, Danny Shahar, Jeremy Reid, Brian Kogelmann, Greg Robson, Hannah Tierney, Jerry Gaus, Sarah Raskoff, Matt Mortellaro, Stephen Stich, Guido Pincione, David Owen, Fabian Wendt, and David Wiens have all read the manuscript in part or in full and their suggestions have made the book better.

To David McBride at Oxford, I owe thanks for taking on the project, sending it to two thoughtful reviewers, and guiding it to publication. To Robert Keohane and Annie Stilz, my reviewers at Oxford University Press, I am indebted for kindly taking the time to read the manuscript several times and for writing detailed comments that have educated me as well as made me understand more deeply some of the philosophical and empirical issues the book confronts. I have not been able to address all of their concerns, but have done my best to engage them in a conversation and keep all of their concerns alive as I made revisions.

Pamela Phillips and Robert Anthony Peters have provided invaluable copyediting assistance. I owe thanks to Gayle Siegel and Rosie Johnson for making it a pleasure to go to work every day. Danny Mannheim's coffee shop, Espresso Art, has been a place of respite and inspiration.

Parts of Chapter 6 have appeared before in a different form, in an article entitled "Normative Conflict in International Law" in the *San Diego Law Review*, issue 46, 2009, copyright 2009 *San Diego Law Review*, reprinted with the permission of the *San Diego Law Review*.

Finally to my children Luca and Carla, and to Ioan for unconditional love.

Carmen E. Pavel

Tucson, Arizona

5.9.2014

Introduction

ALEX BIZIMUNGU WAS stuck for twenty-one days crouched in a small space behind an open door, as the terror of the Tutsi killings by the Hutu unfolded outside his house in Kigali. He did not move much, for fear of tipping off the relentless attackers who meticulously ensured that everyone was dead or dying. Unable to move or rest, the pain of his swollen legs keeping him awake, he witnessed through the crack in the door the killings in the street by the militant wing of the ruling party. The Hutu were ferocious, organized, armed, and thorough. Alex heard the killers go into his neighbor's house and the father cry while his children were shot. The *interahamwe* (meaning "those who attack together") proceeded to kill the father, then shoved his wife and sister into a hole, and killed them both with a grenade.

This was no spontaneous, unorganized enterprise taking hold overnight. Mass killings require extensive advanced planning: carefully shaping a political system that requires total obedience, gathering resources and weapons, disseminating hateful propaganda, and coordinating thousands, perhaps tens of thousands of people, who are single-mindedly motivated by a will to kill and destroy. Escaping this sort of organized massacre is a lucky and rare occurrence. During a lull in the killings, Alex emerged from his house and fled to another house in the neighborhood, where he stayed for another three weeks, incredulous that he could still be alive when most people around him were dead. In that place and time, Rwanda of April 1994, death was near-certain and the chance of staying alive was slim. Death was the fate awaiting all Tutsis and the Hutu moderates who were not wholeheartedly committed to the killings. Despite losing all hope, Alex was just as shocked to discover that his wife, a Tutsi who had earlier secured fake Hutu documents, was also alive.

This is the story that journalist Scott Peterson tells in his wrenching eyewitness account of the Rwandan genocide.[1] It is a story of 800,000 people being killed in less than one hundred days. The killings were premeditated and efficient. Most of them took place during the first month when the daily killing rate was five times that of the Nazi death camps.[2] Like so many stories of its kind, this is also a story that the world is reluctant to hear and unsure what to do about. Sometimes the best the people around the world witnessing such a massacre can conjure is moral outrage.

Yet moral outrage does not help unless we channel it productively into institutional reform. Situations such as that of Alex Bizimungu in Rwanda, and countless others in Sudan, Congo, Cambodia, Somalia, Kosovo, North Korea, and Syria require a new kind of institutional architecture, one that corrects states' dramatic failures to protect their own citizens. This book argues that coercive international institutions can stop these abuses and act as an insurance scheme against the possibility of states failing to fulfill their most basic sovereign responsibilities. It explains why, given ongoing and massive human rights violations such as genocide, enslavement, mass torture, and rape, states must obey the authority of international institutions despite the fact that the former may (still) have an expectation of complete and unfettered sovereignty over their population and territory.

Faith in international institutions may seem misplaced for those who regard these institutions as overbearing bureaucratic beasts that govern but are ungovernable, coerce but cannot be coerced in turn, are harmful at worst and inefficient at best. These skeptics, let's call them "statists," would say that if one is to put money into institutional reform, better to bet on improving states internally rather than on remedies at the international level. Making existing states more democratic, strengthening the rule of law, and enabling constitutional constraints on political power will go a long way toward curbing state abuses.

The statists are correct that improvements in human rights records can be achieved by reforming states internally. But failures such as Rwanda happen because of a more fundamental defect in the theoretical model of the state itself as an adequate guarantor of the rights of its citizens. Defenders of states as supreme authorities over their citizens and territory lack an adequate answer to the question: "How are citizens' basic rights secured if, for whatever reason, their political representatives severely abuse their powers or fail

---

1. Scott Peterson, *Me Against My Brother: At War in Somalia, Sudan and Rwanda* (New York: Routledge, 2001), 249–52.

2. Ibid., 252.

to adequately fulfill their responsibilities?" States are incomplete as a mode of social organization tasked with preserving their citizens' safety and basic rights. The incompleteness of the state model means that state reform alone cannot offer reasonable guarantees that citizens' rights will be protected against abuse.

The argument offered here targets two audiences. On the one hand, it speaks to the statists' skepticism that international institutions are harmful or superfluous, by defending international institutions as an adequate response to the incompleteness of the state system. Appropriately designed and circumscribed, international institutions can serve as effective tools to reign in destructive state behavior and strengthen the protection of the rights of citizens. On the other hand, the book rejects the overly ambitious plans of those who see the state system as obsolete and seek to supersede it by shifting substantial capacities for governance and control at the global level. Members of this second group, let's call them the "globalists," defend global democracy as a comprehensive scheme of institutional reform that would radically remake our political life by requiring states to relinquish large swaths of previously exclusive prerogatives to the international level.

Between the half-hearted skepticism of the statists and the casual optimism of the globalists lies the path of incremental, problem-specific institutional design and change at the international level. But what justifies the authority of particular international institutions against states, individuals, and non-public international actors such as NGOs and private companies? What is the best way to conceive of the structure of international institutions and the scope of such authority? What are the available alternatives? What are the benefits and limitations of each? What role do institutions play in defining, not just implementing, theories of international justice? These are some of the central questions that motivate this book.

International relations scholars have long debated the dynamics that lead to establishing international institutions and the likelihood of instituting international institutions with certain effects.[3] While these causal explanations

---

3. Robert O. Keohane, *After Hegemony: Cooperation and Discord in the World Political Economy* (Princeton, NJ: Princeton University Press, 1984); Robert O. Keohane and Lisa L. Martin, "The Promise of Institutionalist Theory," *International Security* 20, no. 1 (Summer 1995): 39–51; Joseph M. Grieco, "Anarchy and the Limits of Cooperation: A Realist Critique of the Newest Liberal Institutionalism," *International Organization* 42, no. 3 (Summer 1988): 485–507; Kenneth N. Waltz, *Theory of International Politics* (New York: Waveland Press, 1979); Kenneth N. Waltz, *Man, the State, and War*, Revised (New York: Columbia University Press, 2001); John J. Mearsheimer, "The False Promise of International Institutions," *International Security* 19, no. 3 (Winter 1994–1995): 5–49; Joseph S. Nye, "Neorealism and Neoliberalism," *World Politics* 40, no. 2 (January 1, 1988): 235–51.

are important, the purpose of this book is different. It makes a distinctive contribution to normative institutionalism, a field concerned with the moral assessment of institutions and institutional change. My working definition of international institutions is that they are organizations with agential capabilities: social entities with formal structures and collective goals, capable of acting and being held responsible for their actions. The argument is above all concerned with the normative legitimacy of *coercive* international institutions, meaning *institutions that are entitled to make rules and use force or the threat of force against noncompliers.* Thus, it can apply to analyzing both the desirability of existing coercive international institutions, such as, for example, the UN Security Council, which is authorized to use force under Article VII of the UN Charter, and that of future coercive institutions.

The analysis offered here therefore does not address the question "what kinds of international institutions are there and how do they emerge?" (which is a positivist project), but "what kinds of international institutions should there be and how can they emerge consistent with respecting some minimal moral baseline?" (which is the normative focus of the book). In addition, the book discusses the scope for international authority, the features of the international system that can render it consistent with a concern for human rights protection, and the role international institutions should play in articulating an action-guiding conception of global justice.

The beginning of the twenty-first century affords us the opportunity of a new perspective on this set of issues. We have witnessed two significant developments in the last half a century. The first is the crystallization of a global moral public standard against which to judge the actions of governments and diverse other participants in international politics. Despite significant disagreement about their nature, scope, and reach, the public discourse and practice of human rights seek to constrain the parameters in which states interact with individuals and with one another.[4] Current human rights practices are far from able to address all wrongs. The persistence of these wrongs continues to puzzle and frustrate us, due in no small part to an incomplete institutional capacity to interpret and enforce human rights norms at the international level. However precarious, human rights are the standard against which violations of important human interests are measured, and the reason for action invoked by the international community to redress those violations.

---

4. Charles R. Beitz, *The Idea of Human Rights* (New York: Oxford University Press, 2009).

The other significant development is the embryonic and haphazard evolution of networks of international institutions that aim to insert some measure of governance into world politics. Regional economic institutions such as NAFTA (North American Free Trade Agreement) or ASEAN (Association of Southeast Asian Nations), security alliances such as NATO, and the many organizations under the United Nations umbrella correspond to institutional focal points for governing specific problems in international politics. Only against this background of international institutions, themselves beholden to norms of right conduct, can we begin to imagine ways to limit abusive domestic institutions and enhance the agency of individuals dominated by them.

Political philosophers have been almost exclusively preoccupied with determining the appropriate moral response to global challenges, such as poverty and lack of medical care.[5] They have been much less concerned with institutional design questions. This, to be sure, does not depart from the dominant mood in political philosophy, which, with some exceptions, has been that of relegating institutional design to a marginal position.[6] Principles of justice are treated as primary, while institutional design is an afterthought of a well-articulated, self-contained, and comprehensive account of social and political justice. Understanding themselves to hold expertise in the latter but not the former, political philosophers are aware that there is a bridge between ideal theories of justice and actual institutions. But the bridge is rarely crossed.

Yet theoretical models of institutions cannot be advanced responsibly without an empirical understanding of how institutions actually perform their functions. Institutional proposals should not be wholly determined by such knowledge. Still, normative models of institutions can draw on empirical evidence to enhance their richness and credibility. This means that more so than before, theories of justice must become conversant with the

---

5. Peter Singer, "Famine, Affluence, and Morality," *Philosophy and Public Affairs* 1, no. 3 (Spring 1972): 229–43; Thomas W. Pogge, *World Poverty and Human Rights*, 2nd ed. (Cambridge, UK: Polity Press, 2008); Thomas Pogge, "The Health Impact Fund and Its Justification by Appeal to Human Rights1," *Journal of Social Philosophy* 40, no. 4 (2009): 542–69; Simon Caney, "Cosmopolitan Justice, Responsibility, and Global Climate Change," *Leiden Journal of International Law* 18, no. 4 (2005): 747–75; Seyla Benhabib, *Another Cosmopolitanism*, ed. Robert Post (New York: Oxford University Press, 2006); Kok-Chor Tan, *Justice without Borders: Cosmopolitanism, Nationalism, and Patriotism* (Cambridge, UK: Cambridge University Press, 2004); Charles R. Beitz, *Political Theory and International Relations* (Princeton, NJ: Princeton University Press, 1999); John Rawls, *The Law of Peoples: With "The Idea of Public Reason Revisited"* (Cambridge, MA: Harvard University Press, 2001); Gillian Brock, *Global Justice: A Cosmopolitan Account* (Oxford: Oxford University Press, 2009).

6. Jacob T. Levy, "Federalism, Liberalism, and the Separation of Loyalties," *American Political Science Review* 101, no. 3 (2007): 459–77.

institutional background that they seek to regulate. We cannot understand what justice requires without understanding the institutional context to which it applies. For example, should the existence of states make no difference to whether domestic and international ideals of justice are distinct? Should the various possibilities concerning the nature and authority of international agents have no effects on the principles for regulating international politics? To answer these questions, we must recognize institutions as placing constraints on, and helping to orient the goals of international justice. Therefore, understanding the institutional possibilities of our global future is essential for drawing up principles of justice appropriate for the international context.

While the argument is decidedly normative, it is built on interdisciplinary cross-fertilization. It draws on research into the theory of organization, the sociology and politics of bureaucracy, the economic literature on institutions, international relations theory, research on civil war, rule of law experiments in Latin America, and on cases in international law. The book raises philosophical questions about standards of evaluation for international institutions, the limits of state sovereignty, the nature of international law, the nature of anarchy, and the structure of international institutions. In asking these questions, the project refrains from delving deeply into the ongoing debates about the nature of human rights or the scope and content of global justice. Insofar as it touches upon them at all, it is to illuminate the role of institutional thinking in mediating the application of the concept of human rights and the idea of justice to the real world. The following sections of the introduction explain, define, and distinguish different notions of sovereignty, justification, and human rights, as a way of laying out the normative groundwork for the rest of the book.

1. Why Divided Sovereignty?

As I will show in Chapter 1, the argument builds on two distinct notions of sovereignty prevalent in the literature: (1) popular sovereignty, which embodies the collective right of a community of individuals to self-government, and (2) political institutions that carry out the collective mandates of the people, such as the executive or the legislature. The idea of divided sovereignty rests on the second of these notions and implies that the authority to carry out the popular will can be divided among several institutions at the domestic and international level, not just among domestic institutions. Sovereignty can be divided because political authority can be divided.

Many sovereign states continuously and reliably fail in their sovereign responsibilities. The basis for assessing those responsibilities is an important subset of human rights, namely *jus cogens* norms.[7] Human rights, in general, represent protections of morally important human interests, such as physical integrity, freedom, subsistence, and peaceful enjoyment of one's life. Torture, rape, slavery, extermination, or forcible displacement constitute violations of these fundamental interests. But from agreeing that certain kinds of egregious moral wrongs count as human rights violations, nothing follows about the precise content of those rights, their justification, their practical implications, the preventative and reparatory actions required on their behalf, or the character of institutional structures most suited for their enforcement. Human rights are subject to widespread disagreement about their foundational roots, their scope, and their implications for political practice.

Jus cogens norms represent a special category of norms that codify a number of *security, political, and equality rights* in international law. These norms are considered so important that derogation from them is never allowed. The Vienna Convention on the Law of Treaties (VCLT), Articles 53 and 64, defines norms of jus cogens—also known as peremptory norms—as norms accepted by the entire community of states and from which no derogation is acceptable.[8] Norms of jus cogens exist above the will of states and limit what states can do to each other and to their own citizens. A number of commonly accepted jus cogens norms have emerged despite ongoing disagreements over their scope and content: slavery and slave trade, genocide, prohibition of aggression, torture (as defined by the Convention against Torture and Other Cruel, Inhuman or Degrading Treatment or Punishment, adopted December 10, 1984), racial discrimination and apartheid, the right to self-determination, and the basic rules of international humanitarian law applicable in armed conflict.[9] I am going to limit my discussion in the book to this set of norms.

---

7. Least controversial relative to other alternatives, such as the International Covenant on Social, Economic and Cultural Rights (ICESCR, 1966) or the International Covenant on Civil and Political Rights (ICCPR, 1966). Jus cogens means literally "compelling law" in Latin.

8. Vienna Convention on the Law of Treaties, arts. 53, 64, May 23, 1969, 1155 U.N.T.S. 331, http://untreaty.un.org/ilc/texts/instruments/english/conventions/ 1_1_1969.pdf.

9. Alexander Orakhelashvili, *Peremptory Norms in International Law* (New York: Oxford University Press, 2006); Stefan Kadelbach, "Jus Cogens, Obligations Erga Omnes and Other Rules—the Identification of Fundamental Norms," in *The Fundamental Rules of the International Legal Order: Jus Cogens and Obligations Erga Omnes*, ed. Christian Tomuschat and Jean-Marc Thouvenin (Leiden, Netherlands: Martinus Nijhoff, 2006), 21, 27; Evan J. Criddle and Evan Fox-Decent, "A Fiduciary Theory of Jus Cogens," *Yale Journal of International Law* 34 (2009): 331–87.

The VCLT formalizes jus cogens as overriding rules of international law. States cannot "contract out" of jus cogens norms.[10] By their nature, jus cogens norms alter the consensual character of international law by setting boundaries around the substantive rules that states can consent to.[11] They are thus akin to constitutional norms that place substantive limits on the content of statutes passed by national legislators and of contracts created by private parties. Still, although they have the potential to act as constitutional constraints in international law, they are not yet viewed as such by the international community.[12] This set of basic human rights norms has coexisted precariously with an evolving system of international institutions that lacks compulsory jurisdiction and procedures for prosecution that are automatically enforceable.[13]

The focus on a subset and not the whole list of human rights, as defined by some political philosophers or the Universal Declaration of Human Rights, may seem insufficient to those who hope for faster, more radical progress in improving human well-being across the globe. One could, for instance, ground institutional reform on James Nickel's list of six categories of human rights: security rights, due process rights, liberty rights, political rights, social welfare rights, and equality rights.[14] Or one could start with the Universal Declaration's comprehensive list of conditions for individual well-being, including the infamous "holidays with pay." However, given the limited state of our knowledge about how to improve observance with basic moral norms, and the state of the world, which is rife with massive human rights abuses, it seems both prudent and appropriately modest to focus on a subset of standard

---

10. Ian Brownlie, *Principles of Public International Law*, 6th ed. (New York: Oxford University Press, 2003), 488–89. Brownlie estimates that "more authority exists for the category of jus cogens than exists for its particular content" (p. 490).

11. Orakhelashvili, *Peremptory Norms in International Law*, 7–9.

12. Ibid., 10.

13. Brownlie, *Principles of Public International Law*, 485.

14. James Nickel, "Human Rights," in *The Stanford Encyclopedia of Philosophy*, ed. Edward N. Zalta, Fall 2010, http://plato.stanford.edu/archives/fall2010/entries/rights-human/. Nickel defines each category as: "*security rights* protect people against crimes such as murder, massacre, torture, and rape; *due process rights* protect against abuses of the legal system such as imprisonment without trial, secret trials, and excessive punishments; *liberty rights* protect freedoms in areas such as belief, expression, association, assembly, and movement; *political rights* protect the liberty to participate in politics through actions such as communicating, assembling, protesting, voting, and serving in public office; *equality rights* guarantee equal citizenship, equality before the law, and nondiscrimination; and *social (or "welfare") rights* require provision of education to all children and protections against severe poverty and starvation."

and grave threats to individuals as a starting point.[15] Therefore, I understand minimal human rights as defined by jus cogens norms as public reasons for generating justification for action against states, and not as tools for ensuring the creation of a comprehensive list of conditions for individual well-being.

This view accords with the predominant understanding of human rights in the literature. Following Charles Beitz, James Nickel, and Michael Ignatieff, we can say that human rights serve as regulatory principles for international politics.[16] They measure how people are treated by their governments and other political institutions. Violations of these principles constitute reasons for action: to set up international law, to create institutions that can enforce them, and to undertake preventative or punitive actions. These basic human rights are high-priority norms. They are "resistant to trade-offs, but not too resistant," as James Griffin said.[17]

The existing set of peremptory rules does not preclude extending the list in the future to enlarge the basis of institutional reform to include additional human rights violations that result from a failure of the political agency of states. There have been several instances in recent decades when natural disasters with devastating outcomes for millions of people were followed by prompt action by the international community to deliver aid to the people affected. The humanitarian efforts were impeded by those countries' leaders, who acted as malicious gatekeepers for the areas that needed the most help. In the aftermath of a cyclone that killed thousands of people and displaced over 1 million in Myanmar in 2008, the military junta refused to allow foreign aid to reach the affected areas, and at the same time showed profound indifference to the fate of the Burmese people.[18] As a result of international pressure, the military junta relented, but the delays and repeatedly broken promises for open access toward the international community likely caused several thousand more deaths. Shocked at the callousness of Myanmar's political leaders in the face of such massive suffering, some Western nations, including France, considered a humanitarian military invasion to force aid delivery

---

15. Beitz, *The Idea of Human Rights*, 139; Michael Ignatieff, *Human Rights as Politics and Idolatry* (Princeton, NJ: Princeton University Press, 2003), 55.

16. Beitz, *The Idea of Human Rights*, 8, 13, 128; Ignatieff, *Human Rights as Politics and Idolatry*, 5–7, 11–12; James Nickel, *Making Sense of Human Rights*, 2nd ed. (Malden, MA: Wiley-Blackwell, 2007).

17. James Griffin, "First Steps in an Account of Human Rights," *European Journal of Philosophy* 9, no. 3 (2001): 306–27.

18. Andy Newman, "U.N. Pressures Myanmar to Allow Aid," *The New York Times*, May 9, 2008.

to those in need.[19] It is difficult to describe exactly what went wrong in the actions of the Burmese political elites. What duties did they fail to carry out? What rights have they violated? Whether or not this situation constituted grounds for humanitarian military action is debatable, but we can attempt to characterize such actions as violating the Burmese political leaders' fiduciary responsibility toward their people in some important way. We can say that their actions represented a violation of the Burmese people's right to a government that does not unduly interfere with their right to life, or we can describe it as a case of criminal neglect and refusal to uphold the duty to assist. Whatever we settle on as an account of what went wrong, we must develop theoretical and regulatory tools without which we cannot include such abuses of power in the category of jus cogens norms.

Therefore, I set aside such complicated moral and legal matters, and instead focus on jus cogens norms as defined by international law as a first approximation of an international morality whose purpose is to regulate the conduct of states and other participants in international politics. Using jus cogens as a starting point for justifying the authority of international institutions does not preclude either the enlargement of the category of jus cogens norms currently in use or the addition of other regulative principles for the conduct of states. Nonetheless, jus cogens norms enjoy the advantage of eliciting growing support attested by their codification in international law. Bearing in mind that there are still substantive philosophical and legal questions raised by the justification of jus cogens, I will take these norms as the starting point for the justification of coercive international institutions.

2. *Method and Justification*

Political philosophers are increasingly captivated by questions arising in the areas of international justice, law, and institutions. Although there is a long-standing interest in international institutions in political theory, going back at least to Kant's *Perpetual Peace*, the recent attention given in works in political philosophy to international justice and international institutions marks real progress, because these works encourage us to think about the limits of state authority, and about the possibility and pitfalls of international cooperation. [20] Contemporary

---

19. Robert D. Kaplan, "Aid at the Point of a Gun," *The New York Times*, May 14, 2008.

20. Immanuel Kant, *Perpetual Peace, and Other Essays on Politics, History, and Morals* (Indianapolis, IN: Hackett, 1983); James Bohman and Matthias Lutz-Bachmann, *Perpetual Peace: Essays on Kant's Cosmopolitan Ideal* (Cambridge, MA: MIT Press, 1997).

political philosophers such as Charles Beitz, John Rawls, Allen Buchanan, James Bohman, Carol Gould, Andrew Altman, Christopher Wellman, and Matthew Smith have expanded our theoretical horizon in thinking of international institutions as a coordination mechanism that *could be* important for preserving peace and human rights.[21] Some, such as Allen Buchanan and Mathew Noah Smith, have gone further and discussed why coercive international institutions have an important role to play that is distinctive from the role of states. Yet an explanation of why individuals should participate in the creation of international institutions and why states should obey them is missing. This emerging literature explains neither the ways in which power is delegated to *coercive* international institutions, nor the nature of the relationships between individuals and such institutions, given that states have primary responsibility for the protection of their rights and may regard such institutions as dangerous, unjustified impositions that must be resisted.

This book provides that explanation. Using the principal–agent language, the book argues that states provide incomplete mechanisms to protect individual rights due to the very nature of executive power and that, in order to overcome this incompleteness, authority must be divided between states and international institutions in order to better (probabilistically speaking) protect citizens' basic interests. The principal–agent language keeps at the forefront questions about the adequacy of the agency relationship, and prevents complacency and wide-eyed optimism about states and international institutions from the start. Thus, it is markedly different from globalist optimism that tends to obscure the pathologies of delegation and control at the international level, and from the realist skepticism that says international institutions are merely an extension of the dominant states' power.

Although the political science and philosophical literature often use language in distinctive and sometime incompatible ways, they converge on interpreting institutions as a set of rules, norms, principles, expectations, and procedures. In the international relations literature, institutions are identified with regimes and are defined as a "set of explicit or implicit principles, norms, rules, and

---

21. Beitz, *The Idea of Human Rights*, 31–42; Rawls, *The Law of Peoples*, 36, 70; Allen Buchanan, *Justice, Legitimacy, and Self-Determination: Moral Foundations for International Law* (New York: Oxford University Press, 2004); James Bohman, *Democracy across Borders: From Dêmos to Dêmoi* (Cambridge, MA: MIT Press, 2007); Carol C. Gould, *Globalizing Democracy and Human Rights* (New York: Cambridge University Press, 2004); Andrew Altman and Christopher Heath Wellman, *A Liberal Theory of International Justice* (New York: Oxford University Press, 2009); Matthew Noah Smith, "Rethinking Sovereignty, Rethinking Revolution," *Philosophy & Public Affairs* 36, no. 4 (2008): 405–40.

decision-making procedures around which actor expectations converge in a given issue-area."[22] For the purpose of this book, I depart from this consensus and work with a much narrower definition of institutions. I thus distinguish norms, rules, behaviors, and expectations from *organizations*, which are distinct collections of individuals whose relationships are structured around a specific purpose or mission. I use institutions in this latter sense, thereby setting aside some of the ambiguities of referring to institutions as norms or expectations. Organizations have political agency because they have authority to create rules, demand compliance, and be held accountable for failures to act according to their mandate. They are what people generally think of as organized groups that have a formal structure, a mission, a physical location, permanent staff, and letterhead.

International organizations can be coercive or noncoercive. Arguably, most of the international institutions in existence are not coercive. International institutions can be instituted purely for the purpose of coordinating the actions of different states. As such, they are voluntarily entered into, voluntarily complied with, and lack the capacity to coerce member agents who refuse to follow their rules. The International Organization for Standardization (ISO) is one such coordination institution. The ISO's role is to produce standards for products and services "such as quality, environmental friendliness, safety, reliability, efficiency and interchangeability" to its members.[23] It is an independent international agency based in Geneva, Switzerland, with 163 member countries. Individuals and private enterprises are not eligible for membership, but have the opportunity to serve as experts on national panels, become part of consulting committees, or act as liaisons to other international or professional organizations. Membership is optional, and the organization is financed with monetary contributions from member states and from companies that acquire its services.

The Security Council, which is charged with maintaining international peace and security and is based at the UN headquarters in New York, is a coercive international institution. It has the authority to establish peacekeeping missions and to authorize international military interventions. It comprises only fifteen member countries (including five permanent members, with veto power, and ten elected members who serve two-year terms) and some of its

---

22. Stephen D. Krasner, "Structural Causes and Regime Consequences: Regimes as Intervening Variables," *International Organization* 36, no. 2 (Spring 1982): 186.

23. From the International Organization for Standardization webpage: http://www.iso.org/iso/about/discover-iso_why-standards-matter.htm.

rulings are implemented by the use of force or the threat of force. Other international institutions, such as the newly minted International Criminal Court (ICC), have the potential to become coercive if supplemented by a proper enforcement mechanism. It is on this latter type of international institution such as the Security Council or the ICC that I focus.

This project is firmly rooted in the liberal presumption that coercive political power is always in need of justification. Coercion is an imposition on individuals and groups' freedom and, as such, it must be justified in order to be acceptable. The justification must contain accessible, public reasons that people can understand, endorse, and defend as a basis for affirming particular institutions. If people agree with the reasons that support certain institutions, and the processes by which such institutions get created and sustained, they will come to accept them as legitimate, even when disagreeing with these insitutions' particular judgments.[24]

The purpose of coercive international institutions is to constrain the actions of states, individuals, and other agents operating in international politics. But why should there be such institutions at all? What justifies the existence of a layer of supra-national authorities in a world where states have traditionally reigned supreme over their own internal affairs? Such justification has to start with the "natural condition" of states.[25] States have never enjoyed complete freedom in their dealings with each other. Aggressive behavior toward other states has always been subject to retaliation, even if the rules regarding when and what kinds of retaliation are permissible have been formalized only relatively recently. But in their internal dealings with their own citizens and territory, states have enjoyed almost complete, unfettered autonomy for a long time.

We can call this state of nature in which states act only subject to retaliation and free from effective, principled constraints on their behavior the "natural

---

24. John Tomasi, *Liberalism beyond Justice: Citizens, Society, and the Boundaries of Political Theory* (Princeton, NJ: Princeton University Press, 2001); Gerald F. Gaus, *Justificatory Liberalism: An Essay on Epistemology and Political Theory* (New York: Oxford University Press, 1996); John Rawls, *Political Liberalism* (New York: Columbia University Press, 1995).

25. This is how Kant understood the problem of justification in *Perpetual Peace*. Kant said that the state of nature is injurious to states just as it was to individuals prior to the emergence of states. Thus, the only way in which external laws have binding power over states is if they agree to a federation of states whose final point is a lasting peace. Absent such common agreements to regulate war and peace, interference with the government of another state "would render the autonomy of all states insecure." See Immanuel Kant, *Perpetual Peace, and Other Essays on Politics, History, and Morals*, 109, 115; James Bohman and Matthias Lutz-Bachmann, *Perpetual Peace*, intro. 4–5.

condition" of states. International institutions should be justified in terms of permissible transitions from the natural condition of states. Without offering a defense, I take as my starting point a two-dimensional account of justification: (1) An institution is justified if it performs the functions it was set up for and it does so in acceptable ways: uphold the rule of law, provide public goods, and so on; (2) an institution is justified if it arises through a history that is morally acceptable. John Simmons and David Schmidtz have made this distinction salient to discussions of political authority.[26] Building on their theories, I will call the first kind of justification functional and the second kind emergent.[27] Institutions that meet both standards of justification are fully legitimate in their authority to rule.

Expecting all or most insitutions to reach this standard of justification is a tall order. Since so few of them do, we must judge legitimacy as a continuous variable and not a dichotomous one, so we can assess whether institutions meet some threshold of partial legitimacy. I want to leave open what the threshold is. The state of the world is such that we must compromise on our theoretical standards. The distinction between partial and full legitimacy is essential for being able to judge existing and future institutions to be normatively authoritative and practically effective. Requiring that all institutions with authority must meet the full legitimacy standard will leave us with few coordinating and enforcement mechanisms for managing our common social life. Institutions can stay closer or farther from their mandated function and can arise through a history that is more or less morally acceptable. We can thus judge some institutions to be partially legitimate, even as we recognize that the actions of institutions judged partially legitimate require additional scrutiny and justification.

But why is it not acceptable to collapse the two standards and say that international institutions that serve good purposes are fully justified? For Simmons, the problem of collapsing the two evaluative standards is that justifying particular institutions would simply follow from justifying a certain institutional form. The legitimacy of each institution would follow from the justification of the institution type.[28] But as Simmons and Schmidtz point

---

26. A. John Simmons, *Justification and Legitimacy: Essays on Rights and Obligations* (Cambridge, UK: Cambridge University Press, 2000); David Schmidtz, "Justifying the State," *Ethics* 101, no. 1 (October 1, 1990): 89–102.

27. Schmidtz refers to teleological versus emergent justification, while Simmons distinguishes between justification and legitimacy.

28. Simmons, *Justification and Legitimacy*, 136.

out, the general qualities of an institution are one thing, the origins of its authority over particular subjects is another.

This distinction is relevant in international politics. Think of humanitarian intervention. If a humanitarian catastrophe is in progress in state A, another agent B (a state, international institution, or private entity) may be justified in intervening. Still, it matters whether agent B intervened legitimately, that is, whether it had the proper authorization that granted this particular agent,and not another, the authority to intervene to prevent massive harm, even if intervention was the right thing to do. Not accidentally, "proper authority" is one of the basic principles of just war theory.[29] If we just focus exclusively on what agents do, to the neglect of the processes by which the agents acquired their authority to do what they do, we would miss an important dimension of institutional evaluation.[30]

Consequently, this dual standard of justification requires showing that some system of coercive international institutions is preferable on balance to a system of states left to their own devices and that it can emerge in morally acceptable ways. The first justificatory step entails showing that international institutions possess certain qualities or that they supply goods such as criminal justice, which make it a good thing to have them in the world.[31] The second kind of justification requires showing that such institutions can acquire authority through legitimate political processes. That certain type of international institutions can be justified, can arise and function within morally acceptable bounds, and can produce benefits does not prove that any existing international institution is justified.[32] Therefore, the theory of justified international authority provided here must not be interpreted as endorsing any or most of the international institutions currently in existence.

International institutions arise today by state consent. I will make the case that a version of state consent can justify the authority of international institutions under the principal–agent model. But according to the dual justification criteria established earlier, this raises a challenge. According to many accounts, including Simmon's, no state is legitimate with respect to the emergence criterion. Historically, most states originated through oppression,

---

29. Terry Nardin, "Introduction," in *Humanitarian Intervention: Nomos XLVII* (New York: New York Universty Press, 2006), 24.

30. Simmons, *Justification and Legitimacy*, 148–49.

31. Ibid., 126.

32. Ibid., 127–28.

aggression, and brute force.³³ If existing states are not fully legitimate, state representatives could not legitimately authorize international institutions, since they themselves lack the authority to make such authorization. As I pointed out, however, full legitimacy may be too stringent and counterproductive as a criterion for state action. States are partially legitimate when, for example, they meet the functional justification criterion by providing minimal protections of basic rights to their citizens, and since no other alternative may be available for the authorization of international institutions, authorization coming from partially legitimate states will have to do.

Based on these two criteria, we can generate a general theory of legitimacy for international institutions. Coercive international institutions are justified and thus legitimate to the extent that they can arise, acquire goals, and pursue them in morally acceptable ways. These criteria will not be deployed to judge the adequacy of current international institutions, but rather I focus on offering a general theory of justification and legitimacy and the guidelines according to which such analysis could proceed.

The practical upshot of a concern with legitimacy is this: A legitimate international institution has the right to issue legally binding rules, to require compliance with those rules, and to coerce noncompliers.³⁴ Legitimate institutions generate various legal rights and obligations for individuals, states, and other international entities. They exercise authority over individuals, public officials of all ranks, states, NGOs, and other nonpublic bodies.

This account of legitimacy should not be confused with the Weberian understanding of legitimacy, which attributes legitimacy to the beliefs and attitudes people have toward an institution.³⁵ According to this "sociological" understanding of legitimacy, an institution is legitimate if people believe it is. This is an important approach to legitimacy, and its practical importance cannot be denied. Institutions that are normatively legitimate cannot function without being perceived as such by the people who are subject to their rules. Nonetheless, recognizing that people can be mistaken either in supporting or in withholding their support for a certain set of institutions, normative

---

33. Charles Tilly, *The Formation of National States in Western Europe* (Princeton, NJ: Princeton University Press, 1975); Peter B. Evans, Dietrich Rueschemeyer, and Theda Skocpol, "War Making and State Making as Organized Crime," in *Bringing the State Back In* (Cambridge, UK: Cambridge University Press, 1985), 169–91; Martin van Creveld, *The Rise and Decline of the State* (Cambridge, UK: Cambridge University Press, 1999).

34. Adapting from Simmons's definition of state legitimacy. Simmons, *Justification and Legitimacy*, 137.

35. Max Weber, *The Theory of Social and Economic Organization* (New York: Free Press, 1997).

legitimacy must be kept distinct: Do people have good reasons to believe that a certain institution is legitimate? A theory of normative legitimacy offers a set of reasons for citizens living in different countries to comply with the authority of international institutions, and not an assessment of whether people actually comply with them.

The two criteria of legitimacy I have just discussed, functional and emergent, are noncomparative: They provide criteria of assessment that depend on meeting certain moral standards and not on how an alternative institutional system may fare in meeting the same criteria. Noncomparative objections are met by showing that the institutions in question are morally acceptable and that they do not amplify injustice and wrongdoing. However, any general theory of legitimacy for a system of international institutions must meet comparative objections as well, objections that seek to show that a different system of international institutions is preferable to the one put forward.[36]

My conception of what political philosophy and theoretical arguments in humanities and social sciences more generally can accomplish is quite modest. Arguments often come together from a series of considerations for which one gives reasons, takes into account counterarguments, and does one's best to engage the ongoing conversation. This means they are always provisional and open for challenge, refinement, and revision. In political philosophy, as elsewhere, we are hard pressed to find knock-down arguments that vanquish the opponent in one stroke. As Robert Nozick said about philosophical method, "There is room for words on subjects other than last words."[37] This book is offered in that spirit.

3. *Outline of the Book*

Chapter 1 shows that the failure to protect people who are subject to mass violence can be traced to a theoretical failure of the state model. The modern state, which finds its theoretical justification in the social contract theories of the seventeenth and eighteenth centuries, cannot offer reasonable assurance over the long run that it can protect individuals against abuse. The reason is twofold: (1) The government has a monopoly of coercive force as a condition of exercising its power, which it can easily turn against citizens, and (2) the people have no effective institutional channel to assert their authority over

---

36. Simmons, *Justification and Legitimacy*, 124.

37. Robert Nozick, *Anarchy, State, and Utopia* (New York: Basic Books, 1977), xii.

a usurping government. The state model is incomplete, because, as we can begin to glimpse from Hobbes, Locke, and Rousseau's problematic account of the authority of the sovereign, we need an institutional solution that includes external constraints on the power of the state. The answer to the question *Quis custodiet ipsos custodes?* (Who guards the guardians?) consists therefore of an institutional system made up of states *and* coercive international institutions that keep states in check and make sure they do not overstep the bounds of their authority toward their citizens.[38]

But how can citizens be expected to embrace this dual understanding of sovereignty and divide their loyalties accordingly? Citizens have traditionally bestowed their allegiance on one sovereign alone, and sovereign states have cultivated this undivided loyalty as a cardinal condition for exercising their authority. However, if citizens come to understand their domestic institutions as agents with specific purposes and functions, they can also regard international institutions as separate agents whose role is to keep the domestic sovereign in check and fulfill governance gaps in the state system.

In Chapter 2, I argue against the long-standing assumption that collective grants of authority from the citizens of a state should be made exclusively for institutions within the borders of that state. Despite worries that international institutions could undermine domestic democratic control, citizens can divide sovereign authority between states and international institutions consistent with their right of democratic self-governance. External restraints on states' power will have to make sense of the ambiguous and conflicting rules regarding the exercise of sovereign prerogatives in international law. Fundamentally, the problem of deciding which rules apply to state behavior is an institutional problem. States engage in a wide range of patterns of abuses against their citizens and foreign nationals, from small or haphazard daily indignities, to massive violations of rights such as forceful displacement, mass killings, rape, and widespread torture. Judging those patterns requires procedures for making rules, interpreting the rules in light of specific instances of abuse, and determining the appropriate response in each context. Drawing on principal-language theory, the chapter develops a delegation model of political authority for specific international institutions that are empowered to act as fiduciary agents for people living in separate states with respect to a narrow range of human rights norms, namely jus cogens. The chapter then addresses

---

38. The Latin phrase is attributed to the Roman poet Juvenal, and it became familiar in political philosophy via Plato's Republic.

some worries related to the legitimate authority of international institutions to make rules for states.

But what should be the scope of the authority of international institutions vis-à-vis states? What are the issues over which international institutions should be expected to trump states? Chapter 3 applies the principal–agent model to the case of slavery, genocide, and civil wars in failed states to illustrate possible roles for coercive international institutions. The chapter defends a restrictive conception of the authority of international institutions instead of an expansive one. But even a narrow conception of the scope of international institutions' power changes the nature of the authority of states with respect to their citizens and therefore changes the nature of the constitutional compact between citizens and domestic political institutions. In some cases, the delegation of authority to international institutions as secondary agents of justice will require constitutional amendments and/or a reinterpretation of the authority of different domestic institutions with respect to each other and to international agents.

The possibility of a layer of international institutions tasked with keeping states in check alters the nature of the grant of power to state institutions, which can no longer be the supreme and final word on all internal political matters. Therefore, institutional models must play a more central role in theories of political authority and theories of justice more generally. Chapter 4 explains that principles of regulation that structure our political institutions must be sensitive to and grounded in a particular type of facts, namely institutional facts. Institutions transform the relationships among people, the patterns of interaction, and the nature of the problems that arise in social and political life. Thus, regulative ideals of international justice must be path-dependent, sensitive to the institutional context to which they apply, and must attend to trade-offs of moral goals.

Chapter 5 argues against globalists that we have good reasons to doubt that establishing formal political institutions at the global level in the form of a global democracy will generate the benefits associated with democratic institutions in Western liberal democracies. In particular, institutional reform of this type is accompanied by a high degree of variance, and consequently the risk associated with sweeping institutional change is substantial and the benefits uncertain. The empirical literature on rule of law reforms in Latin America and on organizational behavior show that, at the very least, we simply do not know what it takes to create working, effective formal institutions from scratch. Moreover, we have good reason to be concerned that the dysfunctional behavior of existing international institutions and states will be grafted onto and magnified by a comprehensive cosmopolitan scheme for institutional reform.

What alternatives to global democracy are there? Chapter 6 proposes institutional pluralism as one candidate for imagining the structure of international institutions. It argues that we should support, on reflection, a system of institutional pluralism based on authority distributed among many nodes, experimentation with institutional design, competition between institutional forms, and gradualism in the construction of supra-state authority. What is crucial to institutional pluralism is the absence of a central agency or a hierarchy of subordinated agencies that perform all the functions of international cooperation and, in effect, hold a coercive monopoly on power. Drawing on international law, I address conceptual worries related to pluralist institutional orders, such as a lack of consistency of the rules, a lack of institutional coherence, and the possibility of jurisdictional conflict. I also consider and reject a Hobbesian worry against institutional pluralism.

The final chapter discusses a persistent statist worry for a system of international institutions raised by realist international relations scholars: Can international institutions have real effects on state behavior? Drawing on case studies informed by liberal institutionalism and constructivist theories, I show that there is strong and mounting evidence that international institutions limit state action and change the nature of the dynamic of international politics.

In addition, the chapter challenges the self-conception of at least a part of the international relations literature as value-free social science. I show that some of the rational choice models deployed by international relations scholars rely on questionable normative assumptions about state agency, preferences, and goals. Questioning those assumptions opens the possibility of arguing for an international normative order that makes it desirable and prudent for state behavior and the behavior of all other actors in international politics to be guided by shared principles and norms, and to submit to international organizations' authority.

I

Sovereignty, the Social Contract, and the Incompleteness of the State System

THE RWANDAN STATE failed Alex Bizimungu and his fellow Tutsis during the genocide organized by the ruling Hutus in 1994. Instead of protecting their lives, the state became an efficacious killing machine turned against its own citizens. Millions of people were displaced and hundreds of thousands killed in just over three months. No one intervened to stop the Hutus. The United Nations labeled the conflict a civil war and declared outside intervention to be inappropriate and antithetical to respecting the sovereignty of the Rwandan state.[1]

I will argue that failures to protect of this sort can be attributed to a theoretical failure of the state model. Theories that embrace the state as the final locus of justice provide an incomplete specification of the institutional conditions that make the realization of individual rights secure. A system of political institutions is incomplete when it is easy to modify or overturn, undermines its intended goals, or is otherwise unreliable in fulfilling its function. For example, a system of laws and courts with no police force to enforce the law, or a system of police and courts but no procedural guarantees for fair trials and due process constitute incomplete institutional setups.

I will argue that similarly, the state is an incomplete institutional setup, because its institutions cannot offer *reasonable assurance* over the long run that they can secure minimal protections of their citizens' rights. We can trace

1. Michael Barnett and Martha Finnemore, *Rules for the World: International Organizations in Global Politics* (Ithaca, NY: Cornell University Press, 2004), 121–55.

this failure to theories of political authority and theories of justice that justify state power more broadly. Such theories meet the condition of *institutional completeness* when they propose political institutions that adequately realize their values. Perhaps no political theory can be complete in providing a comprehensive account of all the necessary and sufficient institutional guarantees that make the realization of its values possible. Nonetheless, there are some forms of institutional incompleteness that strike at the plausibility of the theory at a fundamental level. Theories can fall short in their institutional specifications in ways that damage their credibility, and I will use the example of social contract theory to show that traditional state models fail to offer adequate guarantees that states alone can secure basic individual rights. Social contract theorists such as John Locke, Thomas Hobbes, and Jean-Jacques Rousseau do not provide a reliable institutional solution to the following problem: How are citizens' basic rights secured if, for whatever reason, their political representatives severely abuse their powers or fail to adequately fulfill their responsibilities?

Undoubtedly, the social contract theorists did wrestle with the challenge that states might fail in their responsibilities to their citizens and sometimes dramatically so. However, the remedies they offered in response to this problem do not provide *reasonable assurance* that citizens' basic rights will be protected. This is because they overlooked the possibility of institutional guarantees *external to the state* that strengthen this protection, and they did so due to a particular view about the authority of the sovereign state. External institutional guarantees compromised what they believed were some of the core functions of sovereign state authority.

Given the stakes, this is a failure worth investigating. Social contract theories are not unique in tying the state model to rights protections or in insisting on the unquestioned supremacy of the state. They merely illustrate a much larger problem afflicting all theories of justice predicated on the state model. Such theories of political authority must confront the question of how to restrain the power of the state from harming its own citizens. I will focus on social contract theories because they capture essential features of the state model and of the relationship citizens have with political rule, and thus offer a good test in assessing the practical challenges of this model.

Social contract theorists confront two separate questions: First, what justifies the authority of the state over individuals who are by nature free and equal? And second, what political institutions best secure civil and political rights? The first question, which has been extensively discussed in the literature, concerns the normative justification of political authority, and the second question focuses on institutional design.[2] My primary concern in this chapter is to look at the institutional design features of social contract theories and to touch on normative justification only insofar as it illuminates these features.

The first section of the chapter offers a schematic overview of the accounts of three classical social contract theories—Locke, Hobbes, and Rousseau's—and identifies some important normative differences that shape their institutional views. Without providing a full account that is sensitive to the historical contexts that inspired these authors, or exploring alternative interpretations of their views, the reading of these theorists will not stray far from standard interpretations of their work. My aim is to emphasize the normative underpinnings of their institutional proposals with a view toward highlighting problematic aspects of the state institutional model in general. The second section shows that the institutional solutions of these theorists are predicated on their views of sovereignty. The third section emphasizes the shared features of their institutional views that render their accounts incomplete. I will suggest that an additional layer of institutions that divides authority to protect basic rights between states and international institutions is a promising way to complement the state system. Finally, I confront some challenges to the idea of divided sovereignty.

1. The Institutions of the Social Contract

Justifications of political authority often build on the contrast between an anarchic state of nature and an organized political association in order to explain how legitimate political rule emerges.[3] Individuals who are free and

---

2. On the question of the justification of political authority, see, for instance, Christopher W Morris, ed., *The Social Contract Theorists Critical Essays on Hobbes, Locke, and Rousseau* (Lanham, MD: Rowman & Littlefield, 1999); David P. Gauthier, *Morals by Agreement* (Oxford: Clarendon Press, 1986); Gregory S. Kavka, *Hobbesian Moral and Political Theory* (Princeton, NJ: Princeton University Press, 1986); Robert Nozick, *Anarchy, State, and Utopia* (New York: Basic Books, 1977).

3. It is generally accepted that the stories provided by social contract theorists are not best understood as socioanthropological accounts of how the modern state came into existence. Rather, social contract theories identify a moral baseline for evaluating laws and social arrangements and for guiding the proper attitude of citizens with respect to the obligations they have toward the state. In this sense, social contract theories are prescriptive, not descriptive. Jeremy Waldron, "John Locke: Social Contract Versus Political Anthropology," in *The Social Contract from Hobbes to Rawls*, ed. David Boucher and Paul Kelly (London: Routledge, 1994), 51, 55, 65; Howard Williams, "Kant on the Social Contract," in *The Social Contract from Hobbes to Rawls*, ed. David Boucher and Paul Kelly (London: Routledge, 1994), 135.

equal in their authority over one another empower collectively the institutions of the state to protect their security, welfare, and freedom. Social contract theorists believed that the agreement requiring individuals to transition from the state of nature to an organized political community is difficult to achieve. Hobbes formulated most clearly the collective action problem that individuals face in the state of nature. Individuals live in a state of total freedom but must act preemptively to survive, which leads to a condition of constant conflict and insecurity. With their reasoning powers sufficiently developed, individuals can perceive that their long-term interest is to obey the law, but each individual loses if she initiates cooperative behavior and limits her freedom while others do not. We can call this the mutual assurance problem: individuals would be better off if they agreed to common rule, yet they cannot agree to limit their own freedom unless they gain assurance that others will do the same. Hobbes argues that to overcome anarchy, rational human beings must simultaneously sign a contract to form a political association, the state. Individuals can protect their lives and interests by committing to each other to submit to the authority of a supreme ruler, who offers protection in exchange for obedience.[4]

There are actually two mutual assurance problems in the state of nature. The first problem concerns the assurance needed by individuals that others will also submit to political authority so that the first individuals who submit do not lose by restraining their behavior when others do not; and the second problem concerns the assurance that in submitting, individuals gain reliable guarantees that their rights will be protected by their collectively appointed ruler. Solving the first assurance problem does not guarantee that the second one has been adequately dealt with. Individuals can collectively trade natural freedom for political freedom without thereby securing adequate political institutions to protect their rights.

Hobbes understood the first as well as the second mutual assurance problem when he claimed that the long-term goal for each rational person is "to assure forever the way of his future desires."[5] This goal requires institutional guarantees, which for the Hobbesian social contract are not very complex.

---

4. Hobbes does not claim that individuals have ever established states in this manner. The lesson of Hobbes's theorizing is that the social contract is a rational solution to a condition of anarchy. Any political authority that can solve the mutual assurance problem is justified in its rule, and individuals are bound to obey it, even if there is no historical point in time in which they explicitly consented to it.

5. Thomas Hobbes, *Leviathan: With Selected Variants from the Latin Edition of 1668*, ed. Edwin Curley (Indianapolis, IN: Hackett, 1994), 57.

All power is vested with one person or group of people, the sovereign, who is the lawgiver and executor of the laws.[6] The interpretation of the laws must be consistent with the intent of the sovereign, and therefore judges cannot interpose their judgment between that of the citizens and the sovereign. On the contrary, they are appointed by the sovereign to ensure fidelity to its will.[7]

Hobbes argues emphatically that the sovereign cannot be part of the social contract. He gives several reasons for this. The first reason is that individuals do not appoint the sovereign as their agent. Rather, they "lay down [their] rights to all things."[8] Because individuals surrender all their rights to the sovereign, Hobbes claims that any action the sovereign undertakes is authored by everyone, either collectively or individually. The subjects cannot claim breach of contract.[9] Thus, Hobbes defended an *alienation* theory of sovereign power, as Jean Hampton showed.[10] Rights are given up and not loaned to the sovereign, as Locke would argue later.

The second reason is that the nature of political authority is determined, in part, by the available institutional options. For example, the sovereign cannot enter a contract with the subjects and thus serve as their agent because there is no higher judge to assess a breach of contract, and no outside power to enforce the contract.[11] The lack of authoritative settling of disputes between subjects and sovereign would lead to conflict and to the dissolution of the Leviathan.[12] These institutional limits raise the most formidable challenge to holding the sovereign accountable for its actions.

The fact that Hobbes could not envision an outside third party enforcing a contract between the sovereign and its subjects is telling. If such third-party enforcement was possible, Hobbes would have had to concede that it would lend support to the idea of a contract between citizens and the ruler. Even if the

---

6. Ibid., 173.

7. Ibid., 180.

8. Ibid., 80.

9. Ibid., 111. Hobbes is cryptic in this passage, but he seems to suggest that if each person enters a contract with the sovereign, then each person is an author of sovereign's acts. All individuals, including the sovereign, are both principals and agents at the same time and there can be no differentiation between their responsibilities. This claim is dubious, because no possible understanding of a contract exists that can render the parties' responsibilities indistinguishable.

10. Jean Hampton, *Hobbes and the Social Contract Tradition* (Cambridge, UK: Cambridge University Press, 1988), 118–20.

11. Hobbes, *Leviathan*, 111.

12. Ibid., 112.

possibility of third-party mediation might not generate all-things-considered support for the idea of the sovereign as part of the social contract, it is likely that this possibility would fundamentally alter the nature of the social contract and the role of the sovereign within it. It is hard to speculate on how Hobbes would have integrated such a possibility into his account of the state, but at the very least, he would have had to impose limits on the power of the sovereign whose actions would consequently be subject to sanction by the citizens *and* by an outside power.

Yet, in Hobbes's view, the sovereign is above the law and has final, absolute, and undivided authority.[13] Dividing power leads to dissension, conflict, and a possible return to the state of nature. The sovereign authority cannot be limited either. The only way to make sense of limits was to consider the sovereign constrained by another power, a condition incompatible with its supreme and absolute power over citizens: "Therefore, where there is already erected a sovereign power, there can be no other representative of the same people, but only to certain particular ends, by the sovereign limited."[14] There can be no delegation of power after the initial delegation to the sovereign, except when and to the extent that the sovereign deems it necessary because "powers divided mutually destroy each other."[15]

Hobbes's political suggestions are outdated in many ways. Societies that protect the rights of their citizens today insist upon limited government power that is divided among several offices and branches (executive, legislative, judicial). However, Hobbesian-inspired contractarian political philosophy is at the heart of many contemporary theories of justice and political authority, and it retains the original focus upon the individual as the primary unit of moral justification. Political arrangements must be justified from the point of view of each person, and must take each person's basic needs and interests into account. Consequently, Hobbes has raised the vital question in political philosophy from an individual standpoint: *What is the most stable, long-lasting set of political institutions that protect my interests and basic rights?*

Famously, John Locke goes further in answering this question. His normative premises are different. Locke says, "[T]he great and *chief end* therefore, of Men uniting into Commonwealths, and putting themselves under Government, *is*

---

13. Ibid., 213, 115–16.

14. Ibid., 119.

15. Ibid., 214.

the Preservation of their Property."[16] Pre-political rights to liberty and property shape the political goals of the social contract and the reach of governmental power.[17]

In the Lockean state of nature, disagreements will arise among individuals over the extent of their liberty and property, and they must serve as judges in their own cases. Giving one individual or a group absolute, arbitrary power to judge, as Hobbes proposes, is both incompatible with self-preservation and with the natural jurisdictional equality of individuals in the state of nature.[18] Locke explains this incompatibility with an attack on Hobbes, whose solution, as far as Locke is concerned, is not an improvement over the state of nature. Instead of the insecurity of the state of nature, individuals are now bound to "one Man commanding a multitude, [who] has the Liberty to be Judge in his own Case, and may do to all his Subjects whatever he pleases, without the least liberty to anyone to question or control those who Execute his Pleasure."[19] Locke is exercised by the fact that the Hobbesian social contract fails to solve the second mutual assurance problem: sovereign power that is unchecked, unsupervised, and unaccountable gives rise to abuses that threaten the lives of individuals, and thus fails in its primary aims of protecting individuals' safety.

This criticism of Hobbes is more far reaching than Locke realizes, because it extends to all social contract theories, including Locke's own. If the problem with the Hobbesian ruler is that he is a judge in his own case, the bearers of executive power will serve as judges in their own cases even in the most well-organized, constitutionally limited states. To anticipate my argument later on, the executive power can hardly be kept in check when it alone has the monopoly on the means of force as a condition of exercising its office.

Locke seeks to restrain the overreach of government power as a precondition for the protection of the rights of the contracting individuals. Instead of total alienation, Locke proposes trading natural liberty for a kind of political liberty that is defined by the will of a constrained legislature whose prerogatives are limited according to the social contract.[20] Individuals transfer limited power to the government and retain the right to dissolve the government

---

16. John Locke, *Two Treatises of Government* (1689), ed. Peter Laslett, 3rd ed. (Cambridge, UK: Cambridge University Press, 1988), 350–51.

17. Ibid., 358.

18. Ibid., 284.

19. Ibid., 276.

20. Ibid., 283.

should abuses occur. A constitutional separation of powers between the legislative branch and the executive/federative branch, where the federative power (the power to create foreign policy) and the executive power combine in the same person, ensures checks on abusive authority.[21] The powers of the legislative and executive branches are fiduciary. The legislative branch is supreme as the body that makes the law and directs the executive, but people retain supreme power to dissolve or alter the legislative when it stops performing according to its trust, due to the "Fundamental, Sacred and unalterable Law of *Self-Preservation*."[22] The executive power is normally subordinated to the legislative.[23] But legislative power can in cases of emergency be entrusted in the executive, which is only to exercise it for the common good.[24] The executive, in fact, enjoys a substantive prerogative, which can be exercised even when there is a working legislature that makes laws. The executive power enjoys an extra-legal prerogative to act against established laws if it deems it necessary.[25]

Yet despite his elevated sensitivity in matters of government abuse, Locke's answer to the question "Who is to ensure the fidelity of executive actions to the grant of power given by the people?" is unsatisfactory. Locke says that when a controversy between the people and the sovereign arises, the body of the people shall be umpire.[26] But if the prince refuses to accept their judgment, there are no ordinary political means through which the people can exercise their authority. In the event of disagreement between the people and the sovereign, there is no appeal left but to heaven, in Locke's view.[27] The community can revolt as a means of last resort to enforce its will. However, the right to revolution is a right without institutional protection, and therefore ineffective as a means to enforce popular will.[28] Locke also fails to solve the second mutual assurance problem, and therefore his institutional proposal is incomplete.

---

21. Ibid., 364–66. Locke did not consider judicial power to be a third separate branch of government. He also worried that further dividing power (say, by separating executive and federative powers) would lead to "disorder and ruin"; therefore, he too aims to keep the power of the government relatively concentrated.

22. Ibid., 366–67, 371.

23. Ibid., 368.

24. Ibid., 372.

25. Ibid., 375; Ross J. Corbett, "The Extraconstitutionality of Lockean Prerogative," *The Review of Politics* 68, no. 3 (2006): 430.

26. Locke, *Two Treatises of Government*, 377.

27. Ibid., 427.

28. Corbett, "The Extraconstitutionality of Lockean Prerogative," 446–47.

Jean-Jacques Rousseau believed that he could render some of these worries inconsequential by relying on direct democracy to make popular will authoritative. Like Hobbes and Locke before him, Rousseau saw the purpose of political association as the solving of a mutual assurance problem, but he was far more ambitious. He did not seek a form of political organization that would merely ensure protection for certain rights and privileges, but one that would reconcile full personal autonomy with political rule. Rousseau wanted to "find a form of association which defends and protects with all common forces the person and goods of each associate, and by means of which each one, while uniting with all, nevertheless obeys only himself and remains as free as before."[29]

The "as free as before" condition is demanding, but full autonomy under political rule is possible in "a free community of equals," Rousseau argues.[30] Freedom for Rousseau means being guided in one's decisions and actions by one's will alone and not by some other person's or group's will. Freedom is a fundamental moral commitment that allows the expression of human agency, and is therefore the most essential requirement of a well-ordered political community. This requirement can be met if citizens see each other as equals in a political community in which they place the protection of their shared interests—the common good—at the core. Political equality depends on constraining the level of economic inequality such that citizens' interests and power do not widely diverge. Equality and the priority of the common good, together with individual autonomy, form the foundational trio of Rousseau's political system. They represent the objectives of the state's institutional system and set limitations on the acceptable range of political relations in society.

For example, a social system that demands complete and irrevocable submission to one person or group is not acceptable for Rousseau, because it denies people's nature as free.[31] Contrast this with Hobbes, who is adamant that personal security cannot be realized without complete submission to the authority of the person or group that is the sovereign. For Rousseau, on the contrary, freedom and obedience to the law are compatible only when individuals submit to laws that are guided by the common good and give equal weight to each citizen's fundamental interests. Thus in his view, participatory

---

29. Jean-Jacques Rousseau, *The Social Contract* (1762), in *The Basic Political Writings*, trans. and ed. Donald A. Cress (Indianapolis, IN: Hackett, 1987), 148.

30. Joshua Cohen, *Rousseau: A Free Community of Equals* (New York: Oxford University Press, 2010), 14.

31. Ibid., 11.

democracy governed by the general will makes freedom and security compatible. Each person is part of the legislature and submits to her own will when she complies with laws that reflect the general will.

But although Rousseau rejects the Hobbesian solution, he offers a different version of the same alienation social contract theory. The original contract involves a total alienation of rights to the community as each member "places his person and all his power in common under the supreme direction of the general will."[32] In placing faith in a social contract that provides a solution to the problem of reconciling political authority and individual autonomy in a way that "requires no sacrifice of the freedom that defines our nature," Rousseau may be overstating the normative payoff of his theory here.[33] Full autonomy is not compatible with political authority. To accept the directives of the state means to abandon to some extent the power to act according to our own individual reasons, and this tradeoff involves a sacrifice of autonomy. This blind spot makes Rousseau unable to think through appropriate institutional guarantees for individual freedom and equality.

The institutional system that gives citizens a guarantee that their freedom and their basic interests will be protected is made up of a legislature in which citizens directly and fully participate in making laws, and an executive that ensures their implementation. However, to fully appreciate what Rousseau means by these institutions, we need to understand his notions of the general will and popular sovereignty. Rousseau envisions a direct democracy in which citizens fully participate in the making of political rule. The general will, which directs the citizens' judgments in political affairs, is not the expression of their particular wills, which give priority to their private interest, but rather a collection of special reasons that reflect the common good and are accessible to everyone with common sense.[34] Thus, exercising self-government in a direct democracy and submitting to political authority are not only compatible with full autonomy, they create the conditions that make the exercise of full autonomy possible, Rousseau believes.

The requirement that all citizens directly participate in making laws in popular assemblies is not suited to the conditions of contemporary political communities with large populations and complex bureaucratic functions. Contemporary societies have transformed the practice of self-government into

---

32. Rousseau, *The Basic Political Writings*, 148.

33. Cohen, *Rousseau*, 32.

34. Rousseau, *The Basic Political Writings*, 203.

a practice of representation. This is one of liberal democracies' "enduring solutions."[35] A division of labor between political officials and regular citizens emerges that is better suited to political life today. Rousseau may have wrongly identified the general will as a principle of legitimacy with the institutional requirement that laws be decided in popular assemblies, as Habermas argues.[36] This apparent oversimplification has deeper roots, though. Rousseau was wary of legislative representation because he worried that it engenders domination by an elite political class, and that it destroys citizens' motivation to support laws guided by the common good, thus undermining the preconditions for equality and freedom. Legislative representation was akin to slavery for him. However, delegation of sovereign authority was not out of the cards for Rousseau, because he believed that executive power must be exercised by delegated officials. The condition of this delegation of authority was that the executive office would be closely scrutinized by the people. Similarly, legislative representation could be compatible with a reconstructed version of Rousseau's theory of political authority, provided that it is complemented with institutional restraints on representatives themselves. As we shall see, the institutional restraints that Rousseau thought available are not quite adequate for this purpose.

In conclusion, Hobbes, Locke, and Rousseau share, above all, a view of sovereignty as final and supreme. Final authority requires the sovereign to have the last word on any political issue, while supreme authority demands that the authority of any institution or agent of the state derives from the sovereign. For Hobbes and Rousseau, sovereign power was also absolute, meaning that the sovereign has complete and comprehensive control over the citizens' rights, laws, and public policy. Because of Locke's particular understanding of the origins and aims of the social contract, he moves away from the absolutist conception of sovereignty, but his view is an exception to the dominant tenor of social contract theories of his time. As historian F. H. Hinsley explains, "At the beginning, at any rate, the idea of sovereignty was the idea that there is a final and absolute political authority in the political community ... and no final and absolute authority exists elsewhere."[37] The difference between the proposals of Hobbes, Locke, and Rousseau can be traced

---

35. James Bohman, *Democracy across Borders: From Dêmos to Dêmoi* (Cambridge, MA: MIT Press, 2007), 4.

36. Jürgen Habermas, *Communication and the Evolution of Society*, trans. Thomas McCarthy (Boston: Beacon Press, 1979), 185–86; Cohen, *Rousseau*, 133.

37. F. H. Hinsley, *Sovereignty*, 2nd ed. (Cambridge, UK: Cambridge University Press, 1986), 25–26; Christopher W. Morris, "The Very Idea of Popular Sovereignty: 'We the People' Reconsidered," *Social Philosophy and Policy* 17, no. 1 (2000): 2.

to the location of sovereignty, a difference that, in part, explains their institutional prescriptions.

2. On Sovereignty and Delegation of Authority

Hobbes, Locke, and Rousseau shared the view that justice can only be achieved in the context of a sovereign state. This view remains the dominant account for the justification of sovereign authority and independence to this day. As Thomas Nagel explains, centralized sovereignty is commonplace among contemporary theories of morality and institutions, even if they differ substantively from earlier social contract theorists in their understanding of what justice requires.

> What creates the link between justice and sovereignty is something common to a wide range of conceptions of justice: they all depend on the coordinated conduct of large numbers of people, which cannot be achieved without law backed by a monopoly of force.... The only way to provide that assurance is through some form of law, with centralized authority to determine the rules and a centralized monopoly of the power of enforcement. This is needed even in a community most of whose members are attached to a common ideal of justice, both in order to provide the terms of cooperation and because it does not take many defectors to make such a system unravel. The kind of all-encompassing collective practice or institution that is capable of being just in the primary sense can exist only under sovereign government. It is only the operation of such a system that one can judge to be just or unjust.[38]

As Nagel emphasizes, justice requires a sovereign state. And we have seen that traditional social contract theorists believed justice requires *only* a sovereign state: the state is necessary and sufficient for justice, and thus a complete institutional form. Since Hobbes, Locke, and Rousseau located sovereignty with different agents within the political community, they identify distinct solutions to the problems of the abuse of political power. Hobbes located the sovereign with the person or group of people that also hold executive power. This has several advantages. It ensures that sovereignty is unlimited, absolute, and undivided: "That king whose power is limited is not superior

---

38. Thomas Nagel, "The Problem of Global Justice," *Philosophy & Public Affairs* 33, no. 2 (2005): 115–16.

to him or them that have the power to limit it; and he that is not superior is not supreme, that is to say not sovereign."[39] The identification of sovereignty with a specific institutional agent makes it effective as the absolute, ultimate, and supreme voice in the political association, but comes at the high cost of an indefensible notion of political authority, one that can easily crush, rather than reliably protect, its citizens.

In contrast, for Rousseau and Locke sovereignty resides in the people understood as a social entity, not a political one. Sovereignty for Rousseau does not refer to any specific institutional agent with the formal power to act and the enforcement power to back up its decisions. For Rousseau, "Sovereignty is merely the exercise of the general will."[40] Sovereignty establishes that the people as a whole have the final word on public law and state institutions, and thus their authority is unlimited, absolute, and undivided. Consequently, each individual finds herself under a twofold commitment, "namely as a member of the sovereign to private individuals, and as a member of the state toward the sovereign."[41] For Rousseau, sovereignty is univocally *popular sovereignty*.

Locke's theory of sovereignty is more complex and indeterminate at the same time. While he is widely and accurately read as a defender of popular sovereignty, Locke actually posits multiple centers of supreme authority: the individual, the community, the legislature, and the executive.[42] Sovereign power is exercised through the legislative and the executive, and each has the last word in political matters in their own sphere of authority. The separation among spheres is not clear-cut for Locke, since the monarch is subject to the rule of law but also has the prerogative to go against the legislative assembly and even suspend it. But if either fails to represent the interests of individuals, the people have a final right to censure. Locke makes it clear that people's sovereignty is a latent power, and it cannot be exercised while the government exists.

Popular sovereignty is expressed through bottom-up authorization. It requires that people rule through intermediary agents to whom they delegate authority in order to represent their interests. Although Locke defends a form of mixed government where nonelected, aristocratic elements, such as a monarch and legislators, coexist with legislative representatives, political power is

39. Hobbes, *Leviathan*, 123.

40. Rousseau, *The Basic Political Writings*, 153.

41. Ibid., 149.

42. John T. Scott, "The Sovereignless State and Locke's Language of Obligation," *The American Political Science Review* 94, no. 3 (September 1, 2000): 547–61.

an act of public trust, and public officials are judged by how well they perform their entrusted functions. The people can grant, withhold, or withdraw authorization for their public officials as an act of popular will. This is consistent with the contemporary prevailing notion that in order to be effectively limited, government power needs to be granted to a multitude of agents and institutions.[43]

Jean Hampton has argued persuasively that this "agency" model of political authorization according to which people loan power to the government, which finds a defender in Locke but not in Rousseau or Hobbes, is the only defensible expression of popular sovereignty. The social contract methodology compels one to advocate political rule as an agency relationship, since people retain a right to private judgment. This right to private judgment is based on the reasons that compel them to enter the social contract in the first place.[44] The reasons for which individuals enter a social contract might differ (e.g., self-preservation, property, autonomy), yet they always serve as a benchmark for judging how well the appointed officials fare in their mandate. In an agency relationship, a person or group of persons appoint an agent to act to further their interests. What is missing in the state model of the social contract is an institutional pathway for subjects to render their private judgments effective against their political agents. The main strength of Locke's and Rousseau's conception of sovereignty is the idea that the people are the ultimate judges of the exercise of political power. The shared weakness of their accounts is the assumption that popular sovereignty is institutionally effective. How can one ensure that the people really are sovereign, if they lack an institutional channel to make their will effective?

3. *Problems of Institutional Design*

Locke and Rousseau believe that the answer lies with popular sovereignty, but they offer an incomplete specification of the institutional setup that would render popular sovereignty effective as the ultimate power in society. Rousseau thought that government representatives must adhere to the laws and be held accountable in periodic assemblies "which have as their sole object the preservation of the social treaty," and are devoted specifically to the purpose of vetting existing administrators.[45] But Rousseau does not

---

43. Morris, "The Very Idea of Popular Sovereignty," 6.

44. Hampton, *Hobbes and the Social Contract Tradition*, 263.

45. Rousseau, *The Basic Political Writings*, 202–203.

explain what the relative status of these assemblies is vis-à-vis the legislature and the executive, as well as how they can enforce their decisions when the administrators *and not the assemblies* are in control of the means of force in the state.

In addition, even if the executive is the perfect agent for a legislative principal, as Rousseau seems to suggest at times, one cannot assume that the legislative assembly itself will offer the best protection of the citizens' interests.[46] Rousseau says that the law is the expression of the general will and the general will never errs; but, of course, the process by which the general will is expressed via law is mysteriously utopian. Even if the people are motivated by the common good when creating laws, there are many competing interpretations of what the common good requires at the level of law and public policy. Where there is room for interpretation, there is room for misinterpretation, for special interests to masquerade as public interests, and for large-scale error and abuse. Moreover, we cannot assume that the lawgivers internalize the motivation to work for the common good, pace Rousseau's implausible reliance on the omniscient, benevolent legislator who authoritatively guides majorities to collective wisdom.[47] A more plausible procedural specification of the general will is majority rule. However, majority rule can lead to severe abuses of minority rights if left unconstrained. Thus, Rousseau leaves the citizens vulnerable to the abuse of the legislature *and* the executive.

Similarly, both the executive and the legislative in Locke's social contract can overstep their bounds. They do so when they make or enforce laws that trample on the natural rights of individuals to liberty and property. Locke's social contract offers a public standard against which to judge such abuses, and that public standard is defined in the constitutional limitations of government power. But the operative value of this standard is undermined by Locke's explicit grant of an extraconstitutional prerogative to the executive who alone decides the conditions in which the exercise of this prerogative is justified. Who is to judge when public power is deployed for the public good? Locke's answer is that the people are the supreme power and the ultimate judges. However, if the prince refuses to accept the determination of their judgment, there is "no *Judge on Earth*."[48] This point is essential and worth stressing: the problem of severe abuse of power is a problem without a solution in Locke's view.

---

46. On the executive as a perfect agent for the legislature, see Cohen, *Rousseau*, 149.

47. Ibid., 162.

48. Locke, *Two Treatises of Government*, 379.

People commonly believe today that certain institutional choices internal to the state can ward off the peril of abuses of power. Indeed, the rule of law, popular supervision of government, constitutional limitations on public power, freedom of the press, rights of free speech, as well as an active and engaged citizenry drastically reduce the number of opportunities for states to violate the rights of their citizens. This is why advanced democracies have not as of late been responsible for the most egregious human rights abuses such as genocide, forceful displacement, mass imprisonment of political opponents, curtailment of minority rights, and so on. In this regard, dictatorships and countries in transition to democracy take the lead.

Yet it is easy to overstate the effectiveness of internal institutional guarantees. Two responses are in order for those who are optimistic about the capability of modern states to ward off such abuses. First, these advances in Western democracies are relatively new, and until the mid-twentieth century, some of them were still engaged in vast human rights violations such as internment, racial discrimination, forced sterilization, and genocide. The United States alone is responsible for systematic racial discrimination, the internment of American citizens of Japanese origin during the Second World War, and forced sterilization, the last policy adopted in a large number of US states and continuing well into the 1970s.[49]

Beyond the relatively recent gains in equal human rights protection in Western democracies, a much more important fact should loom large in our judgment of the institutional completeness of the state system. Many countries have simply never developed the internal checks and balances present in Western democracies, or if they did, these checks and balances were short lasting or ineffective. These countries will not be able for the foreseeable future to ensure that their political leaders are responsive to their citizens' needs, and furthermore that these leaders are discouraged from harming citizens solely for private gains. According to Freedom House statistics, this problem is quite widespread. As of their 2012 rankings, 108 countries representing 55 percent of the world's population were ranked partially free or not free, and 40 of these countries representing a population of 35 percent of the global total were classified as not free. According to Freedom House's definition, a

---

49. Kim Severson, "Thousands Sterilized, North Carolina Weighs Restitution," *The New York Times*, December 9, 2011, sec. U.S., http://www.nytimes.com/2011/12/10/us/redress-weighed-for-forced-sterilizations-in-north-carolina.html; Jeffrey White, "Report: Czechs, Others Sterilize Gypsies," *The Christian Science Monitor*, September 6, 2006; "Sweden Plans to Pay Sterilization Victims," *The New York Times*, January 27, 1999.

"Not Free country is one where basic political rights are absent, and basic civil liberties are widely and systematically denied." In these places, the protection of peoples' rights is fragile at best and nonexistent at worst. Partly free countries fare only slightly better: "Partly Free states frequently suffer from an environment of corruption, weak rule of law, ethnic and religious strife, and a political landscape in which a single party enjoys dominance despite a certain degree of pluralism." In contrast, only 87 countries representing 45 percent of the world's population are ranked as free.[50]

Statistics aside, the problem is intrinsic to the institutional model of the social contract. If popular sovereignty is the most desirable interpretation of the notion of sovereignty and the most plausible in light of the idea of common authorization of political institutions that protect shared interests, the people as sovereign cannot successfully constrain political leaders when the latter overstep the bounds of their delegated authority. This difficulty is due to the fact that the people lack formal power to enforce their will against the institutional representatives who, in fact, have a monopoly on the use of force.

Locke anticipates this problem when he discusses the conditions that lead to the dissolution of the social contract. When the prince usurps political power by unjustifiably infringing on the peoples' rights and when such infringement is grave and cannot be corrected through the existing formal channels such as appeal courts, the social contract is automatically dissolved. The responsibility for the dissolution always lies with the prince, because the sovereign alone has the "Force, Treasure, and Offices of the State" necessary to get his way, and no other power or private individuals can impose their will without his concurrence.[51] The prince has ultimate power, and this means that he is ultimately responsible if the social contract collapses. This responsibility can be traced to the prince's unquestioned supremacy of force, which guarantees that he cannot be easily overturned. The people have no recourse other than the prince's voluntary submission to their will.

A different way to state the fatal flaw of social contract theory is this: if it is plausible to conceive the relationship between the people and their political representatives as a principal–agent relationship in the manner Hampton encourages us to do, the only way to make sense of the state as the sole protector of basic rights is to assume that the supposed "agency contract" between the principal and the agent is self-enforcing. The second mutual assurance

---

50. Freedom House, "Freedom in the World 2012," 3–4, http://www.freedomhouse.org/sites/default/files/FIW%202012%20Booklet_0.pdf (accessed September 8, 2012).

51. Locke, *Two Treatises of Government*, 410.

problem—that individuals need an adequate guarantee that once they leave the state of nature, their basic rights will be protected—is left unresolved. Anarchist thinkers such as Anthony de Jasay rely on this shortcoming to reject the state as a mode of social organization. Dependence on the state as the ultimate enforcer of rights and of the agency contract makes implausible the idea that "power is both transferred to the ruler and retained by the people for the purpose of taking it back from the ruler if he abuses it."[52] The alternative to considering the agency contract self-enforcing is to rely on an external agent to enforce the contract between the people and their state. But we are left with the question of who enforces this new contract between the external agent and the people, and the next contract, and so on, which leads to an infinite regress of contracts for enforcement and adjudication of previous contracts.[53]

We can illustrate this point more dramatically with the right to revolution. The last appeal of the people when faced with abusive power is to rise up in arms and try to remove the offending leader. But if the state alone guarantees citizens' rights, state representatives cannot guarantee a right to revolution, which would lead to the dissolution of political authority and the end of political guarantees for any individual rights. In the absence of some enforcing agent who can guarantee rights above and beyond what the political community guarantees, the right to revolution remains aspirational. Immanuel Kant anticipated this dilemma. According to Kant, a right to revolution is self-undermining, because it involves the destruction of political authority that guarantees rights in general.[54] Therefore, Kant denied there was such a thing as a right to revolution. But we are left to wonder: Can such a right be secured in any other way? In "Rethinking Sovereignty, Rethinking Revolution," Mathew Noah Smith answers affirmatively and dispatches the Kantian challenge to the right to revolution. He justifies the right to revolution by reference to an international institution that would guarantee such a right for the population of a state.[55] Smith explains that the challenge could be solved if a political guarantor for a right to revolution distinct from individual states existed; the institutions of the guarantor would

---

52. Anthony De Jasay, *Against Politics on Government, Anarchy, and Order* (London: Routledge, 1997), 23.

53. Ibid., 19, 22–23, 197, 204; Anthony De Jasay, *Justice and Its Surroundings* (Indianapolis, IN: Amagi/Liberty Fund, 2002), 49–53.

54. Katrin Flikschuh, "Reason, Right, and Revolution: Kant and Locke," *Philosophy & Public Affairs* 36, no. 4 (2008): 375–404.

55. Matthew Noah Smith, "Rethinking Sovereignty, Rethinking Revolution," *Philosophy & Public Affairs* 36, no. 4 (2008): 405–40.

not be the target of revolutionary action and thus would not be susceptible to being thwarted. Smith proposes a solution involving two sovereigns governing the same territory: a traditional national sovereign and a decentralized international sovereign, the purpose of which would be to serve as a political guarantor to a right to revolution, among other things. Smith thus establishes a functional differentiation of sovereign responsibilities between national and international institutions that makes sense in the context of a right to revolution.

De Jasay would, of course, argue that it is fine that the international sovereign guarantees a right to revolution, but would question the availability of guarantees that the international sovereign sticks to its bargain. I will argue in the next chapter that there is a way to conceive of the authority of international institutions that solves the infinite regress problem. International institutions constrain states and can be constrained by states, in turn, in a complicated but feasible reciprocal enforcement relationship. If the argument is successful, it can serve to dismantle, in part, the anarchist objection on which de Jasay relies to reject the state.

In order to explain how these international institutions emerge and exercise their power and how they can be constrained in turn, we must develop a new understanding of sovereign authority that permits a division of authority between domestic and international agents. In the historical imagination of social contract theorists, institutional safeguards against abuses of power have been limited to institutions within a state. This need not be the case, and indeed international institutions can guarantee a more effective expression of popular sovereignty by securing the rights that people have both as a whole and individually against their own government.

I will build on Locke's and Rousseau's conception of popular sovereignty as the collective will of the people to develop a model of international institutions. I will use sovereignty in two senses: (1) to refer to people as sovereign with the ultimate decision power and a right to democratic self-government and (2) to refer to authoritative political institutions that carry out the mandates of the people. Divided sovereignty only makes sense on this secondary account of sovereignty. It means that the authority to express popular will can rest with several institutions at both the domestic and international level. Sovereignty can be divided because political authority can be divided. This focus on institutional authority as sovereignty preserves the idea of the people as the ultimate source of legitimate political power. The foreground notion that sovereignty rests in the people is what makes divided authority possible. On this more primary notion, Rousseau was right that popular sovereignty cannot be alienated. Specific institutional powers flow from it, but people never lose the right to refashion political life on their own terms.

4. Conceptual and Practical Hurdles to Divided Sovereignty

The idea that sovereignty could be divided may seem counterintuitive. After all, traditional political philosophy, as well as states in their ordinary political practice, have insisted that sovereignty bestows unfettered, exclusive, and indivisible authority over a state's territory and citizens. By contrast, a divided sovereignty model sees state institutions as primary authorities, with substantive autonomy over its domestic governing functions, and international institutions as secondary authorities, whose role is to intervene when states fail to fulfill their minimal responsibilities. The worry is twofold. First, it may not make sense *conceptually* to talk of divided sovereignty, because unfettered authority is what defines sovereignty in the first place. And second, it is difficult to imagine how sovereignty could be divided between states and international institutions *in practice*, in a way that does not completely undermine states' ability to run their domestic affairs autonomously.

Hobbes famously claimed that "a kingdom divided cannot stand."[56] By definition, the power of the sovereign must be absolute, because divided power breeds difference of opinion and dissension, and this, in turn, leads to conflict and war. Indeed, one of the poisonous doctrines he sought to weaken was "*that the sovereign power may be divided*. For what is it to divide the power of a commonwealth but to dissolve it: for powers divided mutually destroy each other."[57] Absolute sovereign power was for Hobbes a conceptually internal requirement, and he insists that the natural consequence of dividing the authority is a return to the state of nature.

While it is true that Hobbes and others have argued that sovereignty must be indivisible, in truth, sovereignty does not require absolute authority. Rather than being a binary concept, sovereignty can be understood more like a continuum, or a bundle of different kinds of functions and authority mandates, some of which can be transferred upward or downward. The fact that a state's sovereignty is limited by international institutions does not make that state completely devoid of sovereignty any more than the fact that an

---

56. Hobbes, *Leviathan*, 115.

57. Ibid., 213–14.

individual's autonomy is limited by the laws of a state makes that individual completely devoid of autonomy. Sovereignty, like autonomy, is something one can possess more or less of, over more of fewer areas of decision making.

But even if we think of sovereignty as a continuous concept, how does the division of sovereignty really work in practice? Doesn't the fact that states cede authority upward to international institutions undermine their ability to rule domestically? How can citizens be expected to embrace this dual understanding of sovereignty and divide their loyalties accordingly? Federative political arrangements show that sovereignty can be divided without being dissolved.

Federalism is an example of shared rule in which multiple levels of government (usually two—state and federal) have separate decision-making authority over certain areas in political, social, and economic life. Citizens have their rights secured by the two levels of government and have political obligations to both. Within the US federal system, there is a constitutional allocation of authority between states and the federal government. This allocation of authority sustained changes and bargains over time.[58] Still, both levels of government have their own distinct competencies as well as overlapping ones. For instance, in a series of cases, the Supreme Court has affirmed what is known as the doctrine of "dual sovereignty."[59] This doctrine allows both states and the federal government to exercise their sovereign prerogative and to prosecute the same individual for the same offense under their separate laws, thus avoiding the double jeopardy prohibition.[60] The Court has claimed that "when a defendant in a single act violates the 'peace and dignity' of two sovereigns by breaking the laws of each, he has committed two distinct 'offences.'"[61] The Supreme Court has determined that the federal government, state governments, and Native American tribes are considered separate sovereigns.[62]

---

58. Jenna Bednar, John Ferejohn, and William N. Eskridge Jr., "A Political Theory of Federalism," in *Constitutional Culture and Democratic Rule* (New York: Cambridge University Press, 2001), 223–67; Jacob T. Levy, "Federalism, Liberalism, and the Separation of Loyalties," *American Political Science Review* 101, no. 3 (2007): 459–77.

59. Most notably in *Heath v. Alabama*, 474 U.S. 82 (1985).

60. George Conner Thomas, *Double Jeopardy: The History, the Law* (New York: NYU Press, 1998).

61. Neil P. Cohen and Donald J. Hall, *Criminal Procedure: Post-Investigative Process, Cases and Materials* (LexisNexis, 2008), 675.

62. David Rudstein, *Double Jeopardy: A Reference Guide to the United States Constitution* (Westport, CT: Praeger, 2004), 88–89.

The European Union provides another example of divided sovereignty. The European Union is an intergovernmental union of twenty-eight member states (as of March 2014). The division of sovereignty within the European Union works according to the principle of subsidiarity, which is fundamental to understanding how different levels of government relate to each other. The principle of subsidiarity became European law as part of the Maastricht Treaty signed in 1992, which made the transition from the European Community, a looser, confederate intergovernmental structure, to the European Union, which is intended to work as a federative state.[63] The principle of subsidiarity says that decisions about policy should be made at the level at which they are most appropriate. The formerly independent member states have transferred to the governing bodies of the European Union a part of their sovereignty. There is a single market, a customs union, a common agricultural policy, a single currency and monetary union to which most member states adhere, a common trade policy, and more recently, a common foreign and security policy. States retain important prerogatives, such as responsibility for national defense. Member states are also the masters of the successive treaties that lead to the institutional buildup of the European Union, which means the agencies of the central European government cannot transfer additional powers from the states to themselves without explicit state consent.

Citizens of various European member states of the European Union are learning how to negotiate their multiple identities by remaining participants in domestic politics but also being asked to vote on referenda concerning the principles and laws of the European Union itself. The French may still think of themselves as French first and European second, but they are increasingly called on to shape the character and functions of the larger political union, for example, in deciding whether to accept new members, such as Turkey, and what benefits and responsibilities existing and future members should accrue. The boundaries of these divisions of sovereignty are constantly negotiated and reworked in multilayered political arrangements, and they serve as a demonstration that citizens' allegiance can be realigned to accommodate a nonunitary, distributed practice of sovereign functions.

Neither the European Union, nor the United States are meant as a template for the division of sovereignty between states and international institutions, although they are certainly possible candidates. They merely serve as proof that divided sovereignty is both conceptually possible and practically

---

63. See Andreas Føllesdal, "Subsidiarity," *Journal of Political Philosophy* 6 (June 1998): 190–218, and also Levy, "Federalism, Liberalism," 8–9.

feasible. While the definition of sovereignty as exclusive authority has had a strong hold for a long time on both our conceptual representation of states and on states' practical understanding of their attributes and powers, there is no reason to define sovereignty that way. Citizens have traditionally bestowed their allegiance on one sovereign alone, and sovereign states have cultivated this undivided loyalty as a cardinal condition for exercising their authority. Political philosophers such as David Miller, Anna Stilz, and George Klosko have shown that states cannot function as political agents unless they enjoy their citizens' support.[64] However, if citizens come to understand their domestic institutions as agents with specific purposes and functions, they can also regard international institutions as separate agents, and divide their loyalties accordingly. International institutions as secondary agents do not lead to a suspension of state sovereignty. Such institutions would only undermine state sovereignty if sovereignty required absolute de facto control. But it does not.[65]

5. Conclusion

This chapter has shown that the modern state system, which can trace its roots in the models developed by social contract theorists such as Hobbes, Locke, and Rousseau, is an incomplete institutional system because it does not offer adequate guarantees that citizens' physical safety and liberties can be secured by government institutions alone. The reason is twofold: (1) the government has a monopoly of coercive force as a condition of exercising its power that it can easily turn against citizens and (2) the people have no effective institutional channel to assert their authority over a usurping government. Citizens and states alike have acted on the assumption that states alone can protect individual rights, with disastrous consequences when abuses take place. The political practice of states both domestically and internationally "as if" they are institutionally complete political forms rests on a mistake. This mistake consists of ignoring external constraints on domestic political authority as part and parcel of a defense of popular sovereignty.

The fundamental worry about the incompleteness of the state system stems from the fact that states too often fail to fulfill their most basic responsibilities

64. David Miller, *On Nationality* (Oxford: Oxford University Press, 1997); Anna Stilz, *Liberal Loyalty: Freedom, Obligation, and the State* (Princeton, NJ: Princeton University Press, 2011); George Klosko, *Political Obligations* (Oxford: Oxford University Press, 2008).

65. Jean L. Cohen, "Rethinking Human Rights, Democracy, and Sovereignty in the Age of Globalization," *Political Theory* 36, no. 4 (2008): 593.

to their citizens. One may believe that this is a problem without a solution. Any attempt to modify the state system by adding layers of international institutions or fundamentally changing the nature of the state is bound to misfire, so we had better stick to what we have. But there is too much at stake to be defeatist and passive. This attitude was not acceptable to the people of Rwanda in 1994 and is not acceptable to other people around the globe whose rights are routinely violated by their state. The state model provides an incomplete specification of the institutional arrangements needed to protect people's personal security, so we must examine how state institutions can be complemented in order to enhance the protections of the rights of their citizens. I will take on this question next.

2

Divided Sovereignty

THE PRINCIPAL–AGENT MODEL

CHAPTER I SHOWED that we cannot rely solely on mechanisms internal to states to restrain state abuse of their own citizens. This chapter will argue that external restraints grounded in the collective endorsement of other states will have a better chance of succeeding. Such restraints will have to make sense of the existing ambiguous and conflicting rules regarding the exercise of sovereign prerogatives in international law. Rules defending the unconstrained exercise of state authority within one's territory, such as nonintervention in the internal affairs of a state, sovereign equality, and national self-determination, coexist uneasily with sovereignty-limiting rules such as those prohibiting genocide, crimes against humanity, and other widespread abuses committed by a state against its own citizens. For example, international relations scholar Ian Hurd has shown that according to different sources of international law, humanitarian intervention is legal and illegal at the same time.[1] This is just one instance where international law contains justifications both to restrict states' sovereignty to protect human rights and for those states to resist any intrusion on their authority to keep peace, prosecute criminals, and provide justice. Article 2(7) of the 1945 UN Charter states that there is no right to "intervene in matters which are essentially within the domestic jurisdiction of any state." Since what is and is not properly within a state's "domestic jurisdiction" is not univocally spelled out, state leaders can at any given time draw on conflicting interpretations of state sovereignty to suit their interests. This

---

1. Ian Hurd, "Is Humanitarian Intervention Legal? The Rule of Law in an Incoherent World," *Ethics & International Affairs* 25, no. 3 (2011): 293–313.

condition leads to "organized hypocrisy" and undermines the viability of any existing constraint on what states can do to their citizens.[2]

Overcoming these ambiguities about rules and getting states to comply with widely recognized minimal standards requires international institutions with the authority to create rules and bind states to follow them. Fundamentally, the problem of deciding which rules apply to state behavior is an institutional problem. States engage in a wide range of patterns of abuses against their citizens and foreign nationals, from small or haphazard daily indignities, to massive violations of rights such as forceful displacement, mass killings, rape, and widespread torture. Judging those patterns requires procedures for making rules, interpreting the rules in light of specific instances of abuse, and determining the appropriate response in each context.

Not surprisingly, states are reluctant to cede authority to international institutions for a number of reasons. From the perspective of the states' leaders, international institutions tie their hands and limit their ability to set policy objectives. From the perspective of the citizens, international institutions are distant, elitist bureaucratic machines that undermine democratic self-government. Citizens see themselves as bound to delegate authority, by a process of public deliberation and consent, to domestic institutions only, which they can shape, question, and hold accountable. Delegating authority beyond the nation-state is often regarded as inconsistent with preserving the integrity of domestic political processes.[3]

This long-standing assumption that collective grants of authority from the citizens of a state should be made exclusively for institutions within the borders of that state must make room for a different picture of the relationship between citizens, their states, and international institutions. Despite worries that the international institutions could undermine domestic democratic control, citizens can divide sovereign authority between states and international institutions consistent with their right of democratic self-governance. The *principal–agent model* as a modified consent model can address some of the worries related to the legitimate authority of international institutions to make rules for states. According to this model, coercive international institutions should be conceived as agents of people living in separate states, whose task

2. Stephen D. Krasner, *Sovereignty: Organized Hypocrisy* (Princeton, NJ: Princeton University Press, 1999).

3. Robert A. Dahl, "Can International Organizations Be Democratic? A Skeptic's View," in *Democracy's Edges*, ed. Ian Shapiro and Casiano Hacker-Cordon (New York: Cambridge University Press, 1999), 19–36; Jed Rubenfeld, "Unilateralism and Constitutionalism," *New York University Law Reivew* 79, no. 6 (2004): 1971–2028.

is to keep those states within the acceptable bounds of legitimate behavior by filling in governance gaps in the state system. Supranational authorities should function as an insurance scheme against the possibility that states may fail to fulfill their duties.[4]

The argument is structured in four sections. Section 1 illustrates some of the ambiguities related to the current practice of restricting sovereign authority in international law with reference to the International Criminal Court (the ICC). Section 2 uses the principal–agent model to generate a justification for the authority of international institutions. Section 3 explains how to ensure that international agents serve the interests of their principals. Section 4 defends the principal–agent model as the appropriate way to represent the relationship between citizens, states, and international institutions.

1. Sovereignty-Limiting Norms and Their Current Effects

The ICC is a permanent international tribunal instituted by the Rome Statute that came into effect in 2002.[5] The signatories intended to prevent the necessity of multiple, ad hoc tribunals for massive human rights violations. The role of the ICC is to intervene when national courts are not willing or able to investigate genocide, crimes against humanity, and war crimes, leaving the national courts to exercise primary responsibility.[6] As such, the ICC represents a significant step toward a permanent system of institutions that holds political leaders and regular citizens accountable for extensive violations of human rights.

---

4. I use the term "insurance" here in a loose sense. This follows other references in the literature for international institutions as insurance. For instance, Andrew Moravcsik uses the term "democratic insurance" to explain why emerging democracies committed to the postwar human rights regime in Europe, while Michael Goodhart deploys the idea of insurance or lock-in to discuss constraints that global institutions place on states. Andrew Moravcsik, "The Origins of Human Rights Regimes: Democratic Delegation in Postwar Europe," *International Organization* 54, no. 2 (2000): 217–52; Michael Goodhart, "Human Rights and Global Democracy," *Ethics & International Affairs* 22, no. 4 (December 2008): 395–420.

5. Arash Abizadeh, "Introduction to the Rome Statute of the International Criminal Court," *World Order* 34, no. 2 (2002–03): 19; Jamie Mayerfeld, "The Mutual Dependence of External and Internal Justice: The Democratic Achievement of the International Criminal Court," *Finnish Yearbook of International Law* 12 (2001): 71–107.

6. The ICC jurisdiction can be triggered in three situations: by a state party to the treaty, by the ICC prosecutor, or by the Security Council. The Security Council is the only agency that can refer a case to the Court for states in which crimes were committed that were not parties to the statute. Abizadeh, "Introduction to the Rome Statute of the International Criminal Court," 22–23.

However, the consensual nature of much of international law, including the Rome treaty that led to the creation of the ICC, limits its authority to states that have *expressly agreed* to its charter, unless the Security Council refers a case to it for prosecution. In practice, this means that, if the slow and capricious Security Council machine does not set its gears in motion, the states most likely to commit human rights abuses are exempted from ICC jurisdiction.

A Security Council referral explains how the ICC asserted jurisdiction over Sudan, which is not a member state, and more recently how it came to investigate Libya's president for serious crimes committed against his people during their 2011 uprising. In March 2009 the ICC issued an arrest warrant for the acting president of Sudan, Omar al-Bashir. He was charged with five counts of crimes against humanity, including murder, extermination, forcible transfer, torture, and rape, all committed against Sudan's citizens while in office. The ICC prosecutor Luis Moreno-Ocampo, stated that Bashir had "masterminded and implemented" a plan to destroy three main ethnic groups in Darfur: the Fur, the Masalit, and the Zaghawa. According to the evidence presented before the court, al-Bashir had "purposefully targeted civilians" belonging to these groups, killing 35,000 people "outright" in attacks on towns and villages.[7]

An international arrest warrant has been issued for al-Bashir. Not only has he avoided prosecution, but he has been reelected as head of state following a popular election in the spring of 2010.[8] The ICC does not have its own enforcement mechanism, and it relies on member states to capture individuals with outstanding arrest warrants. If those individuals do not travel to ICC member states, they remain safe from capture. This weak ICC enforcement capability reflects a great ambivalence about its role in a world of sovereign states.

Take the United States, for instance. Although it has signed the treaty that led to the creation of the ICC in 1998, the United States has refused to ratify it, fearing that its own political leaders and citizens could be brought under its jurisdiction, and claiming that the United States alone should have final jurisdiction over crimes committed by its citizens. The United States has gone so far as to threaten withholding military aid for countries that support the ICC with the passing of the American Servicemen's Protection Act in 2002.[9]

---

7. Marlise Simons and Neil Macfarquhar, "Court Issues Arrest Warrant for Sudan's Leader," *The New York Times*, March 5, 2009.

8. Jeffrey Gettleman, "Bashir Wins Election as Sudan Edges Toward Split," *The New York Times*, April 26, 2010, sec. World/Africa.

9. Robert Perry Barnidge, "The American Servicemembers' Protection Act and Article 98 Agreements: A Legal Analysis and Case for Constructive Engagement with the International

It has also pressured the Security Council to exempt its citizens from prosecution by threatening to veto the renewal of several United Nations peacekeeping operations.[10] Finally, the United States has entered various bilateral "immunity agreements" asking individual countries to exclude its citizens and military personnel from extradition to the ICC.[11]

The Obama administration's pledge to cooperate with the ICC has marked a sharp turn in the United States' policy in recent years. It supported the indictment of Libya's Muammar Quaddafi, pledged resources in Uganda to fulfill the outstanding arrest warrant for Joseph Kony and his associates, and participated in the last general assembly that led to amendments to the Rome Statute. This has led legal scholar David Scheffer to claim that the United States has all but become a legal member of the ICC.[12] Nonetheless, the United States is not taking the necessary steps toward becoming an official member, signaling its continued ambivalence toward the ICC.

This ambivalence with respect to the ICC is understandable to some degree, since traditionally, sovereignty has meant that states have supreme authority over their territory.[13] The traditional conception of sovereignty has entailed both de facto power over one's territory and citizens, and the authority to make law and require obedience from the law's subjects.[14] Prior to the Second World War, international treaties rarely, if ever, limited national sovereignty. Treaties were mainly concerned with holding states responsible for trespassing on each other's sovereign prerogatives, such as invading foreign territory or attacking foreign citizens. However, as a matter of international law, states were not ordinarily held accountable for respecting their responsibilities toward their own citizens. The Second World War and the Holocaust have transformed the perspective of international law by bringing front and

Criminal Court," *Tilburg Foreign Law Review: Journal on Foreign and Comparative Law* 11, no. 4 (2004): 738–55.

10. Thom Shanker and James Dao, "U.S. Might Refuse Peace Duties Without Immunity," *The New York Times*, July 3, 2002, sec. World; Carsten Stahn, "The Ambiguities of Security Council Resolution 1422 (2002)," *The European Journal of International Law* 14, no. 1 (2003): 85–104.

11. Brian Knowlton and Thomas Fuller, "Europe Opposes World Court Exceptions: After War, a New Rift between U.S. and EU," *The New York Times*, June 11, 2003.

12. David Scheffer, "America Embraces the International Criminal Court," *Jurist*, http://jurist.org/forum/2012/07/dan-scheffer-us-icc.php (accessed February 15, 2013).

13. Dan Philpott, "Sovereignty," in *The Stanford Encyclopedia of Philosophy*, ed. Edward N. Zalta, Summer 2010, http://plato.stanford.edu/archives/sum2010/entries/sovereignty/.

14. Krasner, *Sovereignty: Organized Hypocrisy*; Jean L. Cohen, "Rethinking Human Rights, Democracy, and Sovereignty in the Age of Globalization," *Political Theory* 36, no. 4 (2008): 593.

center the ongoing and large-scale abuses of citizens by their own states. The International Military Tribunals that convened in Nuremberg and Tokyo had for the first time held political leaders accountable for abuses they committed against their own citizens. These tribunals represented a big first step toward a new understanding of sovereignty.[15]

Since the Nuremberg Trials, ad hoc tribunals and humanitarian interventions have made a considerable dent in the practice of unconstrained sovereignty. But although *in particular cases*, political leaders may agree that the sovereignty of a delinquent state must be curtailed when its abuses are too glaring, they are reluctant to institutionalize *principled, universally binding limits* on sovereign autonomy. This explains in part why the United States can be an enthusiastic supporter of ad hoc tribunals, but a steadfast opponent of the ICC, at least until recently.[16] Yet only by moving beyond soft, noncoercive international legal arrangements, can we make limits on state sovereignty stick. This entails designing and building *coercive* international institutions that have the power to enforce norms to restrict state behavior. Only with extended prosecutorial and enforcement capacity can the ICC become more effective in capturing and prosecuting the Omar al-Bashirs of the world.

Assuming the ICC can acquire such powers, what would justify its authority to limit states in their exercise of sovereignty? To answer this question, we must look at the ICC's mandate. The functional justification for the authority of ICC derives from jus cogens norms. *Jus cogens* norms belong to any plausible set of norms for setting principled constraints on state sovereignty. The Vienna Convention on the Law of Treaties (VCLT), Articles 53 and 64, defines norms of jus cogens as a special category of norms accepted by the entire community of states and from which no derogation is acceptable.[17] Norms of jus cogens exist above the will of states and limit what states can do to each other and to their own citizens. A number of commonly accepted jus cogens norms have emerged despite ongoing disagreements over their scope and content: slavery and slave trade, genocide, prohibition of aggression, torture (as defined by the Convention against Torture and Other Cruel, Inhuman or Degrading Treatment or Punishment, adopted December 10,

---

15. David Held, "Law of States, Law of Peoples," *Legal Theory* 8, no. 1 (2002): 1–44.

16. According to Schabas, in the face of strong reservations from the international community, the United States was the decisive force in establishing the International Criminal Tribunal for the former Yugoslavia. William A. Schabas, *The UN International Criminal Tribunals: The Former Yugoslavia, Rwanda and Sierra Leone* (New York: Cambridge University Press, 2006), 19–20.

17. VCLT, "Vienna Convention on the Law of Treaties," 1155 U.N.T.S. 331 (1969): arts. 53, 64.

1984), racial discrimination and apartheid, the right to self-determination, and the basic rules of international humanitarian law applicable in armed conflict.[18] By their nature, jus cogens norms alter the consensual character of international law, by setting boundaries on what substantive rules states can consent to.

The establishment of jus cogens norms indicates a weak but growing convergence on the importance of limits for sovereign authority among political representatives of states in international politics. They establish a normative hierarchy in international law by overriding conflicting rules, treaties, or customs. Yet in practice, the tension between sovereign authority and jus cogens norms remains the source of much uncertainty. Outside of the ICC, only a handful of cases have addressed this tension. In five cases brought before national courts between 1999 and 2010, the views with respect to the authority of jus cogens over sovereign autonomy have been divided, with three national courts claiming that "state immunity is not available as a bar to jurisdiction in cases concerning jus cogens violations," and the remaining two courts upholding the sovereign immunity for the state leaders whose actions allegedly contravened jus cogens norms.[19]

What complicates this case law is that these trials take place not in international courts but in state courts under the *universal jurisdiction principle*, raising questions about the jurisdictional authority of states serving as impartial forums for judging breaches of international law committed by other states. Universal jurisdiction is a relatively new and controversial principle of international law that allows any state to claim jurisdiction over egregious violations of human rights, regardless of the country of residence of the accused and the victims and the location of the crime.[20]

---

18. Alexander Orakhelashvili, *Peremptory Norms in International Law* (New York: Oxford University Press, 2008), 50–54; Stefan Kadelbach, "Jus Cogens, Obligations Erga Omnes and Other Rules—the Identification of Fundamental Norms," in *The Fundamental Rules of the International Legal Order: Jus Cogens and Obligations Erga Omnes*, ed. Christian Tomuschat and Jean-Marc Thouvenin (Leiden, Netherlands: Martinus Nijhoff, 2006), 21, 27.

19. Lorna McGregor, "State Immunity Jus Cogens," *International & Comparative Law Quarterly* 55, no. 2 (2006): 439.

20. The United States declined to assume universal jurisdiction. In *Samantar v. Yousuf*, in which five foreign nationals of Somalia sought damages from the former Somali defense minister Mohamed Ali Samantar, for the crimes of torture, rape, arbitrary detention, and extrajudicial killing, the Supreme Court decided that the claim of state immunity does not hold under a domestic law, but it refused to pronounce on whether the Somali's defense minister's behavior complied with international law. Sevrine Knuchel, "State Immunity and the Promise of Jus Cogens," *Northwestern University Journal of International Human Rights* 9 (2010–11): 149.

As for international courts, the relevant case law is patchy and uninformative. The International Court of Justice, an organ of the UN, endorsed the jus cogens idea for the first time in 2006 in the Judgment on Preliminary Objections in Armed Activities on the Territory of the Congo (*Democratic Republic of the Congo v. Rwanda*), although it failed to clarify its legal status.[21] The European Court of Human Rights has addressed jus cogens also once, in the case of *Al-Adsani v. The United Kingdom*, when it rejected the argument that jus cogens trumped sovereign immunity. [22] As these cases make vivid, the issue of whether limitations on sovereign authority is justified is still very much in dispute as a matter of international law. The 2004 UN Convention on Jurisdictional Immunities of States and Their Properties stipulates no exception to immunity for violations of peremptory norms, which according to one scholar "reflects the fact that such exceptions do not enjoy broad acceptance in the international community."[23] These ambiguities about what rules states should follow cannot be settled without international organizations that are widely perceived as legitimate by states and their citizens, with the authority to make, interpret, and enforce such rules. Such organizations must meet both the functional and emergent justification. They must both serve appropriate goals and emerge through a process that is acceptable to the people who will end up being subject to their rules.

The necessity of curbing abuses of state sovereignty has received sustained attention in the philosophical literature.[24] Increasingly, political philosophers have reflected on the moral basis of the principles that justify restrictions of

---

21. Evan J. Criddle and Evan Fox-Decent, "A Fiduciary Theory of Jus Cogens," *Yale Journal of International Law* 34 (2009): 346.

22. Ibid., 347; McGregor, "State Immunity Jus Cogens," 443. The United Kingdom's standing to hold Kuwait responsible for jus cogens violations committed against the latter's own citizen, Al-Adsani, rested on the controversial "universal jurisdiction" principle. The European Convention on Human Rights did not, however, make a judgment about the standing of the United Kingdom with respect to Kuwait, but only pronounced on the relative force of different principles of international law. In this case, it claimed that jus cogens cannot supersede sovereign immunity.

23. David P. Stewart, "Immunity of State Officials under the UN Convention on Jurisdictional Immunities of States and Their Property," *Vanderbilt Journal of Transnational Law* 44 (2011): 1064.

24. Larry May, *Crimes against Humanity: A Normative Account* (New York: Cambridge University Press, 2004); Andrew Altman and Christopher Heath Wellman, "A Defense of International Criminal Law," *Ethics* 115, no. 1 (October 2004): 35–67; Allen Buchanan, *Justice, Legitimacy, and Self-Determination: Moral Foundations for International Law* (New York: Oxford University Press, 2007); John Rawls, *The Law of Peoples: With "The Idea of Public Reason Revisited,"* (Cambridge, MA: Harvard University Press, 2001).

state authority. They provided good reasons to believe international institutions could meet the functional justification by serving legitimate goals. But, with few exceptions, they have spent less time thinking about how the institutions that put those principles in practice emerge and what are the legitimate ways in which these institutions can exercise their authority over states. Resolving many of the moral and legal issues surrounding the limits of state authority entails generating a new account of institutional authority that applies to both states and international institutions, and explains how institutions such as the ICC can operate in ways that do not constrain but rather enhance democratic self-governance. I will borrow the principle–agent model familiar from analyses of domestic bureaucratic politics to provide one such account of the emergence and authority of international institutions over states.

2. *Divided Sovereignty:* *The Principal–Agent Model*

2.1. The Origins of the Model

Originally developed as a model for understanding the theory of the firm and the problems of moral hazard in the insurance business, the principal–agent relationship such as lawyer–client, doctor–patient, and broker–investor is typically conceived as a contractual relationship between one party, the principal, and another party, the agent, who is expected to act in the principal's interest.[25] Individuals and organizations enter agency relationships for various reasons, such as lack of specialized knowledge or inability to coordinate on their own with other people. In theoretical accounts of domestic political institutions, a breakthrough occurred in the 1980s when political scientists seized on the principal–agent model to explain congressional oversight of bureaucratic agencies. The model describes congress as a principal when it appoints government agencies to fulfill administrative roles.

Principal–agent theorists have emphasized a problem characteristic of the agency relationship: There is no guarantee that, once appointed, the agent will choose to act in the principal's best interest, or that it will pursue his or her interests as efficiently as possible.[26] The agent has its own interests that may conflict with those of the principal and "is induced to pursue the principal's objectives

---

25. Terry M. Moe, "The New Economics of Organization," *American Journal of Political Science* 28, no. 4 (November 1984): 739–77.

26. Ibid., 756.

only to the extent that the incentive structure imposed in their contract renders such behavior advantageous."[27] The agency relationship is shaped by the independent goals of the agent, by the mandate (contract) that gives power to the agent, and by the environment in which it operates––all of which structure the agent's motivation to stay close to the principal's wishes or stray from them.[28]

The relationship between the citizens of a state and its political institutions more broadly can also be modeled as a relation of agency. Social contract theorists such as Jean Hampton have argued that the relationship between the people and their political officials is best understood as a relation of agency.[29] Scholars of democratic representation such as Jane Mansbridge, or Adam Przeworski, Susan Stokes, and Bernard Manin in their edited volume, portray the relationship between citizens and their representatives in the language of the principal–agent relationship.[30]

Strictly speaking, political officials do not stand in a contractual relationship with citizens. The relationship between the citizens and political officials is a fiduciary relationship, in which the citizens as the principal delegate authority to an agent or agents that are supposed to act in the principal's interest. This relationship is a "conditional grant of authority from a principal to an agent that empowers the latter to act on behalf of the former," circumscribed by constitutional rules defining the extent of the agent's authority.[31] The citizens, as a collective principal, delegate authority to the executive, legislative, and judicial institutions as their agents. These agents can, in turn, delegate authority to bureaucratic and administrative agencies and elongate the chain of delegation.

Scholars have illustrated the unique challenges of political agency as a special agency relationship. For example, George W. Downs and David M. Rocke have modeled this relationship of agency in order to understand how its nature

---

27. Ibid.

28. Barry R. Weingast and Mark J. Moran, "Bureaucratic Discretion or Congressional Control? Regulatory Policymaking by the Federal Trade Commission," *The Journal of Political Economy* 91, no. 5 (October 1983): 765–800; Kenneth A. Shepsle and Barry R. Weingast, "Policy Consequences of Government by Congressional Subcommittees," *Proceedings of the Academy of Political Science* 35, no. 4 (1985): 114–31.

29. Jean Hampton, *Hobbes and the Social Contract Tradition* (Cambridge, UK, and New York: Cambridge University Press, 1988).

30. Jane Mansbridge, "A 'Selection Model' of Political Representation," *Journal of Political Philosophy* 17, no. 4 (2009): 369–98; Adam Przeworski, Susan C. Stokes, and Bernard Manin, *Democracy, Accountability, and Representation*, Cambridge Studies in the Theory of Democracy (Cambridge, UK: Cambridge University Press, 1999).

31. Darren G. Hawkins et al., *Delegation and Agency in International Organizations* (New York: Cambridge University Press, 2006), 7.

influences the executive's actions when the latter acts on preferences in the area of foreign policy potentially different from the preferences of the public.[32] This special agency relationship is plagued by *information asymmetries* (i.e., the executive has more information about foreign policy) and *power asymmetries* (i.e., the executive has coercive power over the principal). In addition, the principal is made up of a large mass of people, the citizens, who exhibit *rational ignorance* and face *collective action problems*. The principal has difficulties controlling, monitoring, and structuring the incentives of the agent. This is in no small part due to the fact that this relationship can be characterized by a reversal of control from principals to agents. It is a feature and not a bug of the model in the political context that agents have coercive powers over the principal.

However, the public exerts some form of control over the executive as they can remove it from office. If the executive engages in wars that are too risky or irresponsible, the public can express its disagreement during an election. Ideally, the threat of this sanction serves to make the executive align its preferences more closely with those of the electorate. But this is an imperfect mechanism of control of the agent by the principal. The citizens often lack sufficient information about the policies of other states to assess the appropriateness of the executive's actions, and the executive can engage in risky and counterproductive foreign policy if the threat of removal from office disappears, as it does toward the end of a presidential mandate. Evidently, the less control the principal has over the agent, the less effective the agency relationship is in protecting the interests of the principal, and the more a state's foreign policy can diverge from the interests of its citizens. In states that lack a democratic tradition and effective constitutional constraints on political power, the chasm between citizens and their political leader is wide. The important question becomes how to make sure political agents' actions serve their principals' interest as closely as possible. The solution lies in oversight by international institutions.

2.2. The Principle–Agent Model for International Institutions

When the citizens of a state have difficulties monitoring and structuring the domestic agent's incentives, one way to ensure that the latter stays within the appointed bounds is by providing external constraints. Supranational

---

32. George W. Downs and David M. Rocke, "Conflict, Agency and Gambling for Resurrection: The Principal Agent Problem Goes to War," *American Journal of Political Science* 38, no. 2 (1994): 362–80.

institutions can provide a second layer of agency and act as an insurance scheme that keeps states in check and ensures that they stay within acceptable bounds of their authority. International institutions can ensure, among other things, that humanitarian interventions proceed from appropriate justifications, criminal responsibility is upheld, a modicum of governance exists in failed states, and mass violence during civil war is restrained.

The principle–agent model is implicit in a number of analyses of the legitimacy of international institutions, but its implications for a normative theory of political authority have not been explored at length.[33] Principal–agent models can enable us to better identify and describe the difficulties arising from the relationship of citizens and political elites and to locate solutions for the tendency of elites to act contrary to the interests of the citizens, a condition also known as agency slippage.

2.3. Delegation

Citizens from several states can conditionally empower international institutions to act on their behalf. Similar to domestic institutions, international institutions have a *collective principal*. But unlike the domestic principal, which is composed of a collection of individuals, the international principal is composed of a collection of peoples. International institutions represent the citizens of different states collectively when such institutions are authorized by a single agreement as in Figure 2.1. Otherwise, they have multiple principals, each of which authorizes the agent to act on behalf of its constituent members for a specific (and different) task.[34]

The collective principal must be able to define and delegate authority to international agents, but also to revoke or to change it. To exert control, the principal can resort to direct delegation, by say, holding elections to elect representatives to international forums, or indirectly, by relying on appointed state representatives who, in turn, appoint representatives to international forums. In the second case, the chain of delegation of authority is longer, but in this respect it is no different than domestic chains of delegation. Keohane and Nye argue, for example, that while delegation to international institutions

---

33. Allen Buchanan and Robert O. Keohane, "The Legitimacy of Global Governance Institutions," *Ethics and International Affairs* 20, no. 4 (2006): 405–37.

34. For more on the distinction between multiple and collective principals, see Daniel L. Nielson and Michael J. Tierney, "Delegation to International Organizations: Agency Theory and World Bank Environmental Reform," *International Organization* 57, no. 2 (2003): 241–76.

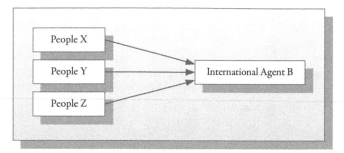

FIGURE 2.1. Each international agent has a collective principal

is indirect, "the chain of connections between elections and the actions of an Undersecretary of the Treasury, an independent Congressional commission, or a federal court is at least as indirect."[35] Thus, delegation to international institutions should not raise questions about democratic authority any more than delegation to bodies indirectly appointed by the legislature or presidency with authority to act in domestic politics does. The citizens as ultimate principals delegate authority to state representatives as their primary agents, who then act as proximate principals to delegate authority to international institutions as secondary agents as in Figure 2.2. In the short to medium term, this is probably the most feasible method of delegation since it builds on existing practices of delegations to international institutions.

2.4. The Role of Consent

Consent serves an important role to legitimate the authority of coercive international institutions on this model, but a very different role than consent currently plays in international law. For the time being, states are only bound by treaties and agreements they consent to. Consent is dispositive. The question arises how to interpret the lack of consent of some states to institutions such as the ICC. The fact that some peoples cannot effectively consent, because their political leaders are not legitimate representatives and because they have no alternate route to authorize international institutions, poses a special problem. Their inability to authorize certain international agents to act on their behalf means they cannot be protected from oppressive rulers. We are left with a dilemma: People in decently functioning political regimes

35. Robert O. Keohane and Joseph S. Nye Jr., "Between Centralization and Fragmentation: The Club Model of Multilateral Cooperation and Problems of Democratic Legitimacy," Harvard Kennedy School working paper, 2000, 20.

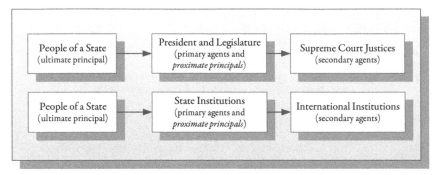

FIGURE 2.2. Complex delegation for domestic and international institutions

can consent and consequently acquire protection from international agents, yet people living in states with oppressive political rule, who need that protection the most, cannot acquire such protection.

Collective (consensual) delegation for the protection of nonconsensual norms can solve this dilemma. Consent is required for international institutions to be legitimately created and authorized. However, there is a category of norms that are nonconsensual, in the sense that their validity does not depend on whether states agree to follow them. Jus cogens norms are certainly part of that category. Collective agreements in which a majority of states, suitably defined, grant authority to a coercive international institution that protects jus cogens norms make that institution authoritative even for nonsignatories. We can further distinguish between *strong authorization*, where a majority of states grant authority to one international organization with the power to act in a certain area of jus cogens enforcement, such as the ICC, and *weak authorization*, according to which less than a majority but more than a small number of states authorize an international institution to act on behalf of jus cogens norms. For example, NATO has a total of twenty-eight member states, and it is a security alliance that occasionally intervenes to protect people against massive human rights abuses. Should it take on the mandate of human rights enforcement more explicitly, as James Pattison for example argues that it should, it will be weakly authorized on my account by the international community to pursue its mandate.[36] Weaker forms of authorization are valuable where stronger forms are not available. Thus, the fact that its authorization is weak does not disqualify an institution from performing essential functions of basic human rights protections, as long as it meets the functional

---

36. James Pattison, *Humanitarian Intervention and the Responsibility to Protect: Who Should Intervene?* (Oxford: Oxford University Press, 2012).

dimension of legitimacy, by providing the right capacity in the right way to enforce goals that are desirable.

Allen Buchanan doubts that consent has any role to play, especially given that many states do not plausibly represent their citizens' interests.[37] But it is not clear how we get any international institutions off the ground without at least some states consenting to their power. International institutions could not meet the emergent justification otherwise. Therefore, consent serves an essential instrumental function for authorization. It does not have to be either a super-norm, or a uniquely appropriate requirement, for the legitimacy of international institutions.[38] Consent is necessary not for establishing the relationship of authority between every people and the international institution that is newly appointed to protect their rights, but for coordinated efforts, even from a limited number of states, to create it, define its mandate, and the limits of its authority. The consent of some states for coordinating purposes is instrumentally valuable, and not intrinsic to the relation of authority established between international institutions and individuals living in different countries.

Thus, we can separate the legitimacy of the way an institution acquires authority from the legitimate scope of its exercise. But why extend the authority of international agents over nonacceding states this way? Recall that the characteristic problem of agency is that the agents will not always act in the principal's interest. Because not all de facto state agents accurately represent the interest of their citizens, their lack of consent cannot exempt them from nonderogable norms such as jus cogens. So, for instance, the fact that the Sudanese president does not sign on to the ICC, because he accurately deems it to be against his own interest to do so, should not mean that the ICC cannot act as a legitimate agent that protects the interests of the Sudanese people. States are not undifferentiated wholes, and when leaders choose not to delegate power to certain political institutions, this cannot mean that those institutions lack authority over them.

For a very narrow type of international agents, that is, those that protect jus cogens norms, international institutions can be legitimate fiduciary agents for people who cannot otherwise consent to their rule. Fiduciary or "surrogate" agency compensates for the substantive failures of agency of the primary agents.[39] Thus, international delegation relies on a modified consent model.

37. Buchanan, *Justice, Legitimacy, and Self-Determination*, 307–09.

38. Ibid., 307.

39. Jennifer Rubenstein, "Accountability in an Unequal World," *The Journal of Politics* 69, no. 3 (July 2008).

International institutions must have the consent of some states in order to exercise authority at all. Organizations cannot become self-appointed international agents; they must be at least weakly sanctioned by the consent of some of the peoples to whom their rules apply. Institutions must themselves acquire their power through legitimate means, and one such mean is a delegation of authority by a collective principal. Once suitably authorized to protect jus cogens norms, international institutions can act as fiduciary agents for the people living in states that have not directly consented to their rule. This is the *consent/fiduciary model of international delegation*. International institutions that protect jus cogens norms derive their legitimacy to act concomitantly from the special, nonderogable nature of these norms, and also from the consent of the other states. The upshot is that once they meet this dual standard of authorization, legitimate international institutions are justified in curtailing the sovereignty of abusive states, even if people living in those states cannot adequately consent to the authority of these institutions. This serves mainly to impede dysfunctional state agents from inflicting further harm on their citizens and to provide some measure of order and security to populations having to endure abuse. To sum up, we can helpfully distinguish between the legitimate creation of international agents, which we can call "initial authorization," and the legitimate scope of the authority of the international agents, which we can call "jurisdictional authorization" (covering both consenting and nonconsenting subjects).

Still, one may object that in the case of decent, liberal democratic states, international agents are redundant, and consequently, the motivation of those states to sign onto an international agreement that limits their sovereignty will be lacking. Why should these states incur the cost of having their sovereignty encumbered while enjoying minimal benefits for their citizens? To answer this question, we must separate the perspective of citizens from that of the 'state,' or state leaders. From the citizens' point of view, international institutions have a purpose even in the case of basically decent states. Democracy gains in most Western democracies are fairly recent, and although the probability of political leaders in those states engaging in massive violations of their citizens' rights is smaller comparatively speaking, it is not zero, and the costs of such violations can be overwhelming. International institutions can act as impartial and authoritative judges and can hold political leaders accountable for failures of the responsibilities entrusted to them by their citizens, even when the likelihood of such failures is small. Thus, even if states such as France withhold consent for the ICC, this fact should not have implications for whether the ICC can exercise jurisdiction over French leaders or its citizens.

This modified consent model is different from the current practice in international politics for authorizing international institutions and deciding what function any given institution adopts, which is state consent. According to the state consent model, states are presumed to be equally entitled to authorize international law and institutions. In practice, this means, of course, that state consent is the consent of state leaders.[40] However, there is no distinction between state leaders who actually respect and represent the interest of their citizens and those who do not. The difference between the state consent model and the principal–agent model can be represented schematically as in Figure 2.3.

In international law, additional mechanisms can be made available to pressure governments to be legitimate representatives of their citizens. Buchanan recommends that a process of recognition be formalized at the international level to recognize new states as legitimate participants in international politics only if they meet certain minimal internal and external justice requirements. Among these criteria, the most important are refraining from committing widespread abuses of human rights among its citizens, acquiring power without a major breach in international law (such as military conquest), and respecting the rights of other states' citizens and their sovereign prerogatives.[41] This seems like the right approach, yet the absence of such additional mechanisms should

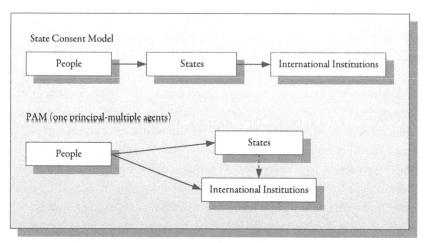

FIGURE 2.3. State consent model versus the principal–agent model (PAM)

40. Allen Buchanan, *Human Rights, Legitimacy, and the Use of Force* (New York: Oxford University Press, 2010), 313.

41. Buchanan, *Justice, Legitimacy, and Self-Determination,* 266–67.

not, for the time being, impede the formation of organizations that can act as surrogate agents for the protection of individuals' basic rights to life and bodily integrity.

Consequently, a hybrid conception of legitimate authority for international institutions is necessary to overcome the problem of countries that refuse to consent on illegitimate grounds. International institutions need the consent of legitimate political representatives to get off the ground, but for certain such institutions, the authorization to act need not be limited only to those that consent. This is because their legitimacy comes simultaneously from *consent*, and from the *special, nonderogable character of the norms* protected by the new institutional body. The ICC is not, and perhaps cannot be, meaningfully authorized by the Sudanese to be their agent, but it can act to protect interests that they share with people in signatory countries, interests in not being persecuted, terrorized, or murdered by their political leaders. This is why it would be legitimate to extend the jurisdiction of the ICC even to states such as Sudan, or the United States, which chose not to sign or ratify the Rome treaty.[42] The Sudanese leader may refuse to ratify it precisely because such refusal is in his interest, but the ICC, acting as a special, nondelegated type of agent that protects the interests of the people of Sudan, can prosecute him because of dramatic failures in his responsibility to protect their interests. The prosecutorial power of the ICC should therefore be extended over nonconsenting states. This extended prosecutorial function can replace the unreliable efforts of the Security Council to authorize prosecutions in cases involving these states.

Legitimacy on this account is different from de facto power. The idea of "recognition legitimacy" contains normative criteria that tell us if a state is legitimate, independent of whether it exercises effective control over its population and territory. Not all states that have effective control over their citizens and territory should enjoy normative legitimacy. Normative legitimacy is also different from sociological legitimacy, meaning that not all states that are perceived as legitimate by their citizens enjoy normative legitimacy according to this view.[43] Citizens can support illegitimate governments based on questionable or self-serving reasons. A majority of citizens can support a country's government even if it is engaged in massive violations of the human rights of a minority, or if it exploits the minority for the majority's benefit.

---

42. Or signed but chose not to ratify the treaty.

43. Allen Buchanan and Robert O. Keohane, "The Legitimacy of Global Governance Institutions," *Ethics & International Affairs* 20, no. 4 (2006): 405–37.

Absent more effective forms of direct authorization for international institutions from each state's citizens, state leaders or legislative bodies may still be the most effective vehicle for delegating authority upward to international institutions. But this conception of legitimate agency is preferable to the status quo for a number of reasons. The fact that the principal–agent model would not accept as dispositive the lack of consent of corrupt political officials has important practical consequences. The authority of international institutions such as the ICC can extend meaningfully to states that refuse to sign its charter. This new understanding of the authority of international institutions as agents of the citizens, directly committed to protecting their interests rather than those of their state representatives, would provide a normative base to give less weight to the lack of consent of unjust political leaders who are not themselves proper primary agents and more weight to the nature of the mandate these institutions adopt.

When applied to international politics, the principal–agent model leaves open both the actual mechanism of authorization of international institutions, and their shape, geographical spread, or domain of authority. However, what makes international institutions different is the fact that there is significantly more scope for a kind of contractarian mode of authorization of international institutions than there is (or was) in the case of states. Since consent to international institutions is an indirect, attenuated form of consent, granted through political representatives rather than directly, it is parasitic on the legitimacy of state agents. Still, individuals living in different countries have broader opportunities to define the mandates of particular international institutions, participate in institutional design, and create mechanisms of accountability for these secondary agents, than they do in the case of states. This process, which allows people to correct agency problems at home by holding severely abusive leaders accountable or removing them from office completely through the actions of international bodies, can enhance, rather than undermine, domestic democratic self-governance. The International Criminal Court is already contributing to that process when it enforces criminal liability for corrupt political leaders.

Coercive international institutions protecting jus cogens norms developed according to the authorization model described here meet the two justificatory criteria outlined in the introduction of the book: functional and emergent. They meet the functional justification when they receive mandates to enforce jus cogens norms against state abuses, and more generally when they mediate between states and their citizens in cases of conflict. Particular international agents also satisfy the emergent justification when authority is expressly delegated to them by a collective principal composed of the representatives of people from different states.

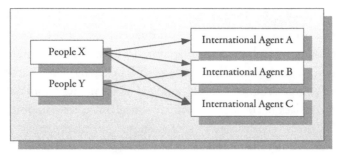

FIGURE 2.4. Each state can have multiple agents

The principal–agent model can serve as a template for a vertical division of sovereignty between states and international institutions. Yet it can also help articulate a horizontal division of sovereignty. International institutions can be responsible to citizens from more than one state, because several principals may have the same agent. But there is no reason why multiple principals should all have one agent, such as the global government, as their supranational authority. International institutions can be responsive to different constituencies, have different functional goals and areas of expertise, as well as different geographical foci, as in Figure 2.4.

Due to the special nature of the agency relationship that forms between the citizens of a state and an international institution, this relationship can impose specific agency costs. International organizations lie at the end of a long chain of delegation that further complicates monitoring, compliance, and control by the principals. The interest of the principal and the agent are never identical—there can be slippage between what the principal's interest requires and what the agent does, and this is just as true for international agents as for domestic ones. Consequently, a defender of divided sovereignty based on the principal–agent model has to confront head-on the following problem: If international institutions are secondary agents meant to correct the agency failure of primary agents, how do we make sure that international agents serve the interests of the principal rather than someone else's? How can individuals from different states delegate authority to international institutions without losing control?

3. Agency Costs at the International Level

International institutions are often regarded as runaway trains whose conductors have lost contact with the station and drive on a destination of their own choosing without due regard for their passengers or freight. While there is some truth to this picture, it misrepresents the extent to which international institutions are responsive to inputs from states and are representative of their interests. There is variance in this regard across international institutions, and while most existing ones are not coercive in the sense used here, the principal–agent model can explain the variance and provide diagnostic tools to make the agency relationship more responsive to principals for coercive and noncoercive institutions alike. Coercive institutions raise specific agency problems that I will address at the end of the section.

The sources of agency slippage can be traced to three major causes: (1) principals that overwhelm international agents with multiple and conflicting goals, (2) institutional design features that fail to maximize agent responsiveness, and (3) environmental factors. The first is not a problem with the agents themselves, but with unrealistic, ambiguous, or incompatible requirements that principals place on them. International bureaucrats face "mission creep," when they are asked to take on new mandates that do not fit easily with their initial ones, and when they are asked to take on more than the organization's capabilities can handle. While they may appear to go against the wishes or interests of their principals, agents may simply be struggling to define their mission in accordance with the demands placed on them and failing to do so because of the nature of the demands or the paucity of resources and powers at their disposal.[44] Principals can make conscious efforts to avoid this problem by delegating a narrow, well-defined set of goals and empowering agents to enact them by endowing the organizations with appropriate resources and powers for accomplishing them.

Second, principals can also resort to institutional design mechanisms that thwart organizational objective, which also creates the impression of misalignment of the agents' incentives with the principal. The principal–agent literature identifies at least five different ways in which principals make design choices that enhance the control of their agents: defining the *scope and means* of the organization, "*screening and selecting*" the personnel to reflect their interests, engaging in *monitoring and oversight*, leveraging *credible commitments to punish*, and instituting *procedural checks and balances* to keep agents in control.[45]

None of these mechanisms works perfectly. People living in separate states can exercise some forms of control over international institutions to ensure that the latter are responsive to their interests and are accountable to them, but there will always be a distance between what principals want or need

---

44. Tamar Gutner, "World Bank Environmental Reform: Revisiting Lessons from Agency Theory," *International Organization* 59, no. 3 (2005): 780.

45. Nielson and Tierney, "Delegation to International Organizations," 246; D. Roderick Kiewiet and Mathew D. McCubbins, *The Logic of Delegation* (Chicago: University of Chicago Press, 1991), 22–38.

and what agents do. This is inherent in the nature of the agency relationship. Agents can diverge from the wishes of their principals and engage in slack. Slack is a cost for the principals, which must decide, given the possibility of slack, whether the benefits of having agents are worth it.

Empirical analyses of existing international organizations document the ways in which states use control mechanisms successfully to increase their ability to reign in international organizations and the circumstances in which they may fail to do so. In the impressive volume *Delegation and Agency in International Organizations*, editors Darren G. Hawkins, David A. Lake, Daniel L. Nielson, and Michael J. Tierney conclude that the evidence shows that in many cases state principals do control their international agents, and delegation problems are not greater at the international level compared to the domestic one.[46] For example, in a chapter in this volume, Andrew P. Cortell and Susan Peterson show that the World Trade Organization (WTO) and the World Health Organization (WHO) are able to engage in slack but do so infrequently, and the extent to which they do can be explained by staffing decisions as well as by the voting mechanism for decision-making procedures. The more the staff is chosen for its special expertise, the more autonomy it demands and receives and the more it can depart from the states' explicit mandates for the organization. Similarly, Mona M. Lyne, Daniel L. Nielson, and Michael J. Tierney find that multilateral development banks are responsive to states that are quite adept at controlling them.[47] Lisa Martin's chapter on International Monetary Fund (IMF) conditionality also explains that the extent to which international institutions gain autonomy is often the result of conscious decisions of member states that find it in their interest to give their international agents leeway to pursue their goals. None of these cases show that international organizations act well, all things considered, only that they can be responsive to their member states; and there is also variance in the degree of responsiveness depending on particular institutional design conditions and choices made by principals, both at the moment of initial delegation and later on while monitoring and reacting to the actions of their agents. Yet these examples dispel the more extreme myth that international institutions are "institutional Frankensteins terrorizing the global countryside."[48]

---

46. Hawkins et al., *Delegation and Agency in International Organizations*, 365.

47. Mona M. Lyne, Daniel Nielson, and Michael J. Tierney, "Who Delegates? Alternative Models of Principals in Development Aid," in *Delegation and Agency in International Organizations*, ed. Darren G. Hawkins et al. (New York: Cambridge University Press, 2006), 73.

48. Hawkins et al., *Delegation and Agency in International Organizations*, 4.

Electoral control is the most direct method for *"screening and selecting,"* and it ensures that political decisions are made by individuals authorized by those to whom the decisions apply. Citizens can vote directly for their representatives to international institutions in general elections (for instance, they could vote for their representative to the UN assembly or the ICC), a practice adopted by member states of the European Union, or resort to indirect electoral representation, when their direct representatives nominate officials (ambassadors, delegations, permanent representatives) in international institutions. This form of indirect representation was typical in the United States before the adoption of the Seventeenth Amendment to the US Constitution, when state parliaments elected representatives to the US Congress.[49] Forms of electoral authorization could be imagined along nonterritorial lines as well.[50]

Yet, electoral control can be so indirect as to ensure no meaningful link between the citizens' needs and interests and those representing them in international institutions. Electoral control of international institutions takes place to a limited extent even now, indirectly. Citizens elect domestic representatives who, in turn, nominate officials (ambassadors, delegations, permanent representatives) in international institutions. But these existing intermediary links are themselves weakly responsive or nonresponsive to the preferences of citizens with regard to the character of international institutions. Therefore, it is not hard to imagine examples in which political leaders are themselves under a weak form of electoral control and appoint officials to international agencies based on whether their interests are served rather than the interests of the citizens.

Even if these obstacles of direct representation are overcome, elections are not always the most adequate route to representation. Indeed, Andrew Kuper, building on previous work in democratic theory, argues that direct electoral representation is a weak control mechanism to ensure reliability, accountability, and receptivity *in general.*[51] Elections guarantee accountability if representatives, in anticipation of the judgment of the electorate, will act to approximate these interests more closely in order to retain office. But if the representatives prioritize their own interests for reelection, they can be rent

49. Wendy J. Schiller, Charles Stewart III, and Benjamin Xiong, "U.S. Senate Elections before the 17th Amendment: Political Party Cohesion and Conflict 1871–1913," *The Journal of Politics* 75, no. 3 (2013): 835–47.

50. Andrew Rehfeld, *The Concept of Constituency: Political Representation, Democratic Legitimacy, and Institutional Design* (New York: Cambridge University Press, 2005).

51. Andrew Kuper, *Democracy Beyond Borders: Justice and Representation in Global Institutions* (New York: Oxford University Press, 2004), 90–96.

seeking, by pursuing self-interested policy choices up to the point at which doing so threatens their chances of reelection. Elections cannot prevent rent seeking, so the pursuit of citizens' interests is likely to be suboptimal.[52] Accountability through elections is simply punishment, and it is not likely to act as a very good deterrent. Representatives have more information, and can discern opportunities for their own gain and act on them in ways that the electorate cannot evaluate. The voters do not know the motivations and cannot accurately monitor the actions of their representatives, or can do so at prohibitive costs. Moreover, the receptivity of the representatives to the principal's preferences is measured only retrospectively in elections, and retrospective evaluation means that the representatives can diverge quite widely from their constituents in the meantime.

I believe Kuper is generally correct. He highlights problems that come largely from studies of domestic electoral representation, but, if anything, they will only be magnified in the case of international institutions. Even in functioning democracies, the link between citizens and their international representatives is so attenuated that there is a serious question if the latter count as representatives at all. Direct representation poses its own special problems. First, it places large demands on citizens to acquire knowledge about the regular agendas, purposes, and effects of international institutions. In addition, deliberating with citizens from other countries prior to electoral choice in order to refine one's interests and take others' interests into account is difficult and costly. Finally, coordinating elections in multiple states is logistically cumbersome. Electoral control is also unavailable as a mode of representation for people living under oppressive regimes. These people cannot adequately participate in the selection of representatives for international institutions.

Nevertheless, if electoral control is a largely blunt instrument, it must not be abandoned, but complemented with other mechanisms and procedures that can make institutions effective at representing the interests of the people affected by their decisions. For instance, the courts serve the interest of individuals in a justice system because they are constrained by *norms and procedures* that ensure due process, fair and balanced weighting of the evidence, and the presumption of innocence.[53] The ICC combines electoral with procedural constraints. Judges are nominated by states' members of the Assembly of State Parties who have signed and ratified the Rome Statute, and they are elected

---

52. Ibid., 93.

53. Michael Goodhart, "Democratic Accountability in Global Politics: Norms, Not Agents," *The Journal of Politics* 73, no. 1 (2011): 45–60.

by the Assembly. In addition to indirect electoral authorization, procedural rules and norms can render the actions of the Court just and fair. For example, Articles 55, 66, and 67 contain procedural rules and principles that grant prosecuted individuals many of the standard protections available in liberal democratic societies, such as requiring that they be provided with counsel, that they be free of arbitrary arrest or detention, and that they enjoy the right to a fair and impartial hearing.[54]

Procedural and substantive norms as control mechanisms for international institutions work best when it is relatively easy to discern objective interests, interests that people have independent of whether they can or do express them publicly, and that do not change with changing circumstances. The interests not to be persecuted, terrorized, or murdered, or the protections of due process are objective interests that can be identified in the absence of anyone explicitly defending them. But a system that relies solely on the identification of all interests *qua* objective interests through independent political agencies is not going to be acceptable, precisely because not all interests are of this kind, and doing so denies individuals the ability to identify their own interests.[55] There must be room in the global institutional scheme for the subjective and direct identification of interests, which is why institutional design mechanisms that focus on building good procedures can supplement, but never fully replace, ongoing forms of agency control by the people over whom their authority is exercised.

All of these mechanisms are endogenous to the agency relationship. There are, however, exogenous environmental factors that can create a third path for improving the alignment of the principal and agent's interests. In international politics, third-party actors are intermediate between individuals, states, and international institutions and can be a potential source of control on the latter by collecting and sharing information and thus enabling *monitoring and oversight*. Nongovernmental organizations (NGOs) and other semiprivate actors can pressure international institutions to justify their operations publicly.[56] NGOs can collect and make available information about bad behavior, as Transparency International does. They can provide new information about the preferences and needs of the individuals who are not able to supply that information themselves, such as political prisoners, and can supply ideas about the most appropriate means to protect people's interests.

---

54. Abizadeh, "Introduction to the Rome Statute of the International Criminal Court," 24–25.

55. Terry Macdonald, *Global Stakeholder Democracy: Power and Representation Beyond Liberal States* (New York: Oxford University Press, 2008), 118.

56. Ibid., 165.

Some international NGOs are afflicted by corruption and capture, or lack an understanding of what is needed on the ground to help people.[57] And the less legitimate, active, or salient third-party actors are, the fewer the opportunities to monitor and pressure international agents to comply. This fact should not disqualify the capacity of NGOs as a distinct form of social organization to offer a unique channel of control and accountability for international institutions, just as the existence of corrupt cops should not disqualify the police as an institution for protection and law enforcement. In addition, there is a burgeoning debate on whether NGOs should be considered representative of the people whose interests they serve or not.[58] Whether they count as proper representatives is a separate question that I will set aside; but NGOs clearly can exert a form of control with the purpose of making international institutions and the system as a whole more responsive to the interests and needs of the people they serve.

The structure of the system, characterized by vertical and horizontal division of authority, induces institutions to check each other's power and reduce asymmetries of information. Institutions that have narrow, well-defined goals that potentially overlap will tend to monitor and constrain one another. Institutional pluralism can act as an international separation of powers in which competing institutions pressure each other to reveal information about themselves. Through this competitive mechanism, voters will gain easier access to information politicians hold, which enhances democratic control.[59] In addition, states can keep international institutions in check. Even small, developing states have been increasingly powerful in influencing existing multilateral international arrangements.[60] Developed states such as the United States have both dominated the creation of these arrangements and influenced their rules and norms. And in some areas of international cooperation, such as financial policy, the powerful states' voice is still louder due to weighted voting rules. However, many international institutions have entrenched the principle of sovereign equality, and have granted small states a much greater

---

57. Michael Maren, *The Road to Hell: The Ravaging Effects of Foreign Aid and International Charity* (New York: Free Press, 1997).

58. Macdonald, *Global Stakeholder Democracy*; Andrew Rehfeld, "Towards a General Theory of Political Representation," *The Journal of Politics* 68, no. 1 (February 1, 2006): 1–21.

59. Kuper, *Democracy Beyond Borders*, 101.

60. Robert O. Keohane, *After Hegemony: Cooperation and Discord in the World Political Economy* (Princeton, NJ: Princeton University Press, 2005); John Gerard Ruggie et al., *Multilateralism Matters: The Theory and Praxis of an Institutional Form* (New York: Columbia University Press, 1993); Stephen D. Krasner, *Structural Conflict: The Third World Against Global Liberalism.* (Berkeley and Los Angeles: University of California Press, 1985).

role in decision making through formal institutional design rules. Thus, small states have been able to pressure large states to adjust their positions to better take into account the former group's interests, influencing the design of voting rules in their favor and successfully blocking undesirable substantive positions advanced by their more powerful counterparts.[61] This does not mean that developed and developing states are functional equals in terms of their influence on the character and goals of international institutions, but it does mean that developing states are able to exert increasingly powerful forms of control and checks on the ability of great powers to get their way.

Coercive international agents raise special challenges, because they (1) can coerce the principal through compulsory jurisdiction, and (2) they receive their authorization from proximate principals, state agents, who may or may not act in the best interest of the ultimate principal, the citizens. The second problem is attenuated, however, when delegation to international authority is grounded in jus cogens norms. International agents are valuable for their coercive capacity, because they deploy it to reign in misbehaving state agents. Coercion, nevertheless, can have widespread and extreme consequences in death and destruction. Thus, responsiveness and accountability are critical for these special agents. As in the case of other agency costs, the solution to this potentially large agency cost is to use all of the institutionally designed mechanisms available, particularly to delegate narrow and well-specified goals, to monitor and evaluate conformity to those goals, and to leverage a credible commitment to punish the officials of these institutions when they misappropriate the authority to act. Such officials must be themselves bound by norms of behavior that are enforceable, and the organization as a whole made subject to the possibility that its mandate will be revoked or its authority dissolved.

To sum up, international agents can be controlled by their principals through direct, electoral modes of authorization. However, electoral control is likely to have a limited impact on those agents' accountability and responsiveness. Other forms of control over the agents can be ensured through institutional design, which means defining and constraining the function of a given agent in advance, and by instituting procedural norms and rules to ensure that agents pursue their functions guided by fairness and an even-handed

---

61. Miles Kahler, "Multilateralism with Small and Large Numbers," *International Organization* 46, no. 3 (Summer 1992): 701–02; Krasner, *Structural Conflict*, 230–63; the formula of weighted voting in the IMF and the World Bank, according to which member countries acquire a number of votes corresponding with their relative share in the global economy, clearly favor economically powerful states. Ngaire Woods, *The Globalizers: The IMF, the World Bank, and Their Borrowers* (Ithaca, NY: Cornell University Press, 2007), 22.

appreciation of the varied interests of their constituents. The pluralist structure of international institutions would also augment the control of principals. International institutions can check and constrain one another to ensure that no one agent is dominant all the time.

4. Why Use Principal–Agent Theory?

Principal–agent theory is not new either to domestic or to international politics. While political theorists have occasionally resorted to the language of agency, principal–agent theory has not made its way into the common vocabulary of political philosophy in the way it has in American or comparative politics. Several advantages make the principal–agent model appropriate for representing the relationships between citizens, states, and international institutions.

First, models of political institutions serve distinctive functions. They focus on the essential features of relationships or phenomena, leave out detracting detail, and make assumptions about the behavior of different parties to the model.[62] As such, they help us understand important features of reality and inform our decisions about whether to accept or change them. The principal–agent model can help us better understand and explain, in particular, the nature and difficulties of political delegation. The model makes vivid the misalignment of interests between citizens and political leaders, and casts light on the inadequacy of the state as the final authority for protecting the individual's rights.

Second, agency theorists have developed detailed accounts of when and under what conditions agents engage in slack, thereby giving scholars and practitioners alike analytical tools to asses solutions to agency slack, to determine when the gains from delegation can compensate the losses, and which trade-offs are worth pursuing.

Third, the principal–agent model has enabled those engaged in institutional design to better understand how to structure the incentives of the agents ex ante in order for them to carry out the desire of the principals ex post. Ultimately, the goal of the principal–agent model is to tell us how particular institutional forms can increase the likelihood of compliant behavior by political officials and bureaucrats.

---

62. For David Schmidtz, models are like maps. They don't tell you where to go but how to get from point A to point B. See his *The Elements of Justice* (New York: Cambridge University Press, 2006), chapter 1.

The normative payoff is plain. Nielson and Tierney make clear that the type of principal–agent model one uses to explain an agency relationship makes the difference between showing that the agent is effective in protecting the principal's interest or not, and therefore makes the difference as to whether we are willing to accept the outcome or mobilize to change it.[63] For example, Karen J. Alter identifies a puzzle in the fact that international judges routinely rule against member states, yet they are not sanctioned by these states for their punitive behavior, as one would expect principals to do with disobedient agents.[64] We need to ask if this is a feature in need of correction, as she suggests, or not. When evaluating whether international judges stray from the interests of states, it is important to explain whether by "state interest" one means the interests of political leaders or the interests of citizens. Straying from the directives of state agents is not the same thing as acting against the best interest of the citizens. Alter demonstrates convincingly that international judges are not subject to reappointment pressures from states, and the latter do not deploy effectively the screening and recontracting tools available to them to prevent judges from imposing costly decisions on them. She implicitly states that this is an undesirable feature of international courts due to careless institutional design and unreflective imitation of domestic legal structures.[65] But whether the relative independence of judges counts as agency slippage cannot be evaluated simply on the basis of how state agents react to them. Even if the latter find the decision of international courts unfavorable, these courts may be doing a good job of imposing costs on otherwise misbehaving state agents. Of course, Alter may be amenable to the suggestion that the normative implication of an agency relationship depends on the model used to explain the relationship. Yet the problem goes deeper still. Whether there really is a puzzle that needs to be addressed—that of agency slack in the case of international courts—or whether judges simply act autonomously to preserve the interests of the ultimate principals, depends on the frame of analysis. Thus, principal–agent theory is a productive way to make transparent the connection between a set of normative aims and the institutional means of realizing them, as Chapter 3 will show we must.

---

63. Nielson and Tierney, "Delegation to International Organizations," 241–76; Lyne, Nielson, and Tierney, "Who Delegates? Alternative Models of Principals in Development Aid," 43.

64. Alter, "Delegation to International Courts and the Limits of Re-Contracting Political Power," in *Delegation and Agency in International Organizations*, ed. Darren G. Hawkins et al. (New York: Cambridge University Press, 2006), 312–38.

65. Ibid., 336–37.

This particular principal–agent model for international institutions helps to address another important objection. James Bohman, for example, worries that the principal–agent model legitimates forms of delegation that end up subverting, rather than enhancing, democratic will. International organizations as agents multiply the centers of authority, thereby extending the antidemocratic tensions within the modern administrative state. In addition, organizations such as the WTO and the World Bank reverse the locus of control from principals to agents. Instead of representing individuals, these agents dictate the terms of the relationship between states and individuals.[66] Principal–agent hierarchies, he claims, exacerbate legal domination by distancing the locus of control from individuals who suffer the consequences of their policies.[67]

Despite Bohman's reasonable worries, nothing in the principal–agent model entails a dominating relationship. Whether the agents dominate the principals or not is not a feature inherent in the agency relationship but depends on the terms of the delegation of authority, the specific design mechanisms that keep the agent's power responsive to the principal's interests and revisable, and factors from the environment that help or diminish the ability of the principals to monitor and control the agents. The principal–agent model is nonspecific about the details of delegation, and there is nothing in the principal–agent theory to suggest that delegation cannot enhance, rather than undermine, popular sovereignty if properly directed. The principal–agent model is simply an abstract way of representing the individuals' relationships with political authorities, whether domestic or international. Delegation can result in agents who act on democratic principles, are reflexive by allowing the principals to change the terms of the delegation, and who are inclusive and even-handed. Choices about the scope of agent authority, the means by which agents can accomplish their goals, and the options for principals to reign them in will shape the possibilities within which international agents act and their likelihood of engaging in antidemocratic, dominating practices.

International institutions can allow individuals to participate in the making of rules at the international level and fortify the normative powers of citizenship. They can do so both by increasing observance of human rights at home and by creating processes of deliberation and inclusion in international agencies themselves. Indeed without such an account of political agency, it

---

66. James Bohman, *Democracy across Borders: From Dêmos to Dêmoi* (Cambridge, MA: MIT Press, 2007), 7–8.

67. Ibid., 153.

is hard to know what to make of the institutional features of Bohman's own account, that of a decentralized transnational democracy. Bohman proposes multiple transnational demoi as inclusive publics that can define and rede-fine the rights of their members. Far from being an alternative to his account, the principal–agent model can actually be a friendly complement to it. Otherwise, how can we tell whether the different demoi are made institution-ally effective by their publics? How do they come into being and what kind of powers do they have over what issues? Only a principal–agent account that explains how power is delegated by individuals and domestic publics at a higher level and how different institutions and publics interact with each other can sort out the confusion that can result from ushering in multiple and overlapping demoi. A guiding model of political agency is necessary for many other groundbreaking accounts of institutional pluralism that have emerged in recent years. Without such a model, these new accounts lack a more fine-grained appreciation of the challenges of institutional design at the international level and of the condition for effective performance in pluralist systems.

5. Conclusion

The divided sovereignty model is predicated on a certain understanding of state sovereignty as the agent of the people under its rule. But like any agent, the state does not always act in the best interest of its citizens. To ensure that the state remains within legitimate bounds of its authority, its citizens can delegate some authority for the protection of their interests to international institutions as secondary agents. The ICC is one such secondary agent, because it has jurisdiction to try individuals for genocide, crimes against humanity, and war crimes when states are unable or unwilling to do it and is the first standing international institution with the express authority to do so.[68]

In international law, the commitment to limiting state sovereignty for egregious violations of human rights is selective. This selective commitment is akin to a domestic situation in which individuals claim that the autonomy of other individuals should be limited on an ad hoc basis when the latter cause harm but that there should be no *general, autonomy-limiting rules* that apply

---

68. This distinguishes it, for instance, from the International Court of Justice, an organ of the UN, which only has jurisdiction over states. The ad hoc criminal tribunals have had jurisdic-tion over individuals; however, the ICC is the first *permanent* international institution with the authority to do so.

to all. To overcome this condition of haphazard norm creation and enforcement, states such as the United States cannot consistently uphold the idea that other states' sovereignty should be limited when super-crimes are committed within their territories or by their citizens, but that its own citizens should be exempt from prosecution. All states must submit to universal, principled limits on state sovereignty.

The argument does not settle which other international institutions, apart from the ICC, fit the model I describe here. Therefore, in thinking about the ICC and ICC-like institutions, we should be careful not to idealize the potential of international institutions. I do not advocate for the proliferation of international institutions, precisely because setting up formal institutional arrangements is a process ridden with uncertainty, and high expectations about the performance of international institutions are often thwarted. Design choices and conditions from the larger environment in which they operate determine how effective institutions are in reaching their goals; but as it turns out, we still do not understand very well what kinds of institutional features will produce the best results and under which circumstances.[69]

The agency model developed here has a number of advantages. First, it explains the authority of at least some international institutions as a means to correct the problematic relationship of agency between the citizens of a state and their political leaders. Second, the reliance on a collective principal that represents a majority of states explains why lack of consent from individual countries to the authority of international institutions should not be dispositive. International institutions can and should protect the interests of people living in repressive regimes, despite their leaders refusing to grant authority over them to those institutions. Third, this understanding of international institutions as agents of people living in different states can serve to broaden rather than subvert domestic democratic authority. Hence, it adds to and extends recent arguments that show the ways in which international institutions can be an expression, rather than a diversion, of democratic will.[70]

---

69. Michael N. Barnett and Martha Finnemore, "The Politics, Power, and Pathologies of International Organizations," *International Organization* 53, no. 4 (1999): 699–32.

70. Robert O. Keohane, Stephen Macedo, and Andrew Moravcsik, "Democracy-Enhancing Multilateralism," *International Organization* 63, no. 1 (2009): 1–31.

3

Domestic and International Implications

SLAVERY, GENOCIDE, AND CIVIL WAR

THE INTERNATIONAL CRIMINAL Court (ICC) wrestles away from states a small part of a previously exclusive sovereign prerogative, namely criminal jurisdiction for a special group of crimes. Should coercive international institutions do more? What should be the scope of the authority of international institutions vis-à-vis states? What are the issues over which international institutions should be expected to trump states?

There may be no complete and irrevocable answer to this set of questions, but the agency problems highlighted in previous chapters suggest minimal guidelines for the scope of authority for international agents. In particular, they favor a restrictive conception of authority instead of an expansive one. But even a narrow conception of the scope of international institutions' power changes the authority of states with respect to their citizens and therefore changes the nature of the constitutional compact between citizens and domestic political institutions. In some cases, the delegation of authority to international institutions as secondary agents of justice will require constitutional amendments or a reinterpretation of the authority of different domestic institutions with respect to each other and international agents.

The chapter starts with a list of reasons in support of a restrictive conception of the authority of international institutions. Second, I discuss the constitutional challenges that a multiagent structure of political authority creates for traditional states. The final three sections apply this multiagent approach to the problems of modern slavery, genocide, and civil wars.

1. The Scope and Limits of International Authority

Judgments about the proper scope of the authority of international institutions must be responsive to four factors: the independent role states must play with respect to their citizens, the importance of preserving the stability of existing arrangements, the ability of international institutions to provide effective constraints on states, and concern for agency slippage. Views about the responsibilities of states vary, yet they overlap in one respect: The protection of the citizens' lives and personal security is one of the central, if not the central function, of any state.

This is the state capacity with which the citizens must be the most concerned, and they should support institutional structures that are more likely to offer reasonable assurance over the long run that their lives and security are protected. For reasons emphasized in Chapters 1 and 2, states alone do not offer adequate guarantees that they can fulfill this function without supervision and restraints from the outside. Therefore, individuals cannot entrust final and complete authority over the protection of their rights to their own states. States bear primary responsibility for the lives and security of their own citizens and each state must have wide powers to decide what the best way to discharge that responsibility is. The division of authority between states and international institutions must be such that the latter intervene only in situations of massive and widespread state failure to protect human rights, when their governments perpetrate harm, or when states are ineffective at preventing internal abuse inflicted by one group against another.

This high threshold of massive and widespread rights violations has several justifications. First, as primary agents, states require a large degree of independence to decide the best way to discharge their responsibilities toward their own citizens. This is both a functional requirement and a normative one: A state cannot have responsibility without authority, and broad sovereign independence is required by the right to self-government held collectively by the citizens of the state. Second, this threshold is justified as a relatively minor departure from the existing practice of states and international institutions. The value of preserving the stability of the existing institutional system precludes any radical change in the states system or the authority of international institutions. Otherwise, the cure risks becoming worse than the disease, by unraveling existing patterns of compliance with a relatively stable system of institutions. Large parts of the global population still rely on the existing system to provide them with substantial guarantors for peace, order, and security.

Preserving these hard-won gains requires a modest approach to international institution building to prevent the deterioration of law and order in parts of the world where they are the norm, and a worsening of conditions in parts of the world where they are scarce.

Third, the high threshold reflects a preoccupation with the ability of international institutions to successfully enhance the protection of human rights. Supra-state structures of any kind are a relatively new phenomenon if one takes a long-term historical perspective. Most have arisen out of peace settlements following World War II. The record of these structures of inducing states to behave according to widely shared norms is mixed. Of the many different international organizations states have experimented with over the last century, very few have had coercive capacities, and one of them, the ICC, is so new that we do not yet know how well it will perform its function. Of the remaining noncoercive organizations, some have been moderately successful at constraining state behavior while others have utterly failed. For example, the UN's record is not promising in many of its ambitious programs, particularly monitoring and protecting human rights.[1] The existing record of international institutions should inspire caution and skepticism for grand institutional schemes at the international level.

Adding to this concern about institutional capacity is the fourth issue: agency problems that invariably result from delegating authority to international institutions. Agency problems are bound to occur when citizens have difficulty monitoring and controlling the actions of their secondary international agents. Delegation often must pass through state representatives and their appointees; information about the actions of international institutions is costly and difficult to obtain; and electoral mechanisms for holding international representatives accountable are not always reliable. The more ambitious the institutional scheme, the harder it is to keep agency problems in check.

Consequently, coercive international institutions should enjoy a restrictive area of authority over states, limited to the protection of human rights identified with jus cogens norms. In the range of issues covered by jus cogens, state sovereignty must be limited and subject to external constraints. The balance of reasons suggests that citizens from different countries must divide authority between states and international institutions along these lines. But there

---

1. Thomas G. Weiss, *What's Wrong with the United Nations and How to Fix It*, 2nd ed. (Cambridge, UK: Polity, 2012); Michael Barnett and Martha Finnemore, *Rules for the World: International Organizations in Global Politics* (Ithaca, NY: Cornell University Press, 2004); David L. Bosco, *Five to Rule Them All: The UN Security Council and the Making of the Modern World* (New York: Oxford University Press, 2009).

may be a significant difference between what people in different countries *on balance have reason to do* and the division of authority *they actually consent to*. People could, for instance, grant international institutions too much authority or not enough, just as they could do the same in the case of various state institutions. The limits outlined here for the authority of international institutions serve as normative guidelines that aim to orient deliberation about the purpose and reach of international coercive arrangements and their institutional design.

States have and will enter international agreements for many purposes such as trade regulation, mutual aid, scientific cooperation, the preservation of historical sites, economic assistance, or the protection of marine life. Most of these agreements are noncoercive in the sense I have described them here, namely enforced by organizations with the ability to use force or the threat of force. An important feature of these agreements is their common "opt-out" clause, which allows individual states to withdraw from the agreements or organization. These agreements are similar to private contracts among individuals. States can choose whether or not to enter agreements, just as individuals do when they contract with each other, and can exit at will consistent with the requirements of the contract. By contrast, the authority of international organizations designed to enforce jus cogens norms must be nonoptional. Respecting the prohibition against genocide, war crimes, and crimes against humanity cannot be left to the discretion of individual states. Only in this way can international institutions play their role as insurance agents for individuals' rights in cases of massive state failure. Perhaps a case can be made that the range of norms that limit the behavior of states should be larger. But whatever the set of norms over which coercive international arrangements have authority, we can distinguish between lawlike international agreements that have nondiscretionary, universal applicability, and optional, consensual ones that have attributes more similar to private contracts among individuals than to public law. Such a new institutional order requires that many, if not most, states change the presumption in favor of the supremacy of domestic law and domestic political institutions. In practice, the process of shifting this presumption will be difficult and protracted. But it is necessary in order to make the division of labor between states and international institutions consistent with the interests and wishes of a self-governing citizenry, when the citizenry chooses to remove the exclusive prerogatives of states institutions. To make the authority of international institutions over states effective may require on occasion constitutional changes or changes in constitutional juridprudence. The United States is a telling case in that regard.

2. *Constitutional Interpretation and Change*

In some countries, constitutional clauses that make the state the supreme and final authority in all internal matters have reinforced the traditional understanding of sovereignty as ultimate, exclusive control over national boundaries. Such clauses have cultivated undivided loyalties among the citizenry aimed at supporting state power as the ultimate agent of justice. Consequently, individuals who embrace a dual or multiagent conception of sovereignty must shift their loyalties as well. While most states have relied on their citizens' unquestioned and undivided commitment in the past, they must now share the allegiance of their members with international institutions. This shift has important domestic institutional consequences.

For instance, the Constitution of the United States is interpreted by some as taking precedence over any international law or rule that it comes in conflict with. Constitutional scholar Michael Stokes Paulsen has argued that as a matter of constitutional interpretation, the US Constitution is always supreme over international law, and no external control can be exercised over the powers delegated to the three branches of government to decide when and if international law bears weight domestically. Only US officials, including the president, have the power to "interpret, apply, enforce—or disregard—international law," which means that the United States is bound by international law only if it chooses to be.[2] Under this interpretation, the only way that international law becomes binding in the United States is if the legislature adopts international treaties as domestic law, or if the president signs an executive statement in favor of the treaty having domestic legal power. In his controversial article, Paulsen is adamant that the implications of this domestic supremacy are clear. Nothing in international law constrains the law-making power of the United States, the manner in which it wages war, the treatment of its enemy combatants, or the treatment of its own citizens, despite the United States being party to the Hague and Geneva Conventions, VCLT, and a host of other international agreements whose explicit purpose is to regulate such conduct among states.[3] For example, "If Congress passes a Military Commissions Act of 2006 (MCA) that contradicts, or interprets narrowly, the Geneva Conventions or the Convention Against Torture, the MCA prevails over the Conventions as a matter of U.S. law."[4] The implications of this

---

2. Michael Stokes Paulsen, "The Constitutional Power to Interpret International Law," *Yale Law Journal* 118 (2008–09): 1762.

3. Ibid., 1769, 1795–96, 1826.

4. Ibid., 1776–77.

line of argument are significant, as Paulsen himself argues. Most treaties to which the United States is a signatory party have no force over the US government and its citizens, unless the Congress or the president make an explicit declaration to the contrary.

According to the divided sovereignty view, this understanding of the supremacy of domestic institutions and legal authority is misguided because it sabotages the ability of citizens to keep domestic institutions in check by resorting to the authoritative, compulsory, and automatic jurisdiction of international forums. Moreover, the text of the Constitution itself leaves room for a more sanguine perspective on the relationship of domestic law to that of international law. Article VI of the US Constitution states, for example, that "this Constitution, and the Laws of the United States which shall be made in Pursuance thereof; *and all Treaties made, or which shall be made, under the Authority of the United States*, shall be the supreme Law of the Land; and the Judges in every State shall be bound thereby, any Thing in the Constitution or Laws of any State to the Contrary notwithstanding."[5] This "supremacy clause," as it is known, was adopted in order to preempt conflicts between state law and federal law. Presumably intended also to protect the encroachment of a foreign power on the popular will, and the possible interference with democratic self-government by US citizens, this clause states expressly that international treaties *are* the supreme law of the land, allowing citizens to override domestic law by grants of authority to international treaties, which upon accession have domestic force.

The jurisprudence of Article VI is complicated, and scholars and judges disagree about the force of international law and about the extent to which international treaties into which the United States enters are self-executing—meaning they automatically become US law—or not. Many believe, with Paulsen, not only that international law and the decisions of international courts are not binding, but that they are moreover irrelevant to what US domestic institutions should do. For example, the International Court of Justice (ICJ) found twice that the United States was in violation of the Vienna Convention on Diplomatic Relations for not notifying the consulates of foreign officials charged with crimes in the United States. The individuals prosecuted argued that they were not able to get adequate legal representation in court due to this disregard for their rights of consular notification. Every member of the UN, including the United States, had agreed to comply with the decisions of the ICJ to which they are party. Despite this prior commitment

---

5. Emphasis mine.

to ICJ jurisdiction, the US courts refused to recognize the ICJ ruling as binding, and Chief Justice John Roberts said in a majority opinion that "nothing in the structure or purpose of the ICJ suggests that its interpretations were intended to be conclusive on our courts."[6] Demanding that when domestic and constitutional law conflict with international law, "U.S. government officials must, as a matter of legal obligation, side with the Constitution and against international law" forces us to ask whether this position is consistent with the plain meaning of Article VI of the US Constitution.[7]

Oona A. Hathaway, Sabria McElroy, and Sara Aronchick Solow show that the hostile attitude toward international law represents quite a reversal of the presumption *in favor* of international law that has operated throughout most of US history.[8] Between 1790 and 1947, the Supreme Court found that international treaties were self-executing in at least twenty-two cases.[9] The shift in jurisprudence occurred after World War II, when courts began to take a more skeptical approach to treaties regulating relations among states or between states and their citizens. Hathaway et al. speculate that this reversal is, in part, due to a "backlash against the emerging human rights revolution and the threat some feared it posed to racial segregation and Jim Crow."[10]

Whatever the source of the skepticism that feeds the current interpretation of the unconditional supremacy of the different branches of the US government over international law, such skepticism entrenches the authority of the federal government to the detriment of international institutions and ultimately that of US citizens, which are deprived of an important channel of political accountability. The jurisprudence that makes this skepticism possible is the mark of "extreme deference to national executive power and political institutions, and resistance to comity or international law as meaningful constraints on national prerogatives," as international law scholar Harold Hongu Koh has noted.[11] This division of authority between the federal government

---

6. *Sanchez-Llamas v. Oregon*, 548 U.S. 331 (2006) at 354.

7. Paulsen, "The Constitutional Power to Interpret International Law," 1765.

8. Oona A. Hathaway, Sabria McElroy, and Sara Aronchick Solow, "International Law at Home: Enforcing Treaties in U.S. Courts," *The Yale Journal of International Law Yale Journal of International Law* 37, no. 1 (2012): 53, 71.

9. Ibid., 57.

10. Ibid., 63.

11. Harold Hongju Koh, "International Law as Part of Our Law," *The American Journal of International Law* 98, no. 1 (January 1, 2004): 52.

and international institutions must be redrawn for the latter to function as secondary agents of the American people.

Remapping of the boundary of authority between states and international institutions cannot succeed if citizens themselves do not see divided sovereignty as vital to the protection of their own interests and the interests of other people around the world. And it seems there is a long way to go on this score. In November 2010 Oklahoma residents voted to amend their state constitution to prohibit judges from using international law in their decisions.[12] Such attempts by individual states or courts to block the applicability of international law make vivid the fact that citizens are very much wedded to the idea of the national authority as exclusive, supreme, and final.

Since the Constitution does say explicitly that both US law and international law are the law of the land, but does not say how conflicts between these two bodies of law must be resolved, the legislature and courts enjoy *at most* interpretive leeway to settle how international law may be best accommodated. But such leeway does not give courts the power to ignore, go against, or repeal the United States' commitment to international law, or otherwise reverse the Constitution on this issue. If the argument for divided sovereignty is right, this interpretation must lean more strongly toward the presumption of giving key international agreements, especially those that protect jus cogens norms, supremacy over domestic law.

When a people, engaged in another exercise of democratic self-government, appoint international agents as insurance against the failure of their primary agents, a conflict can arise between a constitutional clause that insists on the supremacy of domestic institutions and a grant of power to an outside organization that is permitted to override them. For example, the ICC statute allows it to override states that choose not to prosecute alleged criminals without adequate justification. If a head of state spearheads massive human rights violation while in office, and the national courts subsequently refuse to prosecute her based on, say, a constitutional clause that confers heads of state immunity, the ICC can override the national decision. In order to render the authority of coercive international institutions compatible with the exercise of domestic sovereignty, this conflict must be resolved by changing either the immunity-granting constitutional clause, or the constitutional jurisprudence that insists on the supremacy of the state institutions. Since the US Constitution is permissive on this issue, it seems that instead of a constitutional amendment, a

---

12. Garrett Epps, "Constitutional Myth #10: International Law Is a Threat to the Constitution," *The Atlantic*, July 28, 2011.

new constitutional jurisprudence that embraces the divided sovereignty perspective is called for.

Adopting the divided sovereignty perspective with respect to the authority of states and international institutions may thus transform the relationships citizens have to their own states by altering the constitutional compact in cases where such compact insists on the supremacy of domestic law. A new constitution can still delegate supreme authority to state institutions in most matters relevant to its citizens. But in addition, it must enumerate the powers over which specific international institutions precede or override the authority of the state, and the conditions under which they can do so. A constitutional amendment that would implement a new, dual conception of sovereignty represents a momentous shift in the perception of the role of state power with respect to the citizens of any given state. Moreover, constitutional changes are notoriously difficult, especially in the United States, partly by design and partly because of electoral apathy, but they are an essential step to ensure a more adequate protection of citizens' rights against abuse.

And while difficult, constitutional amendments or changes in constitutional interpretation are not an insurmountable obstacle. In fact, some countries had to contend with such change following accession to the ICC. As one would expect, accession is more difficult in countries that have constitutional constraints that conflict with international law. Such conflict creates additional delays for ratification, but ratification takes place nonetheless.[13] Japan had stringent constitutional constraints drafted following World War II that prohibited its support of any international treaty regulating the conduct of war. The inclusion of war crimes in the Rome Statute of the ICC has made the debates for the accession of Japan especially difficult and protracted within its national legislature, the bicameral Diet. Even after legislative changes in which Japan started slowly to recognize international agreements prosecuting jus cogens norms, a series of crimes remained unrecognized by Japan's criminal code. Japan resolved this issue by resorting to the ICC principle of complementarity, and deciding to refer crimes that its legal code does not recognize to the ICC for prosecution.[14] Rather than change its domestic laws, Japan opted to adopt procedural legislation that detailed the conditions

---

13. Jens Meierhenrich and Keiko Ko, "How Do States Join the International Criminal Court? The Implementation of the Rome Statute in Japan," *Journal of International Criminal Justice* 7, no. 2 (May 1, 2009): 233–56; Beth A. Simmons and Allison Danner, "Credible Commitments and the International Criminal Court," *International Organization* 64, no. 2 (2010): 245.

14. Meierhenrich and Ko, "How Do States Join the International Criminal Court?," 252–53.

under which it can turn individuals over to the ICC. While in the end, Japan's accession to the ICC did not require constitutional amendments, it did involve the renegotiation of fundamental principles of Japan's post–World War II jurisprudence in order to accommodate the new legal requirements of the ICC.[15] In this way, Japan was able to reconcile the conflicting imperatives of domestic and international law. The case of Japan shows that if individuals support and actively promote a dual conception of sovereign authority, they will be required to endorse a different perspective on the role of the state, the nature of the constitutional authority entrusted to state institutions, and limitations on that authority.

It may be that in the United States, as well as in other countries, changes in jurisprudence will be sufficient to accommodate the authority of international law more effectively than constitutional amendments. Whatever the ultimate path, jus cogens norms must act, substantively and procedurally, as a kind of supra-constitutional value system, constraining domestic constitutions and resolving any conflicts with domestic law in favor of the principles of international law they protect. That they are still far from achieving that function is illustrated by massive human rights abuses still taking place around the world: slavery, genocide, and severe violations of the rights of innocent civilians in times of civil war.

3. Slavery

Ethan A. Nadelmann has argued that "no other international prohibition regime so powerfully confirms the potential of humanitarian and similar moral concerns to shape global norms as does the regime against slavery and the slave trade."[16] Until a few centuries ago, slavery was both legal and commonplace. The United Kingdom, led by a strong coalition of domestic abolitionist forces, placed itself at the forefront of a global policing effort to abolish slavery. In the 1840s, the British Royal Navy employed between a sixth and a quarter of all its ships to stop the slave trade in international waters and it resorted to force when necessary. For example, when Brazil, the world's leading importer of African slaves, was reluctant to respect one of its bilateral agreements with Britain to refrain from transporting and dealing in slaves, "British naval vessels seized and destroyed slave ships in Brazilian harbors and threatened to

---

15. Ibid., 255.

16. Ethan A. Nadelmann, "Global Prohibition Regimes: The Evolution of Norms in International Society," *International Organization* 44, no. 4 (October 1, 1990): 491.

blockade Brazilian ports."[17] According to Nadelmann, the United Kingdom accomplished its aim of making Brazil reduce its involvement in the slave trade. The abolition of slavery and the slave trade was a success in persuading the world to officially denounce slavery as a scourge of a morally regressive past.

That past is back to haunt us. Slavery has been revived as a worldwide phenomenon of large proportions. Men, women, and children are bought and sold as property and work as forced labor, despite the fact that these practices are criminalized in most countries and in international law. The Walk Free Foundation, an Australian nonprofit that produced the first *Global Slavery Index* in 2013, estimates the total number of enslaved persons at 29.8 million.[18] These persons are lured by new and often fictitious job prospects in their own countries or abroad, and subsequently held against their will and coerced to work without pay on farms and in factories as forced labor, in private residences as domestic servants, and in brothels as sex slaves.[19] Torture, deprivation of food, degrading living conditions, rape and physical violence, and the threat of more abuse are hallmarks of human trafficking. They make the victims pliable and more likely to comply with the demands placed on them.

Slavery is big business today and a highly profitable one. Revenues are estimated at between $20 billion worldwide (ILO) and $31 billion (UN).[20]

---

17. Ibid., 492.

18. Walk Free Foundation, *Global Slavery Index 2013*, http://www.globalslaveryindex.org/ (accessed December 23, 2013). Other estimates place the total number at 27 million (US Department of State) and 21 million, respectively (International Labour Organization, ILO). On the challenges of estimating accurately the extent of illicit activities across borders, see Peter Andreas and Kelly M. Greenhill, eds., *Sex, Drugs, and Body Counts: The Politics of Numbers in Global Crime and Conflict* (Ithaca, NY: Cornell University Press, 2010); and Frank Laczko, "Data and Research on Human Trafficking," *International Migration* 43, nos. 1–2 (2005): 5–16. For a skeptical take on official estimates, see Ronald Weitzer, "The Social Construction of Sex Trafficking: Ideology and Institutionalization of a Moral Crusade," *Politics & Society* 35, no. 3 (September 1, 2007): 447–75 and David A. Feingold, "Trafficking in Numbers: The Social Construction of Human Trafficking Data," in *Sex, Drugs, and Body Counts: The Politics of Numbers in Global Crime and Conflict*, ed. Peter Andreas and Kelly M. Greenhill (Ithaca, NY: Cornell University Press, 2010), 46–74.

19. There is some debate about whether coercion is a necessary part of the definition of trafficking and forced labor. Jo Doezema, "Who Gets to Choose? Coercion, Consent, and the UN Trafficking Protocol," *Gender and Development* 10, no. 1 (March 1, 2002): 20–27. I consider coercion necessary for the definition of slavery.

20. ILO, *The Cost of Coercion*, May 12, 2009, http://www.ilo.org/declaration/WCMS_106268/lang--en/index.htm. See also http://www.unglobalcompact.org/docs/issues_doc/labour/Forced_labour/HUMAN_TRAFFICKING_-_THE_FACTS_-_final.pdf.

According to one source, the cost of a sex slave is, on average, $1,895 worldwide, while the yearly profit generated by a slave is around $29,000.[21] This represents a staggering rate of return of more than 15 times or 1500 percent. Human trafficking is so profitable, in fact, that some claim that unless drastic measures are taken to prevent human trafficking, it will surpass drug and arms trafficking in incidence and profitability to criminals.[22]

Human trafficking is facilitated by the lack of viable economic options, gender bias, and low cultural valuations of women. The victims come from countries afflicted by deep poverty and deprivation. Some victims are kidnapped, others deceived, and yet others are sold by their own families. The families who sell their children, especially girls, for money are sometimes misled by the possibility of better prospects, but often know full well the kind of abuse to which their children will be subjected. Girls as young as 4 years old are sold for prostitution and, if they later manage to escape their tormenters and return, they are rejected by their families who regard them as "damaged goods." According to ILO estimates, 55 percent of forced labor victims and 98 percent of sex trafficking victims are women and girls.[23] These dynamics are complemented by a large and increasing demand for slaves as domestic workers, in manufacturing, agricultural labor, and the sex industry.

Sex trafficking is a worldwide phenomenon and has received the greatest amount of attention. Women and girls are trafficked from Nepal to India, from Eastern Europe into Western Europe and the Middle East, and from Africa all over the world. Slavery outside of the sex industry is a larger problem in terms of absolute numbers and is no less disturbing.[24] One of the tragic stories of girls and women who are enslaved told by Sidharth Kara is that of Aye, who was 4 years old when she left with her mother from their Burmese village that had been attacked by government soldiers bent on eradicating her Shan hill tribe.[25] In Thailand, her mother looked for work. Both went to the factory of a Burmese couple they believed would offer them safety from hunger and abuse. Instead, they were separated, beaten, and enslaved. The girl worked in the factory for the next ten years, until she escaped during a period of particularly

---

21. Siddharth Kara, *Sex Trafficking: Inside the Business of Modern Slavery* (New York: Columbia University Press, 2010), 19.

22. Edward J. Schauer and Elizabeth M. Wheaton, "Sex Trafficking into the United States: A Literature Review," *Criminal Justice Review* 31, no. 2 (June 1, 2006): 146–69.

23. ILO, *The Cost of Coercion*.

24. David A. Feingold, "Human Trafficking," *Foreign Policy* no. 150 (September 1, 2005): 26–32.

25. Kara, *Sex Trafficking*, 216.

savage beating and physical abuse. In the factory, she was made to work from four in the morning until one in the morning. The goods she made were sold on the local market and traded aboard. Aye was kept sleep deprived and famished, without a bed or other basic necessities. In the shelter she eventually made it into at 14, she suffered nightmares, fits of anger, an eating disorder, and could not come to grips with the cruelty inflicted on her and other defenseless children like her.[26]

Slavery is one of the largest government institutional failures today. Many countries are failing dramatically in their responsibilities to protect their citizens' rights against enslavement by serving as countries of origin, transit, or destination for victims. In some of these countries, government officials are complicit in, facilitate, and benefit from trafficking. In a 2005 memorandum, President George W. Bush cited the Cambodian and Myanmar governments for failing to address the complicity of high political officials and the military in forced labor. The document also listed Ecuador, Kuwait, Saudi Arabia, and Venezuela for failing to devote "sufficient attention" to the problem of human trafficking.[27] Other countries are known to be deeply implicated. For example, Eritrea practices state-sponsored slavery by refusing to release those drafted into military service after the required 18 months, and by forcing them to perform forced labor for government officials as domestic servants.[28] North Korea represents an especially brutal case of state-mandated enslavement through its political prison camps.

North Korean prison camps house common criminals, along with people imprisoned for "hostility to the regime," and people who commit "famine-induced" crimes. The continuous mismanagement of the economy by North Korean leaders has ensured a more or less chronic state of food deprivation for the entire population, with periodic famines, persistent food shortages, and strict rationing.[29] Many individuals, desperate in search of food, engage in

26. Ibid., 216–19.

27. Ethan B. Kapstein, "The New Global Slave Trade," *Foreign Affairs*, November 1, 2006.

28. World Report, 2012. Human Rights Watch, Eritrea report, 2012. http://www.hrw.org/world-report-2012/world-report-2012-eritrea.

29. According to Rhoda E. Howard-Hassmann, during the famine from 1994 to 2000, between 3 to 5 percent of the population is estimated to have died. "State-Induced Famine and Penal Starvation in North Korea," *Genocide Studies and Prevention* 7, no. 2 (2012): 150. See also Marcus Noland, Sherman Robinson, and Tao Wang, "Famine in North Korea: Causes and Cures," *Economic Development and Cultural Change* 49, no. 4 (July 1, 2001): 741–67; Daniel Goodkind and Loraine West, "The North Korean Famine and Its Demographic Impact," *Population and Development Review* 27, no. 2 (June 1, 2001): 219–38.

"illegal" activities such as cultivating their own small crops, foraging for food, and selling food on the black market.[30]

Political prisoners are often imprisoned along with family members up to three generations. Their children are sometimes born in prison and never experience life outside it.[31] All prisoners are used for the production of food, commodities, and the manufacture of illegal drugs. This is done at the behest and considerable benefit of the political elites, who sell their products on the internal market and abroad. While they are not bought and sold for money, people in these prisons are summarily charged with farcical crimes and made to work in appalling conditions at starvation-level rations.[32] According to conservative estimates, out of 200,000 prisoners contained in camps, which represents 1 percent of North Korea's population of about 22 million, around 10 percent of these die of malnutrition and abuse every year.[33]

India is also a special case given the absolute number of the population enslaved within its borders. According to the Walk Free Foundation report, almost half of the world's slaves, or around 14 million, are trapped in debt bondage, bonded labor, and sexual slavery in India. Mauritania also stands apart. It is ranked number one in the index because it has the highest prevalence of slavery. Out of a population of only 3.8 million, between 120,000 and 140,000 people are estimated to be enslaved, and hereditary slavery is deeply entrenched.[34]

Pursuant to the Trafficking Victims Protection Act (TVPA) passed in 2000 by the US Congress, the United States ranks countries according to their willingness to address the problem of human trafficking. Tier 3 countries are those that do very little in light of available resources to address problems stemming from forced labor and sexual trafficking and are therefore at the bottom of this

---

30. Howard-Hassmann, "State-Induced Famine and Penal Starvation in North Korea," 152; Rhoda E. Howard-Hassman, "State Enslavement in North Korea" (unpublished manuscript, n.d.).

31. For a personal account of the only person born in prison known to have escaped, see Blaine Harden, *Escape from Camp 14: One Man's Remarkable Odyssey from North Korea to Freedom in the West* (New York: Penguin Books, 2013).

32. Howard-Hassman, "State Enslavement in North Korea."

33. Jasper Becker, *Rogue Regime: Kim Jong Il and the Looming Threat of North Korea* (New York: Oxford University Press, 2005), 87; John Feffer, "The Forgotten Lessons of Helsinki: Human Rights and U.S.-North Korean Relations," *World Policy Journal* 21, no. 3 (October 1, 2004): 33. See also Amnesty International, *Annual Report 2013: North Korea*, http://www.amnesty.org/en/region/north-korea/report-2013 (accessed December 24, 2013).

34. Walk Free Foundation, *Global Slavery Index 2013*.

ranking. Mauritania, China, Russia, Saudi Arabia, Libya, Syria, Democratic Republic of the Congo Zimbabwe, and North Korea are currently Tier 3 countries.[35] Surprisingly, India did not make the list. Although the countries ranked as Tier 3 do not have the largest number of slaves in absolute terms, they are considered the most unwilling to make efforts to reduce the problem within their borders.

Given these facts, what principles of regulation are appropriate for curbing slavery at the international level? The first thing to note is that slavery and human trafficking persist despite being prohibited by a number of international documents, including the Universal Declaration of Human Rights (1948), the jus cogens norms of VCLT (1969), the Rome Statute of the ICC (1998), and more recently in the UN Protocol to Prevent, Suppress and Punish Trafficking in Persons, Especially Women and Children, known as the Palermo Protocol (2000). Many international organizations have special task forces or rapporteurs dedicated to gathering data and making policy recommendations on human trafficking. For example, Ralf Emmers, Beth Greener-Barcham, and Nicholas Thomas report that in Southeast Asia a number of regional and transregional efforts such as the ASEAN (Association of Southeast Asian Nations) Regional Forum, Asia-Europe Meeting, and Bali Process are vehicles dedicated to sharing intelligence and expertise and coordinating anti-trafficking operations across borders.[36]

The second thing to note is that although the norms prohibiting slavery are robust and widely accepted, many of the international and domestic laws remain seriously underenforced, which is why the problem continues to be widespread in some parts of the world, particularly Southeast Asia, the Middle East, Eastern Europe, and Africa. Not only are laws poorly enforced, but also enforcement is often heavy-handed and hurts the victims of trafficking instead of helping them. Victims are treated like common criminals and arrested, imprisoned, deported, and humiliated by judicial and law-enforcement processes in which their special circumstances and vulnerabilities are poorly understood.[37]

35. US Department of State, *Trafficking in Persons Report: Tier Placements*, Office of Website Management, Bureau of Public Affairs, http://www.state.gov/j/tip/rls/tiprpt/2013/210548. htm, accessed June 19, 2013).

36. Ralf Emmers, Beth Greener-Barcham, and Nicholas Thomas, "Institutional Arrangements to Counter Human Trafficking in the Asia Pacific," *Contemporary Southeast Asia* 28, no. 3 (December 1, 2006): 490–511.

37. Dina Francesca Haynes, "Used, Abused, Arrested and Deported: Extending Immigration Benefits to Protect the Victims of Trafficking and to Secure the Prosecution of Traffickers," *Human Rights Quarterly* 26, no. 2 (May 1, 2004): 221–72.

Since the persistence of slavery is a state failure in the extreme, international organizations are justified in pressuring states to reduce the incidence of enslavement and to improve the observance of human rights. But what kinds of measures are available to international enforcement efforts given the modern characteristics of the crime? Given the diffuse and hidden nature of modern slavery, military intervention is a disproportionate and potentially counterproductive measure, yet many other responses remain available. Such responses require trade-offs with other international policing and cooperation efforts. First, global policing efforts resting with regional and international policing treaties can prioritize reducing the incidence of slavery and human trafficking by shifting resources away from the policing of drugs, terrorism, money laundering, and arms trafficking, or from military and economic aid, toward efforts to stop slavery and human trafficking.[38] International policing pacts can help states coordinate enforcement across borders and design enforcement strategies that are sensitive to the special needs of the trafficking victims.[39] Second, the ICC could pursue more aggressively private individuals and politicians who engage in human trafficking, such as North Korean or Eritrean political leaders, brothel owners in Mumbai who traffic in thousands of sex slaves, or the heads of mafia networks that operate across Europe and the Middle East. And third, states in which large numbers are trafficked or enslaved, such as India, should be asked to shift resources into policing human trafficking and be held accountable when they fail to do so at the International Court of Justice or a similar forum.

Some, such as David Feingold, doubt that stricter enforcement will reduce the incidence of slavery and human trafficking. "Convicting a local recruiter or transporter has no significant impact on the overall scale of trafficking," he argues. Given the nature of the trafficking business, "*if the incentives are right,*

---

38. Moral entrepreneurs who seek to make a dent in the practice of slavery and trafficking could take a page from the US guidebook in mobilizing worldwide support for the criminalization of drugs. Often misguided, heavy-handed, and ineffective, the process by which the United States socialized the international community into taking drug trafficking seriously and coordinating enforcement procedures across borders in the 1960s and 1970s is a good model of how to coalesce support for a contested issue. In fact, the United States was so successful that the modern transnational architecture for policing crime that now deals with terrorism, counterfeit products, guns, toxic waste, and money was built on early efforts to monitor and suppress the drug trade. See Peter Andreas and Ethan Nadelmann, *Policing the Globe: Criminalization and Crime Control in International Relations* (New York: Oxford University Press, 2008), 37–46.

39. These policing efforts could be modeled after the weapons inspection programs currently undertaken by the UN and member countries. Kara suggests that such a force can conduct "aggressive investigations and raids" on locations of forced prostitution and slavery. Kara, *Sex Trafficking*, 210–11.

he or she is instantly replaced, and the flow of people is hardly interrupted."[40] Feingold's pessimism is not warranted, however. Effective policing works precisely by changing the incentives of those who engage in criminal activities.[41] Increasing the costs to human traffickers would help to invert their risk–reward calculation and reduce the attractiveness of slavery and bondage. For genocide and crimes committed during a civil war, the stakes are different.

4. Genocide

If no one advocates humanitarian intervention to end slavery, few deny that it is justified in the case of genocide. According to the UN Genocide Convention of 1948, genocide is defined as "any of the following acts committed with intent to destroy, in whole or in part, a national, ethnical, racial or religious group, as such: killing members of the group; causing serious bodily or mental harm to members of the group; deliberately inflicting on the group conditions of life, calculated to bring about its physical destruction in whole or in part; imposing measures intended to prevent births within the group; [and] forcibly transferring children of the group to another group." The first draft of the Convention included the purging en masse of political opponents, but due to pressure from the Soviet Union the language referring to politically motivated genocide was removed.[42]

The actual occurrence of genocide or its likelihood does not constitute an all-things-considered reason to intervene. Rather, the occurrence or likelihood of genocide meets one of the five criteria for just war: *just cause*. For intervention to be legitimate, the other criteria must be met, such as *right intent, proportional force, last resort, reasonable prospect of success*, and *right authority*. The empirical record shows that especially the last two of these conditions are difficult to accomplish, which means that even in the case of mass killings, intervention may not always be available.[43]

---

40. Feingold, "Human Trafficking," 30, emphasis added.

41. Elizabeth M. Wheaton, Edward J. Schauer, and Thomas V. Galli, "Economics of Human Trafficking," *International Migration* 48, no. 4 (2010): 114–41. This point is valid ceteris paribus, that is, assuming that the demand for slavery is elastic to price changes and that other conditions won't affect the demand in the opposite direction.

42. Robert Gellately and Ben Kiernan, eds., *The Specter of Genocide: Mass Murder in Historical Perspective* (New York: Cambridge University Press, 2003), 267.

43. Taylor B. Seybolt, *Humanitarian Military Intervention: The Conditions for Success & Failure* (New York: Oxford University Press, 2007).

The most pressing issue concerning intervention at present is right authority. The institutional basis for intervention in the case of genocide is weak, with the UN and its Security Council assuming ultimate responsibility to intervene. NATO or coalitions of member states typically contribute military power to enforce the Security Council mandates. Several reasons make this institutional setup unreliable. First, the mandate of the Security Council according to the UN Charter is not to protect individuals against violence but to preserve international peace and security.[44] Yet many cases of genocide do not threaten international peace, strictly speaking, as the exchange between Larry May on one side, and Andrew Altman and Christopher Heath Wellman on the other side illustrates.

Larry May has defended a sophisticated principle of regulation that justifies intervention along the lines of the Security Council mandate. May argues that constraining or even invading another state is only justified if the latter has failed to uphold the "international harm principle."[45] In addition to wars, May argues that genocides and crimes against humanity also fall under the international harm principle to the extent that they cause harm to the international community, and affect humanity as a whole. For instance, on this account, to contemplate as a failure of international law the genocide perpetrated by a state's political authorities against its citizens, one would have to make the case that the genocide is such a grievous crime that it victimizes humanity as whole. This is how the international prosecution of the Nazis during the Nuremberg Trials was, in part, justified.

But as Andrew Altman and Kit Wellman observe, this justification is not successful insofar as it fails to make a case that crimes committed by governments against their own citizens, such as the Nazi crimes against Jewish people, victimize humanity as a whole. Most of the world was unaffected by the genocide taking place in Germany. The crime harmed the humanity of the Jewish victims, but it is a leap to argue that it hurt humanity as a whole.[46] The point is not that Germany should be allowed to do whatever it wants, or that the Nazi crimes should have been immune from prosecution under international law, but that the principle of regulation grounded in international

---

44. Article 24 of the UN Charter states that "its Members confer on the Security Council primary responsibility for the maintenance of international peace and security."

45. Larry May, *Crimes against Humanity: A Normative Account* (New York: Cambridge University Press, 2004), 80–95.

46. Andrew Altman and Christopher Heath Wellman, "A Defense of International Criminal Law," *Ethics* 115, no. 1 (October 2004): 41–42.

harm does not allow international agents to take action in cases of harms that governments commit against their own citizens.

Altman and Wellman analogize May's understanding of sovereignty, according to which interference or limitation is only justified in cases of harm to outsiders, to Joel Feinberg's analysis of the moral limits of domestic law. For Feinberg, the state can punish those who harm others, but they cannot punish individuals for harm to themselves, because that would be an unjustified restriction of individual autonomy. If one conceives of state autonomy in these terms, the authority of states should be protected against paternalistic interference until and unless they harm persons outside the state.

Altman and Wellman reject this view and rightly so.[47] States are not analogous to individuals because they are not undifferentiated wholes. Citizens of the state can harm one another, or can be harmed by state institutions. States have authority over their citizens by virtue of protecting their security and their basic rights, at a minimum. If the government of a state fails to prevent, prosecute, and punish such violations, it has failed to take seriously one of its main legitimate functions. When states are unwilling or unable to exercise the prerogative of their sovereignty and curb internal abuse, their inaction provides a rationale for limiting sovereignty from above. Stopping or preventing ongoing genocides within a state, on this account, is not justified by the harm genocide causes to humanity as a whole, but by the failure of a state to fulfill its responsibility to its citizens.

The mission of the Security Council, that of preserving first and foremost international peace, can be read as an application of the international harm principle. Genocides do not always or in most cases threaten international peace. They take place inside national borders, and therefore the Security Council can always excuse itself by arguing that it lacks the justification to intervene, as indeed it did in the case of Rwanda, leaving people exposed to massive human rights violations. Moreover, protecting human rights through humanitarian intervention and protecting international peace can come into conflict, since humanitarian interventions to stop genocides are, in effect, international wars. Therefore, the stated mission of the Security Council can work against intervening in cases of genocide.

If the mandate of the Security Council is a first obstacle to preventing or stopping massive human rights violations, the voting structure of the Security Council, with veto power allocated to its five permanent members, is a second obstacle. More often than not, this veto system has resulted in paralysis when

---

47. Ibid., 45–46.

intervention to prevent genocide would have been warranted. The veto power has been used to prevent military action in countries where one of the council members has strong economic interests. For instance, in February 2012, as the Syrian government was brazenly carrying out attacks on the civilian population in the city of Homs, Russia and China were the only states to veto a Security Council resolution that backed an Arab League peace plan aimed at ending the violence. Russia and China claimed that such a resolution would represent an unjustified interference with the sovereignty of the Syrian state.[48] However, both nations have economic and security interests in the area. According to reports, Russia has signed a $550 million deal with Syria for the supply of aircraft, and has billions of dollars' worth of defense contracts in the country, including a naval base.[49] At the time of the first rejected resolution, the toll of the Syrian conflict was estimated to be around 5,000 deaths, including women and children. Even this early on, it was clear to anyone willing to pay attention that the Syrian civil war was a train wreck that was going to result in massive devastation and suffering. Two years later, at the end of 2013, the death toll has surpassed 100,000, the number of refugees 2,000,000, and the number of internally displaced persons 4,250,000.[50] The actions of the Syrian government have not yet been declared jus cogens violations liable to trigger ICC prosecution and humanitarian intervention, but according to multiple accounts, the atrocities committed very likely qualify as such. This fact does not make much difference at the Security Council, where veto power means that even in cases of massive abuses, any action can be derailed if deemed disadvantageous to the interests of one of the five permanent members.

The third obstacle is the fact that UN forces are staffed by the militaries of developing countries that are poorly trained and equipped, and that these militaries occasionally engage in human rights violations themselves. For instance, UN forces have been reported on more than one occasion to engage in sex trafficking and to trade protection and food for sexual favors.[51] In the

---

48. Neil Macfarquhar and Anthony Shadid, "Russia and China Block U.N. Action on Syrian Crisis," *The New York Times*, February 4, 2012.

49. Harvey Morris, "Russia's Reasons for Saying 'No' on Syria," *International Herald Tribune*, January 31, 2012.

50. Norimitsu Onishi, "Syria Seen as Most Dire Refugee Crisis in a Generation," *The New York Times*, November 23, 2013.

51. Warren Hoge, "Congo Peacekeeper Sex Scandal: Investigators Said to Be Threatened," *The New York Times*, December 17, 2004; Colum Lynch, "U.N. Faces More Accusations of Sexual Misconduct," *The Washington Post*, March 13, 2005.

absence of a reliable military force to intervene, genocides and crimes against humanity are problems without a solution.

The institutional setup at the international level must change if massive violations of human rights are to be effectively reduced. At the very least, the structure and voting rights of the Security Council must be revised, and its mission must more clearly prioritize action for massive human rights abuses, including intervention in countries that are unwilling or unable to prevent such abuses. Given the path dependence of institutional change, it is unlikely that the Security Council will radically alter its character. Alternatively, a new institutional arm of the UN, or an organization outside of it, could be empowered to make judgments about the legitimacy of intervention in specific cases and to assemble the military force to intervene. Whatever the institutional choice, a secondary agent at the international level must more effectively embody the power to prevent states from killing their own citizens or step in when the latter are incapable of defending citizens against genocide.

5. Civil Wars and Failed States

If the case for intervening in instances of genocide is relatively straightforward, the case for intervention in civil war is more ambiguous, despite the fact that civil wars are rife with massive human rights violations. Civil wars are military conflicts between domestic groups that fight for control of political power within a country. They have been traditionally considered internal matters for which outside intervention is not justified. This is how the UN secretary-general justified the organization's policy of nonintervention during the Rwandan genocide, for example.[52]

Despite the general rhetoric, civil wars often meet the "just cause" threshold for military intervention, because the costs to innocent human life are practically indistinguishable in situations of civil war from other situations in which massive human rights violations occur *and* control over political power is not at stake. But this is not the view of political philosopher Michael Walzer, who insists that civil wars are tests of collective self-determination and, as such, must preclude the engagement of outsiders. Yet civil wars are often excuses for each party in the conflict to target tens of thousands or more innocent civilians from the opposing camp for slaughter or abuse. Talk of the importance of self-determination during civil war only obscures the large problems of state failure to protect human life during civil war.

---

52. Barnett and Finnemore, *Rules for the World*, 121–22.

Walzer defends the presumption against noninterference in the case of civil wars by arguing for protecting the integrity of the political community engaged in an act of self-transformation. The integrity of the community must be protected, Walzer says, because it reflects "the rights of contemporary men and women to live as members of a historic community and to express their inherited culture through political forms worked out among themselves."[53] Political institutions reflect this long-standing process of identity formation for a community, and outsiders must presume a fit between them and the values and interests of the citizens.[54] When outsiders intervene, they deny communal integrity and thus the rights of men and women living in that community to shape their own history and political institutions. Outsiders can only intervene when the absence of a fit between the citizens and the government is "radically apparent."[55] The lack of fit is apparent when a government massacres or enslaves its own citizens.[56]

Walzer claims that during a civil war, it is difficult to discern for outsiders if there is a lack of fit between the government and its people. With the exception of the case in which one foreign power intervenes on behalf of one side, and therefore intervention would be justified on behalf of the other side, civil wars should be left to unfold without outside interference. Walzer uses the example of Nicaragua in 1978–1979, when revolutionary forces had used the brief period in between two successive civil wars to regroup, re-arm, and broaden their support base. Had they not been left to their own devices, it would have been difficult for "this internal process of bargaining and commitment" to take place and come to a conclusion.[57] Therefore, intervention "would have violated the right of the Nicaraguans as a group to shape their own political institutions and the right of individual Nicaraguans to live under institutions so shaped."[58]

In civil wars, it is impossible to know whether the people support the government or the rebels, Walzer argues. If a government stays in power long enough, that may be a sign that it finds widespread support among the population. "There is no point," Walzer says, "at which foreigners can point to a

53. Michael Walzer, "The Moral Standing of States: A Response to Four Critics," *Philosophy and Public Affairs* 9, no. 3 (Spring 1980): 211.

54. Ibid., 212.

55. Ibid., 214.

56. Ibid., 217.

57. Ibid., 219.

58. Ibid., 220.

tyrannical regime and say, 'Self-determination, has clearly failed; there is nothing to do but intervene.'" [59] The right of self-determination places constraints on justified intervention and most civil wars fit within those constraints.

Against Walzer, I want to argue that the lack of fit is not the right criterion to assess whether intervention is justified. This is certainly not because a right to self-determination does not matter. Walzer is right that it does, but it cannot trump the concern for large groups of innocent bystanders who are at risk of being killed and who often are killed. Moreover, there are plenty of situations in which a fit exists between the people and their government, in the sense that a majority supports the government in power or at least does not actively oppose it, and they also support (or fail to oppose) the elimination of a minority through genocide.

Thus, Walzer is wrong to resist intervention in civil wars for two reasons: (1) The government has a monopoly on the means of force and therefore an undisputed advantage to squash and fight off any internal challenges to its legitimacy, no matter how justified, and (2) civil wars often involve large-scale violations of human rights. William Reno has found that in Sierra Leone, Revolutionary United Front (RUF) insurgents attacked 1 child for every 3.89 adults.[60] The conflicts in Kosovo, Rwanda, and Syria show how wrong civil wars can go when left to follow their own path and what can happen when a carefully timed intervention takes place, as it did in Libya. In those cases, self-determination must become a side issue.

In Syria, the government is deploying its monopoly on the means of aggression to subdue a population that is revolting against dictatorial rule, the lack of civil and political rights, and low standards of living. The conflict that has now lasted two years has produced over 100,000 dead, millions of refugees in neighboring countries and displaced persons, and continuing chaos, insecurity, and instability. While the opposition movement is responsible for some of the violence and deaths, the majority is attributable to the government of Bashar al-Assad, who is holding onto power at all cost. Allowing the parties to this conflict to duke it out, as Walzer recommends, would result in many more victims. The imbalance of power between the government in possession of fighter jets, cluster bombs, and torture chambers and the opposing forces that have few resources and sporadic access to foreign weaponry would ensure

---

59. Ibid., 222.

60. William Reno, "Persistent Insurgencies and Warlords," in *Ungoverned Spaces: Alternatives to State Authority in an Era of Softened Sovereignty*, ed. Anne Clunan and Harold Trinkunas (Stanford, CA: Stanford University Press, 2010), 64.

many more deaths among those who are not loyal to the ruling elites. Amidst the chaos, the UN Security Council refuses to take action.

By contrast, in Libya, early on during the civil war, the Security Council placed sanctions, an arms embargo, and an asset freeze on Libya. It had also referred Quaddafi's crimes against humanity to the International Criminal Court in The Hague. On March 17, 2011, the Security Council, at the request of the Arab League, imposed a no-fly zone and mandated "all necessary measures" to protect civilians.[61] NATO assumed command of the intervening forces, and within a few months of the beginning of the revolt, it saved thousands of lives in likely casualties from a protracted civil war and it allowed the opposition forces in Libya to organize and defeat Quaddafi's regime. Operation "Unified Protector," which is the name of NATO's mission in Libya, was successful in its three tasks: policing the arms embargo, patrolling the no-fly zone, and protecting civilians. It cost much less than similar interventions and ended within months.[62]

Not all civil wars are triggered by genuine grievances, as the Syrian or Libyan conflicts were. According to economist Paul Collier's research, the warring parties in many civil wars use the language of oppression, democracy, and civil rights, but want nothing more than to usurp political power in order to take turns preying on national resources. "A flagrant grievance," Collier says, "is to a rebel movement what an image is to a business."[63] Political scientist Robert H. Bates confirms this finding. Civil wars are often triggered by the ruling elites when widespread predation of national resources rather than taxation produces higher benefits for them.[64] Whatever the reasons people engage in civil wars, they last an average of seven years, inflict tremendous loss of life and mental harm on the populations caught in them, and take the countries in which they occur twenty-one years backward in terms of economic development. A country such as DR Congo, which has been mired in

61. Ivo H. Daalder and James G. Stavridis, "NATO's Victory in Libya," *Foreign Affairs*, March 1, 2012, http://www.foreignaffairs.com/articles/137073/ivo-h-daalder-and-james-g-stavridis/natos-victory-in-libya.

62. Alex J. Bellamy, "Libya and the Responsibility to Protect: The Exception and the Norm," *Ethics & International Affairs* 25, no. 3 (2011): 263–69; James Pattison, "The Ethics of Humanitarian Intervention in Libya," *Ethics & International Affairs* 25, no. 3 (2011): 271–77; Thomas G. Weiss, "RtoP Alive and Well after Libya," *Ethics & International Affairs* 25, no. 3 (2011): 287–92.

63. Paul Collier, *The Bottom Billion: Why the Poorest Countries Are Failing and What Can Be Done About It* (New York: Oxford University Press, 2007), 24.

64. Robert H. Bates, *When Things Fell Apart: State Failure in Late-Century Africa* (New York: Cambridge University Press, 2008).

civil war for decades, will need fifty years of uninterrupted peace to get back to the income level it had reached in 1960.[65] For many of the already poor African states that experience cyclical periods of internal military conflict, the effects are devastating. Going through one civil war doubles a country's chances of relapsing into civil conflict later, after the initial hostilities have ceased.[66]

Civil wars lead to the breakdown of law and order and ultimately to failed states. The Fund for Peace produces a yearly index that ranks countries according to twelve groups of indicators. States are scored on a series of functional indicators related to human security, public health, infrastructure, group grievances, policing, administration, and governance functions. The higher the score, the higher they rank on the failed state index. In 2012 at the top of this ranking one finds states such as Somalia, DR Congo, Chad, Afghanistan, Sudan, Burundi, and Ivory Coast. These states have either disintegrated or lost control over significant portions of their territory due to internal struggles between insurgencies, often directed at the government.[67]

What principles of regulation can guide international institutions in the case of states affected by civil wars? A number of different answers have surfaced: (1) stop ongoing and mass violence and protect innocent bystanders caught in the trap of civil war (military intervention); (2) rebuild state capacity of the preexisting state (state building); (3) divide the territory into ethnically homogeneous, self-governing wholes (partition); and (4) foster shared governance among the parties to the conflict (power sharing). Not all of these solutions are compatible, since rebuilding the capacity of the existing state comes into conflict with state partition. The last two (partition and shared governance) require negotiated settlements or treaties. All solutions demand the involvement of some international agents.

Military intervention to stop massive human rights abuses during civil war has all the potential and pitfalls of any military intervention. The solutions for civil wars in failed states must include, just as in the case of genocide, efforts to stop the killing and displacement of vast populations, to provide security and humanitarian corridors, and to protect the indigenous or minority rights of those who may be especially targeted during conflicts. Intervention can only succeed when international agents show a strong commitment to curbing

---

65. Collier, *The Bottom Billion*, 34.

66. Ibid., 27.

67. Jens Meierhenrich, "Forming States After Failure," in *When States Fail: Causes and Consequences*, ed. Robert I. Rotberg (Princeton, NJ: Princeton University Press, 2003), 4–5.

abuses and deploy the necessary force to back up that commitment. But assuming that intervention to prevent genocide and crimes against humanity succeeds (a high bar), civil wars and failed states present many other challenges. For one, under civil war circumstances order breaks down completely and anarchy takes root. Even if the fighting temporarily stops due to outside military intervention, long-term solutions are required to reduce the likelihood that it will start again. This is why for a long time, rebuilding state capacity looked like a desirable goal for international peacekeepers.

State building goes beyond preserving ceasefire, peacekeeping, and supervising a negotiated settlement. It requires those who intervene to engage in long-term capacity building for government institutions in order to restore the state to normal functioning. As recently as 2005, Stephen D. Krasner and Carlos Pascual urged the United States and other Western nations to take a more active approach in state building in failed and collapsed states, by adopting a gradual process of state reorganization that must culminate with "the creation of law and institutions of a market democracy," which includes "tax systems, banks, regulatory policies...constitutions, political structures, parties and electoral processes,...courts, police and penal systems to create the rule of law."[68] Others similarly urge the United States to serve as a "reluctant imperialist" and bring good governance to places that lack it, and argue that international institutions should reconstruct state structures to ensure stability and prevent a relapse into internal conflict and disorder.[69] The UN trusteeship system was set up by the UN Charter and has evolved, in part, to oversee state building in postconflict societies and offer governance in societies that are unable to govern themselves.

Many analyses show that this approach is misguided. Developed nations have engaged in various programs of state reconstruction in the past decades, and the results have been uniformly disappointing. The motivations to engage in such programs have been various. At one end, Western nations are concerned that failed states threaten their own security and welfare, primarily by acting as incubators of terrorism. Although the point is still disputed, some research

---

68. Stephen D. Krasner and Carlos Pascual, "Addressing State Failure," *Foreign Affairs* 84, no. 4 (2005): 159. See also Susan Rose Ackerman, "Establishing the Rule of Law," in *When States Fail: Causes and Consequences*, ed. Robert I. Rotberg (Princeton, NJ: Princeton University Press, 2003), 182–221.

69. Sebastian Mallaby, "The Reluctant Imperialist: Terrorism, Failed States, and the Case for American Empire," *Foreign Affairs* 81, no. 2 (2002): 2; John R. Heilbrunn, "Paying the Price of Failure: Reconstructing Failed and Collapsed States in Africa and Central Asia," *Perspectives on Politics* 4, no. 1 (2006): 135–50.

shows that states facing chronic state failures are more likely to host groups that engage in transnational terrorist attacks.[70] At the other end, many are worried for the people living in failed states. Somalia, the poster child of failed states, continues to struggle with widespread lawlessness, crime, terrorism, and insecurity, and has placed at the top of the failed state index for five years in a row. State failure can also be contagious, dragging neighboring states into instability, chaos, and military conflict. The DR Congo failure in 1998 spread violence to seven other neighboring states.[71] The weakening of state institutions in Ivory Coast is attributed, in part, to problems in Liberia and Sierra Leone and has had effects on many of its close and more distant neighbors.[72]

State building has not gone the way foreign intervenors want for a variety of reasons. Unlike traditional peacekeeping, which focuses on restoring peace and security, state reconstruction aims to recapture the monopoly of force and rebuild state institutions. Reconstruction projects have applied a one-size-fits-all model by using the bureaucratic and policy blueprints of Western states that were a poor fit for the local conditions in failed states. Electoral competition has seldom resulted in representativeness and accountability, but rather has served to usher in authoritarian politicians who have replicated the patterns that led to conflicts in the first place.[73] Political elites often have vested interests in maintaining instability and disorder because they benefit from it, and without changing the incentives they face, they cannot be counted on as partners who will promote the long-term institution building that leads to peace and prosperity.[74] Transitional political institutions may compete with local institutions or undermine the conditions for their legitimacy. Top-down institutional building that dismisses the contribution of local solutions to law, security, and economic development alienates the population from rebuilding workable institutions and subverts popular representation and accountability.

---

70. James A. Piazza, "Incubators of Terror: Do Failed and Failing States Promote Transnational Terrorism?" *International Studies Quarterly* 52, no. 3 (2008): 469–88; Ken Menkhaus and Jacob N. Shapiro, "Non-State Actors and Failed States," in *Ungoverned Spaces: Alternatives to State Authority in an Era of Softened Sovereignty*, ed. Anne Clunan and Harold Trinkunas (Stanford, CA: Stanford University Press, 2010), 77–94.

71. Adekeye Adebajo and Ismail Rashid, eds., *West Africa's Security Challenges: Building Peace in a Troubled Region* (Boulder, CO: Lynne Rienner, 2004).

72. United Nations Development Program (UNDP), "The Conflict in Côte d'Ivoire and Its Effect on West African Countries: A Perspective from the Ground," July 2011.

73. Pierre Englebert and Denis M. Tull, "Postconflict Reconstruction in Africa: Flawed Ideas about Failed States," *International Security* 32, no. 4 (2008): 112, 115–18.

74. Ibid., 121.

A more fundamental question raised by these analyses is whether states should be resurrected at all in places where they fail or collapse. As many scholars point out, the Western state model has never been successful in other parts of the world. It is difficult to argue that states have "failed" in Africa in particular, since following decolonization, they hardly ever succeeded.[75] With artificial boundaries, bureaucratic organizations inherited from colonists, and cultural and socioeconomic structures that did not mesh well with the new forms of governance, most of the newly independent African states have struggled to gain control over their territory, function democratically, promote development, provide security, and maintain peace. Given the historical record, it may be better to explore alternatives to rebuilding existing failed states. Peacekeepers must create conditions for a negotiated settlement that leaves space at the table for alternative forms of governance and for the reorganization of political units. Such a process must particularly recognize and harness local institutional solutions for order, governance, and the rule of law coming from domestic groups.[76]

One of these institutional solutions is shared governance. Shared governance consists of apportioning decision-making rights in government among two or more warring factions. Bosnia, the Philippines, and Northern Ireland are cited as cases of successful power-sharing arrangements post–civil war.[77] Carolin Hartzell and Matthew Hoddie have looked at thirty-eight civil wars concluded since World War II and argued that the more dimensions in which power is shared (political, economic, military and territorial), the more likely the negotiated settlement will last. Power sharing promotes moderate and cooperative behavior and restores a sense of security and trust among former enemies.[78]

---

75. Ibid., 111–18; Christopher Clapham, "The Global-Local Politics of State Decay," in *When States Fail: Causes and Consequences*, ed. Robert I. Rotberg (Princeton, NJ: Princeton University Press, 2003), 77–93.

76. Rosa Ehrenreich Brooks, "Failed States, or the State as Failure?," *The University of Chicago Law Review* 72, no. 4 (October 1, 2005): 1159–96; Meierhenrich, "Forming States After Failure," 153–69; Jeffrey Herbst, "Let Them Fail: State Failure in Theory and Practice," in *When States Fail: Causes and Consequences*, ed. Robert I. Rotberg (Princeton, NJ: Princeton University Press, 2003), 302–18; Phil Williams, "Here Be Dragons," in *Ungoverned Spaces: Alternatives to State Authority in an Era of Softened Sovereignty*, ed. Anne Clunan and Harold Trinkunas (Stanford: CA: Stanford University Press, 2010), 34–54.

77. Caroline Hartzell and Matthew Hoddie, "Institutionalizing Peace: Power Sharing and Post-Civil War Conflict Management," *American Journal of Political Science* 47, no. 2 (April 1, 2003): 318–32.

78. Ibid., 318, 320, 321.

Some are skeptical that shared governance is workable, because civil war permanently undermines the possibility of cooperation among warring parties. Chaim Kaufmann argues that more often than not, the solution lies with partition, which requires separating opposing groups into demographically homogeneous, defensible enclaves.[79] This solution often involves large population transfers so that ethnic minorities do not become trapped in enclaves with majorities from the opposing sides. By contrast, power sharing amounts to rebuilding the state, but it does nothing to increase trust among the parties or to reduce their tendency to undermine one another once the peacekeepers leave, in Kaufmann's view. Although partition involves large costs, it is still a better overall alternative because it is the only way to stop violence and maintain a lasting peace. "Separation," Kaufmann says, "is the worst solution, except for all the others."[80]

Although these studies seem to provide conflicting recommendations, a more nuanced analysis of the empirical record reveals that partition and power sharing can both work, but they require different background conditions in order to be successful.[81] In fact, different societies require markedly different solutions to conflict resolution based on their history, institutional culture, and intergroup attitudes.[82] Thus, international agents that facilitate and monitor negotiated peace settlements face complexity and uncertainty related to the best course of action for each individual conflict situation.[83]

The most important role international agents can play is to facilitate the commitment of parties to a conflict to whatever solution they come to endorse. Barbara F. Walter has argued that third parties can provide essential guarantees that the groups in a negotiated settlement will abide by their

---

79. Chaim Kaufmann, "Possible and Impossible Solutions to Ethnic Civil Wars," *International Security* 20, no. 4 (April 1, 1996): 137; James D. Fearon, "Testimony to U.S. House of Representatives, Committee on Government Reform, Subcommittee on National Security, Emerging Threats, and International Relations on 'Iraq: Democracy or Civil War?'" September 15, 2006. For a critical take on partition, see Nicholas Sambanis, "Partition as a Solution to Ethnic War: An Empirical Critique of the Theoretical Literature," *World Politics* 52, no. 4 (2000): 437–83.

80. Kaufmann, "Possible and Impossible Solutions to Ethnic Civil Wars," 170.

81. Alan J. Kuperman, "Is Partition Really the Only Hope? Reconciling Contradictory Findings About Ethnic Civil Wars," *Security Studies* 13, no. 4 (2004): 314–49.

82. Sammy Smooha and Theodor Hanf, "The Diverse Modes of Conflict-Regulation in Deeply Divided Societies," *International Journal of Comparative Sociology* 33, nos. 1–2 (March 1, 1992): 26–47.

83. Stephen John Stedman, "Spoiler Problems in Peace Processes," *International Security* 22, no. 2 (1997): 5–53.

promises.[84] In the absence of a third party to monitor and enforce the terms of the settlement, at least temporarily, negotiated settlements fail because a ceasefire that requires parties to put down their weapons also eliminates their ability to self-enforce the agreement.[85] In the absence of outside guarantees, no side wants to make itself vulnerable to the noncompliance of the other side, and belligerents either refuse to negotiate or walk out if a third party cannot commit itself to enforce the agreement. Otherwise, enemies in a civil war almost always choose to fight until the end.[86]

To sum up, the lack of fit between a government and its people is not an adequate criterion for intervention. What matters is whether the civilian population is in immediate and foreseeable danger, whether thousands or tens of thousands of people are likely to lose their lives, and whether whole states can be expected to descend into chaos and terror and ultimately to fail their citizens. Interventions in cases of civil war work best when they have modest aspirations and focus on preventing the ongoing violence and on enforcing peace settlements, rather than reflect the more ambitious goal of helping states rebuild their former political structures or create new structures based on the Western state model. The first of these, preventing violence and ensuring lasting peace, is difficult enough, without the extra burden of helping to create institutions from scratch based on models that may not be suited to the culture and history of the place experiencing the strain of conflict.

6. Conclusion

Slavery, genocide, and civil war do not lend themselves to easy solutions. But as long as states engage in these practices or turn a blind eye to those inside their borders that do, there is a role for international institutions to reduce the human costs of such activities. Existing institutional schemes that purport to address these problems are inadequate due to the ambiguous nature of the

---

84. Barbara F. Walter, "The Critical Barrier to Civil War Settlement," *International Organization* 51, no. 3 (July 1, 1997): 335–64.

85. Ibid., 336; Michael W. Doyle and Nicholas Sambanis, "International Peacebuilding: A Theoretical and Quantitative Analysis," *The American Political Science Review* 94, no. 4 (December 2000): 779. This is consistent with both Hartzell and Hoddie's results that power sharing is more likely to be stable when third-party enforcement is present and with Kaufmann's view that international institutions must monitor partition and assist in population transfers. Hartzell and Hoddie, "Institutionalizing Peace," 322; Kaufmann, "Possible and Impossible Solutions to Ethnic Civil Wars," 167.

86. Walter, "The Critical Barrier to Civil War Settlement," 342, 350–51.

relationship between states and international institutions and the role that traditional conceptions of sovereignty play in shaping this relationship.

Making states and international institutions more effective in protecting individuals against mass abuse requires significant changes. At the state level, constitutional grants of supremacy to domestic law and institutions must be replaced with a divided sovereignty view in which international institutions take over sovereign functions when states are unable or unwilling to fulfill their basic functions. Such constitutional changes can only take place when the general population is aware of and supports institutional possibilities beyond the nation-state that can improve institutional performance and enhance the respect of individual rights.

At the international level, representatives of people from different states could create and design structures with real coercive powers. This entails either strengthening existing institutions or creating new ones where existing structures fall short. There is significant room for strengthening international institutions' capacity for preventing slavery and human trafficking, genocide, and other massive harms caused by civil wars, and for them to fulfill a governance vacuum left by state incapacity or indifference.

4

Theories and Institutional Facts

I HAVE ARGUED that we should support the creation of international institutions able to enforce essential prohibitions against massive violations of human rights, such as genocide, torture, or indiscriminate attacks on civilians in war. I have advanced this proposal with an assumption in the background: that we can imagine the range of institutions, such as the ICC, that can carry forward this mandate, and that we can envision them doing so consistent with respecting significant parts of the existing institutional stock of rights and obligations. This chapter makes this assumption explicit. We cannot answer the question of what the goals of new institutional agents should be without taking into account institutional facts such as existing legal and social conventions and the institutional design options available to us.

Following G. A. Cohen, I call rules for regulating our social practices *principles of regulation* (or *regulative ideals*). They are "a certain type of social instrument, to be legislated and implemented" by social or political institutions, either at the domestic or international level.[1] Regulative ideals guide social practice by setting the standards for law and public policy. An example of a regulative ideal is "respect the autonomy of a patient by informing her of her treatment options and their likely consequences," or "respect the sovereignty of another country by refraining from intervening in the normal exercise of its sovereign prerogatives." I contrast principles of regulation with abstract moral ideals, which I take to be general, unspecified values and principles such as "promote equality," "respect autonomy," or "prevent harm to

---

1. G. A. Cohen, *Rescuing Justice and Equality* (Cambridge, MA: Harvard University Press, 2008), 265; G. A. Cohen, "Facts and Principles," *Philosophy & Public Affairs* 31, no. 3 (2003): 211–45. I do not take any position here on Cohen's distinction between fact-sensitive principles of regulation and fact-insensitive ultimate principles. I want to leave open that moral ideals can be fact-sensitive all the way down.

others." General moral norms such as these are severely limited in their ability to provide guidance for regulating social practice, unless we say more about what kind of equality is worth promoting, when the circumstances require us to promote or infringe autonomy (we limit the autonomy of thieves, for example), or about what counts as harm. More important, I will argue that such general ideals cannot provide practical guidance absent an understanding of the institutional context they aim to regulate.

It follows that there are two types of theorizing about justice. One is concerned with identifying and clarifying the nature and relationships between our more general moral ideals and values. Another provides an account of the principles of regulation that seek to rectify harm and of their application to our existing modes of social interaction. This second type of theorizing must be sensitive to and grounded in a particular type of facts, namely institutional facts. Institutional facts are descriptions of social reality that include an account of the organizations that regulate social life, together with an account of the rules, rights, and obligations they create, and the ways in which these rules, rights, and obligations structure the interactions among people. Theories that purport to provide causal explanations linking certain institutional rules with expected behavioral changes will also count as facts on my account.[2]

Facts about institutions shape regulative ideals. Certain regulative ideals are not attainable no matter what institutional system is implemented. Perfect international peace, just as perfect compliance with domestic law, relies on unrealistic expectations about institutional performance and about the ways individual behavior interacts with institutional constraints. Some principles may be attainable under a specified set of institutions only if other principles fall short. Different institutional systems will require different trade-offs, and regulative ideals must specify these trade-offs in context. Regulative ideals are *institution-dependent*, in that they allow possible institutional options to shape or constrain their content. Institutions transform the relationships among people, the patterns of interaction, and the nature of the problems that arise in social and political life.[3] Principles of regulation will consequently vary from one institutional context to the next. It is thus reasonable to expect that principles of regulation for healthcare will be different than principles of

2. For a defense of the idea that complex causal claims must be part of the justification of public policies, see Guido Pincione and Fernando R. Tesón, "Rational Ignorance and Political Morality," *Philosophy and Phenomenological Research* 72, no. 1 (2006): 71–96.

3. Andrea Sangiovanni, "Justice and the Priority of Politics to Morality," *Journal of Political Philosophy* 16, no. 2 (June 2008): 137–64.

regulation for criminal law. We can also expect that principles of regulation for international politics will be different from principles of regulation for domestic politics.[4]

Institution-dependency is, in fact, more demanding than this. It will not do for a set of regulative ideals to be realizable in just any plausible institutional setting. It has to be plausible given the institutional context *already in place*. The starting question for judging feasibility must be: Can the principles and values of this theory be achieved in an institutional system to which we can get from where we are today without prohibitive costs? If there is no foreseeable path to a future scheme that achieves the values of a theory of justice, or if the costs of getting there are too great, then the ideals must be modified in light of these constraints. It thus follows that two political systems with different starting points will require different principles of regulation.

Without explaining in detail the relationship between principles of regulation and general moral ideals, I will argue that to obtain principles of regulation from general moral ideals, we require a *two-step process*.[5] The first step is to ascertain existing patterns of behavior and social interaction, identify injustice, and summon general moral ideals relevant to establishing benchmarks for reform, such as equality, human rights, or a duty to aid. In the second step, we analyze moral ideals in light of the institutional background as well as future institutional possibilities, and translate them into concrete regulative ideals. Institutional facts can shape regulative ideals by providing information about feasible combinations of moral goals, about the transition costs of reform, or about how reforms affect the stability of the institutional system as a whole. We aim to change institutions in light of regulative ideals, yet we also modify ideals in light of institutional options. Theorizing about justice and institutional analysis are thus mutually constraining.[6]

Although many accept that regulative ideals are fact-sensitive in this way, international justice theorists have been insufficiently attentive to the demands it places on them. These theorists seem to embrace an *institution-blind* view

---

4. While not widely accepted, the view that principles of international and domestic justice must respond to different institutional context is growing in support. See, for example, Laura Valentini, *Justice in a Globalized World: A Normative Framework* (Oxford: Oxford University Press, 2011).

5. On certain understanding of what justice requires, there need not be relationship between moral ideals and principles of regulation. My arguments only apply to theories of justice that have as one of their main aims practical guidance.

6. David Wiens, "Prescribing Institutions Without Ideal Theory," *Journal of Political Philosophy* 20, no. 1 (2012): 47.

of justice. The institution-blind view says that justice is invariable with institutional context and is not shaped by it. Yet this approach is mistaken. Insofar as philosophers intend to provide principles of regulation for international politics, they must render their theorizing fact-sensitive in the way that I explain here. Theories of international justice must incorporate the two-step process. In order to become practice-guiding and move beyond theories as accounts of general moral norms, these theories must translate their fact-insensitive norms in light of the institutional constraints on the ground as part of the two-step process. The upshot is that regulative ideals of international justice must be path-dependent, sensitive to the institutional context to which they apply, and must attend to trade-offs of moral goals.

The argument proceeds in three parts. The first part offers a reading of cosmopolitan theorizing as institutionally blind theorizing about justice. It argues that in order to provide principles that regulate our social practice, cosmopolitan theorizing requires a second step in which regulative ideals are made consistent with institutional facts and the available institutional options for reform. The second part provides a model of how to theorize about regulative principles with institutional constraints in mind, drawing on the defense of humanitarian intervention developed by the responsibility to protect doctrine. The last part addresses objections to institutionally sensitive theorizing, particularly the worry that such moral theorizing is unacceptably conservative.

1. One-Step Theorizing: Cosmopolitan Justice

Prevailing views about global justice see theorizing about the values and principles that guide the behavior of different actors at the international level (e.g., states, nonstate groups, international organizations) as a one-step process: The role of the political philosopher is to identify some problematic feature or features of the world and debate the nature and content of moral ideals (values and principles) that can accurately diagnose these features. For example, many cosmopolitan theorists use as a starting point of their theorizing the vast inequalities in material resources or political and civil rights that obtain across the globe. Theorizing about justice in the international context amounts to explaining why equality matters, or assuming that it matters and explaining how our political and social arrangements depart from it. This egalitarianism is the dominant mood in much of the cosmopolitan theorizing about global justice. To achieve justice is to treat all human beings as moral equals and to take equal care to satisfy their fundamental interests and needs.

A cosmopolitan theory of justice works out the general implications of the equal worth of all human beings or of ensuring the protection of vital human interests and needs, irrespective of the position individuals occupy within an institutional system at a given point in time.

Although cosmopolitans argue that individuals are entitled to equal moral concern regardless of contingencies like membership in particular political communities, they differ about what equal moral concern entails.[7] On the one hand, utilitarian versions of cosmopolitanism, such as Peter Singer's, ask that we consider the welfare of each individual equally. In a world of severe poverty and vast inequalities in wealth, the implication for Singer is that we ensure equality of moral concern by transferring from the rich to the poor up to the point where their relative material holdings become comparable.[8] Deontological conceptions of cosmopolitanism, on the other hand, start with a notion of individual rights whose protection needs to be equalized globally. Rights generate entitlements and corresponding claims that all people have against each other, such as negative claims against physical violence or positive entitlements to subsistence and assistance.[9] The utilitarian and deontological versions of cosmopolitanism share the view that the institutional context does not change what individuals *qua* individuals are owed. Institutions are explained away.

In order to urge people to help with the Bengali famine and other similarly catastrophic situations, Singer seeks to justify the principle that we are morally required to help. He conjures the image of a child drowning in a shallow pond and argues that if it is within our power to prevent the child from drowning, without sacrificing anything morally significant, we ought to do it.[10] He famously says that "it makes no moral difference whether the person I can

---

7. Charles R. Beitz, "Review: International Liberalism and Distributive Justice: A Survey of Recent Thought," *World Politics* 51, no. 2 (January 1999): 269–96; Kok-Chor Tan, *Justice without Borders: Cosmopolitanism, Nationalism, and Patriotism* (New York: Cambridge University Press, 2004).

8. Peter Singer, "Famine, Affluence, and Morality," *Philosophy and Public Affairs* 1, no. 3 (Spring 1972): 229–43.

9. Thomas W. Pogge, *Realizing Rawls* (Ithaca, NY: Cornell University Press, 1989); Beitz, "Review."

10. Singer offers a strong and a weak version of the principle. The strong version asks people in wealthy nations to sacrifice their material well-being to the point where they come close to the material holdings of the poor. A weaker version does not propose that people impoverish themselves in order to raise other people out of poverty, but only that they sacrifice just short of the point at which they have to give up "something morally significant." Singer believes that the first principle is the morally justified one but the second has a better chance of being

help is a neighbor's child ten yards from me or a Bengali whose name I shall never know, ten thousand miles away."[11] Singer is referring mainly to physical distance, but he argues by implication that national boundaries are also irrelevant to our duties to distant others.

Cosmopolitans who take their cue from John Rawls's *Theory of Justice* make a similar point. Rawls argues that a person's race, gender, talents, and wealth are arbitrary from a moral point of view and therefore not morally weighty considerations in determining the principles of justice. Although Rawls himself resisted the extension of justice as fairness on a global scale, some theorists who follow Rawls argued that just like race, gender, and natural talent, membership in a nation is just another morally irrelevant characteristic.[12] The existence of states is not relevant for determining what we owe to each other at the global level. The requirements of justice are invariable from the domestic to the international level or from country to country. For instance, Simon Caney and Pablo Gilabert believe that the principles of justice can be derived in the abstract by thinking about universal attributes that all human beings share, such as a capacity for rational thought, about general human needs and interests, or about minimal conditions for individual well-being.[13]

Other cosmopolitans are not reluctant to use the language of institutions when they explain why we should care about people around the world equally. Associational cosmopolitans such as Thomas Pogge, Charles Beitz, and Darrel Moellendorf claim that global institutions produce strong causal interdependence between all the people in the world, and this "fact" warrants adopting global distributive principles to correct for the unequal effects of such a system.[14] Indeed, their views are labeled "institutionalist" for this reason. Yet whether the description of strong causal interdependence mediated

---

implemented because it is less demanding. Singer, "Famine, Affluence, and Morality," 231, 234–35.

11. Ibid., 237.

12. John Rawls, *The Law of Peoples: With "The Idea of Public Reason Revisited"* (Cambridge, MA: Harvard University Press, 2001), 119–20.

13. Simon Caney, *Justice beyond Borders: A Global Political Theory* (New York: Oxford University Press, 2006); Pablo Gilabert, *From Global Poverty to Global Equality: A Philosophical Exploration* (New York: Oxford University Press, 2012); Simon Caney, "Humanity, Associations, and Global Justice: In Defence of Humanity-Centered Cosmopolitan Egalitarianism," *Monist* 94, no. 4 (2011): 506–34.

14. Thomas W. Pogge, *World Poverty and Human Rights*, 2nd ed. (Malden, MA: Polity Press, 2008); Charles R. Beitz, *Political Theory and International Relations* (Princeton, NJ: Princeton University Press, 1999); Darrel Moellendorf, *Global Inequality Matters (Global Ethics)* (New York: Palgrave Macmillan, 2009).

by international institution can be appropriately characterized as a fact is debatable. In any event, whether some cosmopolitans take institutional facts to matter in their diagnosis of the problem, such facts seem to vanish at the pre-scription stage. The cosmopolitan institutionalism is still fact-insensitive in crucial respects, since institutional facts such as the existence of states do not change what individuals are due in practice.

However, it is not always clear that cosmopolitan ideals are meant as prin-ciples of regulation to guide existing practice at all. Cosmopolitans may be simply describing certain general moral standards deployed to diagnose the problems of social life that lack direct prescriptive value.[15] The precise role such standards serve has yet to be explained by those who wield them to pass judg-ment on global patterns of interaction. I am speculating that at a minimum, cosmopolitans seek to offer some moral baseline against which to assess pat-terns of social interaction, and from which themselves or other theorists can subsequently derive more concrete prescriptions, without cosmopolitans them-selves needing to take sides on what these prescriptions are.

A more ambitious interpretation of cosmopolitanism is that it aims to provide principles of regulation. And this is how some cosmopolitans under-stand their own project. Singer, for example, takes the avoidance of harm and equality to lead directly to the redistribution of wealth from the rich to the poor. Similarly, David Luban in his defense of humanitarian intervention sees a straight path from a commitment to human rights and equality, to a com-mitment to equal enforcement. According to the maximalist interpretation of equality and human rights protections he favors, every individual has the right to security and subsistence, regardless of status as a member of a particular political community: "Human rights accrue to people no matter what country they live in and regardless of history and traditions."[16] Furthermore, these rights are essential for the enjoyment of all other rights. Because rights as such are universal, they respect no political boundaries and, consequently, "require a universalist politics to implement them." Thus, "the entitlement to intervene derives from the cosmopolitan character of human rights."[17] The benchmark

---

15. Although a minority view, some prominent philosophers such as David Estlund defend theorizing that does not aim at producing, or cannot be converted into principles of regu-lation and therefore has no practical value. See, for example, David Estlund, "What Good Is It? Unrealistic Political Theory and the Value of Intellectual Work," *Analyse & Kritik* 2 (2011): 395–416.

16. David Luban, "The Romance of the Nation-State," *Philosophy and Public Affairs* 9, no. 4 (Summer 1980): 396.

17. Ibid., 392.

favored by many in the human rights literature for extraordinary cases of large-scale violence sets the bar too high for intervention. In Luban's view, by refusing to intervene even in cases of ordinary oppression, we fail to take rights seriously. The more appropriate response is to go all in, and protect any and all individuals against abuse.

Luban's concern with the rights of all individuals is fundamentally sound. It encourages us to think of the institutional system that can in the aggregate offer the most reliable protection for the rights of each person, one that approximates equality in the best way possible. But equality as a principle of regulation for the protection of human rights cannot be interpreted in the maximalist fashion Luban proposes, because it ignores two kinds of institutional facts. First, it is difficult to imagine what kind of global policing institutions would be capable of rooting out ordinary cases of oppression and small-scale rights violations. Second, and more important, Luban misses the distinct moral constraints that the existence of states places on enforcing rights. States are institutionalized forms of political self-rule, with legal protections under international law. The norms of international law rightly place limits on the permissible ways in which outsiders can interfere with state authority.

The larger point is that, as Aaron James has argued, regulative ideals must be addressed to existing agents and must take into account their roles and regulatory powers. "Although we can in theory address hypothetical normative principles to hypothetically situated and empowered agents, such hypothetical principles do not necessarily tell us anything about what justice requires in the circumstances of actual social and political life."[18] Therefore, we must ground our principles of regulation both in facts about existing agents who have the power to make individuals better or worse off, and in the institutionalized relations and roles that define and circumscribe these agents' acting capacities.

One could argue that the mere fact that certain relations are institutionalized does not create a constraint on one's actions, only a practical obstacle. After all, slavery has been institutionalized in the past and afforded legal protection to slaveholders, but this does not mean that those institutions should be respected. This is a strong point. But if there is a case to be made in this form for the irrelevance of institutions, it is missing from Luban's account for when humanitarian intervention is appropriate. Even so, I doubt that such a case can be made. The move from the claim that illegitimate institutions do

---

18. Aaron James, *Fairness in Practice: A Social Contract for a Global Economy* (New York: Oxford University Press, 2013), 114.

not place any constraint on what one morally ought to do, to the claim that institutions *as such* place no constraints on action, is indefensible.

Luban is right to caution against "the Romance of the Nation State," by which he means turning the state into an object of worship for being the site where moral unity through collective decision making inevitably takes place. But he is wrong to insist that the state therefore has no moral and legal rights that shield it from outside intervention. Luban hints that states are significant in one sense, as agents of actual and potential oppression. But states are more than that. They are the expression of groups of people's collective rights for self-determination. The right of sovereign independence and noninterference is both a fact of international law and a prerogative granted to self-governing independent political communities. They impose significant duties on outsiders that can only be overridden with good reason.

Luban's reliance on equality and human rights falls short of addressing pressing questions about who should receive protection, what agent is required to guarantee it, and the extent of that protection. In order for ideal concepts to guide practice, they need to be applied and specified in concrete institutional contexts. In these contexts, we determine how we may discriminate between competing uses of scarce resources for the realization of different ends, and how and to whom we assign responsibility for protecting a particular right. Moral ideals are silent when it comes to making choices such as these. Views such as Luban's must be accompanied by a second step in which moral ideals are circumscribed and shaped by existing institutional possibilities and their morally relevant features.

John D. Arras and Elizabeth M. Fenton illustrate the pitfalls of one-step theorizing with respect to the human right to health.[19] One-step theorizing consists of identifying injustice in existing patterns of behavior and social interaction, and recruiting general moral ideals relevant to establishing benchmarks for reform. Without a second step that specifies these ideals in light of existing institutional constraints and possibilities, they cannot serve as principles of regulation appropriate for the existing institutional system. The International Covenant on Economic, Social, and Cultural Rights (ICESCR) articulates a human right to "the highest attainable standard of physical and mental health."[20] Understood as a principle of regulation, this way of articulating a human right to health has unpalatable implications. Without keeping in view

---

19. John D. Arras and Elizabeth M. Fenton, "Bioethics and Human Rights: Access to Health-Related Goods," *Hastings Center Report* 39, no. 5 (2009): 27–38.

20. Article 12.1.

real-world constraints such as scarcity, the necessity of allocating resources to multiple uses, and institutional capabilities, it is difficult to define reasonable specifications for such a human right. Think of a resource-poor country that has managed after concerted, costly efforts to raise life expectancy from fifty years to sixty years. But the country in question has many other pressing concerns such as poverty, education, and infrastructure. A rigorous reading of a human right to health requires the government to continue to spend more on healthcare until the citizens reach not just a sufficient level of health, but the highest attainable level, comparable with that of the most developed, advanced, and healthiest countries in the world. However, no human right should be conceived in this maximalist fashion. The highest attainable standard of physical and mental health "is not even a reasonable social objective, let alone a right."[21] Rights play different functions within different institutional structures, and those functions "condition the content and scope of the right," as Andrea Sangiovanni argues.[22] Without attending to the institutional structures in which these rights regulate human behavior and allow those structures to mold their scope, we cannot deploy them as regulative ideals.

Simon Caney may not be moved by this worry, since he has distinguished between principles that are independent of people's membership in associations such as states, and the "*substantive implications of those principles.*" He argues that the latter will be affected by institutional facts, but cosmopolitans are primarily concerned with the former.[23] Caney is merely using a different language to distinguish between general moral principles and principles of regulation. His reply reveals at the very least that cosmopolitans must (1) be as explicit as he is about the aims of their theorizing, and (2) engage in additional theorizing in order to show how their theories can guide practice to avoid the charge that they engage in idle armchair theorizing.

This conclusion requires modesty about the ability of unmediated moral ideals to offer practical guidance. Improving the fate of many cannot proceed by simply asking what equality or human rights demand of us. We must start by clearly identifying the problems and then determining what possible institutional changes can address them productively within the existing context. We may find that we have to adjust our expectations of what can be achieved depending on the institutional alternatives available to us. Ideals can serve as

21. John D. Arras and Elizabeth M. Fenton, "Bioethics and Human Rights," 31.

22. Andrea Sangiovanni, "Justice and the Priority of Politics to Morality," *Journal of Political Philosophy* 16, no. 2 (June 2008): 23.

23. Caney, "Humanity, Associations, and Global Justice," 526.

"a common set of reference points," a system of walls with which to build a theoretical edifice.[24] But they cannot by themselves create a durable structure meant for habitation. Structural beams are required to support it, and institutions serve that supporting role. Depending on the available technology, the size and shape of the beams will influence the size and shape of the building. Institutions create relatively fixed points in our theorizing about justice. Understanding the institutional context can help us provide a more finely grained account of justice in order to address the real problems that confront us today. Theories of humanitarian intervention are typically more sensitive to the institutional context and therefore can offer adequate examples of how to theorize with institutional constraints in mind.

2. Two-Step Theorizing: The Case of Humanitarian Intervention

The missing second step in accounts of cosmopolitan justice is to specify ideals based on the institutional constraints of international politics and law. The scope and reach of the ideals depend on what institutional options are available. Take, for instance, the protection of an individual's right to life. When the life of a citizen of a certain state is threatened, that state is justified in intervening coercively to minimize the threat and stop the violence. In liberal democracies, the state has a responsibility to do so for every individual, in keeping with its function of providing equal protection for individual rights. Even if in practice state action often falls short of this equal standard, in principle the state cannot favor individuals for any arbitrary reasons such as their social or economic status or the color of their skin. Every life is valuable and is equally valuable in the eyes of the state.

Is coercive action in the form of humanitarian intervention in cases where a single individual's or a few individuals' right to life is violated an appropriate goal for international institutions? The answer is no. It is not that international institutions cannot recognize that all human beings are of equal worth. They certainly can and should. It is, rather, that when intervening to protect basic rights at the international level, the existence of a system of states changes the conditions in which coercive interference is justified. The necessity of respecting the sovereign prerogatives of states, of refraining from upsetting the normal exercise of sovereign responsibilities, and of guarding against the potential

---

24. Michael Ignatieff, *Human Rights as Politics and Idolatry* (Princeton, NJ: Princeton University Press, 2001).

loss of more human life are morally weighty considerations that must be balanced against protecting individual rights. These institutional facts impose feasibility constraints on principles of regulation for humanitarian intervention, principles that cannot demand both that every human rights violation be corrected and that state sovereignty be respected. The constraints will tip the balance against interfering in order to protect individual rights by raising the threshold for the number and severity of violations that warrant the action of international agents.

Theories of humanitarian interventions are typically produced in stages from a more abstract, idealized set of principles to a set of principles and values specified for the set of institutions operating in the international realm. The first stage is to identify the relevant ideals, and the second is to explain how existing institutional conditions determine, in part, what the moral ideals mean in practice and how they guide the actions of different agents in a humanitarian intervention. This two-stage sequence is implicit in the Responsibility to Protect document (RtoP) produced by a commission of UN member states organized by the Canadian government in 2005 under the name of the International Commission on Intervention and State Sovereignty. The aim of the commission was to produce a policy guide in order to prevent "gross and systematic violations of human rights."[25]

The two normative starting points for the commission were respect for basic human rights, such as the right to life, and the Samaritan duty to help. "Never again!" was the collective call after the horrors of the genocide campaigns in Europe and Asia during World War II were uncovered. The international community has struggled ever since to find appropriate responses to human rights violations internal to states. More recent humanitarian tragedies in Rwanda and the former Yugoslavia have tested the resolve of the community of states to curb such harms.

While the twin commitments of respect for human rights and the Samaritan duty to aid are a good starting point, they are not sufficient to guide action in the case of human rights violations, pace Luban. They are ideal norms setting the stage for the second step in the analysis. Humanitarian intervention takes place in an institutional context with certain features, which are morally relevant to setting limits on the legitimate ways to

---

25. The commission took as its own task answering the question posed by Kofi Annan: "If humanitarian intervention is, indeed, an unacceptable assault on sovereignty, how should we respond to a Rwanda, to a Srebrenica—to gross and systematic violations of human rights that affect every precept of our common humanity?" Alex J. Bellamy, "The Responsibility to Protect and the Problem of Military Intervention," *International Affairs* 84, no. 4 (2008): 615.

intervene. Two of these features of the international landscape have special relevance: the existence of states and the fact that, at least for now, the Security Council of the UN is the only body that can legitimately authorize the use of force internationally. But why would these facts about international politics be *morally relevant* to a theory of humanitarian intervention?

Defending the idea that they are morally relevant could focus on the fact that states embody the right of collective self-determination, and such a fact must enter any judgment about appropriate action at the international level. I believe this is one of the strongest defenses that one can give to taking states seriously. But I want to focus on a related but less appreciated feature of states: A rich and long history has endowed states with *legal standing*. This means both that they have the power to create rights and obligations for their citizens, including rights with respect to state action to protect their interests, and that states themselves have rights and obligations with respect to other states that are codified in international law. Among the former, states define and consider themselves responsible for the basic rights of the individuals living in their territory; among the latter, states vow in international law treaties to respect each other's sovereign prerogatives and to refrain from interfering in each other's domestic affairs.

Legal conventions are a particular kind of institutional fact with relevance for what we should do. They offer solutions to problems of social cooperation, solve coordination dilemmas, and minimize conflict. They also protect morally important interests. The requirement for doctors to disclose information to patients about possible courses of treatment and their likely consequences is grounded in respect for the autonomy of the patient. And the requirement is itself a convention that has further implications for new principles of regulation, for example, those that ground appropriate treatment of surrogate decision making in medical practice.

Nobody who upholds the value of conventions believes that all conventions are equal. Bad, pernicious conventions must be questioned and challenged just as bad organizations and social practices are. So, for example, limited support for the principle of sovereign independence and the principle of nonintervention does not imply an endorsement of all the other practices of international law such as those of recognizing new states. For reasons that Allen Buchanan and Fernando Tesón have made compelling, the existing practice of state recognition lacks criteria of minimal moral acceptability, and must be replaced with new practices that recognize the extent to which states are morally legitimate in claiming authority over a certain territory and population.[26] Recognizing that certain conventions are misguided does not, however, challenge the importance of conventions in general in shaping the content of principles of regulation.

The matrix of international legal rights and obligations creates special relationships between citizens and their states, and among different states, that help coordinate their goals, solve conflict, maintain peace, and shape everyone's expectations about appropriate action. Legal protection for states gives citizens legitimate expectations that their ordinary political practices will not be disrupted by outsiders. This is why they are morally significant. Cosmopolitan theorists must either explicitly reject this significance or explain how they incorporate these institutional features as part of their regulative ideals.

The authors of the RtoP report offer a good example of how to establish just goals with institutional constraints in mind. They have addressed a two-pronged question: When is intervention legitimate, and who is responsible for authorizing intervention? On the question of whether intervention is ever consistent with respecting the sovereign prerogative of independent states, the answer of the commission is a qualified yes. Intervention is not consistent with sovereignty understood as the unlimited, exclusive, and final authority of the state over all matters related to their population and territory. However, intervention is consistent with a limited and conditional sovereign prerogative that includes substantive internal autonomy for state institutions to fulfill the bundle of responsibilities they have with respect to their citizens. The sovereign prerogative is conditional because when states systematically fail to uphold their responsibilities to their citizens, states lose the presumption of noninterference in their internal affairs.

The RtoP doctrine marked an important shift from earlier understandings of international law, which defined sovereignty as state control. Instead, the commission redefined sovereignty as a matter of state responsibility.[27] Borrowing from just war theory and established norms in international law, the commission relied on a *just cause threshold* to set limits to intervention. The commission argued that intervention is only appropriate in extreme cases of "large scale loss of life" and "large scale ethnic cleansing." The document seeks clarity regarding what this threshold does and does not include.

---

26. Allen Buchanan, *Justice, Legitimacy, and Self-Determination: Moral Foundations for International Law* (New York: Oxford University Press, 2004); Fernando R Tesón, *A Philosophy of International Law* (Boulder, CO: Westview Press, 1998).

27. "The Responsibility to Protect," *Report of The International Commission on Intervention and State Sovereignty,* http://responsibilitytoprotect.org/ICISS%20Report.pdf (accessed June 9, 2010).

Intervention can proceed in cases that involve the threat or actual occurrence of large-scale loss of life as defined in the 1948 Genocide Convention, the systematic killing of members of a particular group, systematic rape as part of an ethnic cleansing campaign, crimes against humanity, other crimes of war defined by the Geneva Convention, situations of civil war resulting in massive human casualties and starvation, and catastrophic natural disasters with which the state concerned is unable or unwilling to cope.[28]

The commission also lists actions that do not warrant intervention. The list is not exhaustive, but is meant to be a rough guide to help distinguish situations in which it is appropriate to intervene from those in which it is not. Anything short of "outright killing or ethnic cleansing" is excluded, such as systematic racial discrimination, systematic imprisonment, or oppression of political opponents.[29] Also, cases of military takeover after a democratic election, or rescuing one's own nationals on foreign territory do not constitute adequate grounds for coercive military action.[30] The document claims that these may be appropriate grounds for punitive diplomatic measures and sanctions but not for intervention. And according to the ICC statute, some of them can also be grounds for international criminal jurisdiction. Consistent with the logic of the commission, small-scale human rights violations and even outright but isolated killings would not serve as valid justifications for intervention.

But why not go "all in," as Luban suggests? Why should the scope of justified international intervention be limited in this way? The commission's answer focused on the importance of respecting the sovereign prerogatives of states, which creates a presumption against noninterference. In the case of humanitarian intervention, the presumption against interference can only be outweighed by large-scale loss of life or potential loss of life. The commission briefly mentions other considerations that must be taken into account in assessing the justness of intervention in particular cases. One of the more important factors is the reasonable prospect for success. There may be cases in which, even if the loss of life is massive, military action cannot protect the potential victims. In these situations, intervention is likely to make things worse for the victims, or the projected costs in terms of human lives for the interveners is likely to be unreasonably high.[31] In addition, interventions are politically disruptive, undermining the opportunities for self-government

---

28. Ibid., 32–33.

29. Ibid., 34.

30. Ibid., 35.

31. Ibid., 37.

and thus the chance for order, security, and predictability, leading to more violence and death. These considerations all speak against undertaking military action except in the most egregious cases of human rights violations.

In addition to intervention, the commission's recommendations also focused on the prevention of human rights abuses and on postintervention reconstruction. In light of these concerns, the commission stressed that intervention is never a first option and always a last resort. Despite stressing the critical importance of prevention, the commission's main focus was on intervention, since intervention raises the thorniest moral and political issues. In answer to the first prong of the question, the commission proposed just cause thresholds ("large scale loss of life" and "large scale ethnic cleansing") and four precautionary principles ("right intention," "last resort," "proportional means," and "reasonable prospects"), claiming that satisfying these principles would severely limit the likelihood of intervention to cases where intervention is genuinely warranted. Regarding the institutional prong, the commission stated that the Security Council has the primary responsibility to act when gross human rights violations occur. Should the Security Council fail to act, the commission argued that the General Assembly should be next in line, and the relevant regional organizations and willing states should be last in the decision hierarchy. RtoP has garnered substantial public attention and scrutiny, and was also endorsed by the General Assembly in 2005 and unanimously reaffirmed by the Security Council in 2006 (Resolution 1674).[32] Yet, since no concomitant efforts to replace or clarify existing prohibitions against intervention in key documents of international law have taken place, the timid attempts to embrace RtoP have aggravated the confusion about the applicable norms.[33] This is why the initial effort to embrace the RtoP doctrine was followed by indecisiveness in the face of humanitarian crises such as Syria.

Another reason for indecisiveness is the question of legitimate authority. There are no international institutions tasked explicitly with authorizing humanitarian intervention and, despite the received view, the Security Council does not look like a plausible candidate for it. For international law and RtoP, the Security Council is the default mechanism of authorization because it is the only institution regarded as having the authority to sanction the use of force, but its many deficiencies prevent it from being the right institutional choice, at least absent major reforms. Its main purpose is to protect

---

32. Bellamy, "The Responsibility to Protect and the Problem of Military Intervention," 615.

33. Michael W. Doyle, "International Ethics and the Responsibility to Protect," *International Studies Review* 13, no. 1 (2011): 72–84.

international peace, which often conflicts with authorizing humanitarian intervention; its decision-making process is captive to poor design choices that often lead to inaction, such as the veto power of permanent members; and countries with a long record of extensive human rights violations (China and Russia) have significant power within the organization. Human rights violators are not themselves appropriate judges of other countries' human rights records, the council stalls at the worst of times (Rwanda, Bosnia, Sudan, Chechnya, Indonesia being prime examples), and if it took on humanitarian intervention as an explicit mandate, it would have conflicting goals with no clear way to prioritize them. The Security Council cannot be relied upon to make the decision to intervene in a morally responsible way, and because of this, the question of legitimate authority remains wide open.[34]

Resolving the question of a legitimate authority to intervene is a tall order, and the RtoP does not come close. Still, one need not endorse either the institutional hierarchy that the RtoP recommends for authorizing intervention or the precise line it draws for when intervention becomes acceptable in order to see that the document makes an exemplary case that the decision to protect human rights is inextricably linked to the existing institutional constraints (the system of sovereign states) and the available institutional possibilities (the institutions available to authorize intervention).

The implication of this new approach to intervention undertaken under the RtoP umbrella is still unclear. Scholars, however, agree that it marks a significant shift in the doctrine of coercive human rights protection.[35] It reinforces the commitment, however delicate, of the international community to basic security rights, even as it introduces new questions about legitimate authority, the possibility for abuse, and postintervention responsibilities.

---

34. See also James Pattison on this point, *Humanitarian Intervention and the Responsibility to Protect: Who Should Intervene?* (Oxford: Oxford University Press, 2012), 54–57, 188. Pattison proposes a "moderate instrumental approach" to assess among other things the effectiveness of the potential intervener, and he concludes that of the existing organizations NATO comes closest to fulfilling the criteria that must be met by an intervener.

35. See, for example, the special issue of *Ethics and International Affairs* on the Libya intervention with articles by James Pattison, "The Ethics of Humanitarian Intervention in Libya," *Ethics & International Affairs* 25, no. 3 (2011): 271–77; Thomas G. Weiss, "RtoP Alive and Well after Libya," *Ethics & International Affairs* 25, no. 3 (2011): 287–92; Simon Chesterman, " 'Leading from Behind': The Responsibility to Protect, the Obama Doctrine, and Humanitarian Intervention after Libya," *Ethics & International Affairs* 25, no. 3 (2011): 279–85; Jennifer Welsh, "Civilian Protection in Libya: Putting Coercion and Controversy Back into RtoP," *Ethics & International Affairs* 25, no. 3 (2011): 255–62; Ian Hurd, "Is Humanitarian Intervention Legal? The Rule of Law in an Incoherent World," *Ethics & International Affairs* 25, no. 3 (2011): 293–313; Alex J. Bellamy, "Libya and the Responsibility to Protect: The Exception and the Norm," *Ethics & International Affairs* 25, no. 3 (2011): 263–69.

In sum, the RtoP takes the existence of states and the legal protection accorded to their sovereignty to serve as a weighty institutional constraint against intervention to protect the right to life. This provides just one example in which the principles of regulation for international institutions will differ from those of domestic institutions for the simple reason that international institutions operate in a different context of rules and relationships. This way of thinking about the demands of justice represents a methodological shift. It requires taking note of the institutional facts on the ground, and the way they create new normative goals or shape existing ones at the level of theory construction. The document also shows that normative theorizing that starts from existing institutional practices can be morally progressive, and need not lead to moral conservatism. The next section explains in more detail why the charge of moral conservatism leveled against an institutions-sensitive approach to regulative ideals is misplaced.

3. Objections

One could reasonably object that the view I defend here grants too much to the status quo by placing normative weight on merely descriptive features of the international system. The existence of sovereign states should impose no more limitations on protecting individual rights than the existence of fences between neighbors should impose limitations on protecting innocent children from the abuse of their parents. The existence of states may pose practical barriers to protecting individuals from violence, but they should not affect what we morally *ought to do*.

Such an objection misses the point of borders and fences. Borders and fences are not merely visual reminders of our separation into distinct political communities and families, respectively. They are symbols of the institutional protections of the rights of political communities and of families to organize their internal affairs as they see fit without undue interference. Various norms that recognize the status of states have accumulated over time to cement the functions that state institutions play domestically and internationally, and such norms are deeply embedded in our political practice. States are political entities whose legal rights and responsibilities belong to any conception of global justice. The protection of families under domestic law and of states under international law can only be overridden if states and families misuse or abuse their power in significant ways, and the limits will be specified differently for domestic and international law. But the underlying logic is the same.

We might have good reasons to challenge any of the institutional protections granted to states and any other organization or agency that play a role in realizing a set of moral ideals. This book is just an example of such a challenge: It is an exercise in further weakening the absolutist reading of the norm of state sovereignty. Starting from where we are in a path-dependent way does not require us to endorse the status quo blindly. The evaluation of the institutional framework can also become part of the regulative ideals that we call on to guide reform. For example, one can conclude, as I have, that for the purposes of humanitarian intervention, the Security Council is plagued by so many structural design issues so as to be unreliable to act appropriately in the event of a crisis. The veto power that the five permanent members have (China, United States, Russia, France, United Kingdom) has often been used for posturing, for the protection of corrupt allies, and for the preservation of illicit economic gains. Perhaps transferring authority to authorize intervention to a different existing institution or to a new one created for this purpose is the right way to go. Such a shift can be accomplished conditional on the transition costs not being prohibitive, and on there being a feasible path from here to there given other goals that we seek to accomplish, like stability, peace, and the protection of basic human rights.

Acknowledging the status quo does not entail being enslaved to it. It means selecting the appropriate principles of regulation based on concrete problems, being alive to the institutional realities of the present, and planning reforms with these realities in mind.[36] The conventions regarding state sovereignty are institutional facts that are normatively significant because they embody protections of important interests. Many conventions do so by solving coordination or collective action problems in ways that stabilize social practice and minimize conflict. To the extent that they are deficient, we are entitled to question and change them. But ignoring or rejecting wholesale the institutional landscape of international politics in advancing a set of moral ideals does not produce regulative ideals for our world, but for one with a very different institutional landscape.

It is not clear how a feasible path can be charted in the existing landscape by those who raise what I call the "anarchist" objection: States are significant at present, but this significance should be revisited by restructuring the state system itself. According to this objection, a radical revision of our political landscape is in order, and the state as a social and political form should give

---

36. David Miller, "Two Ways to Think About Justice," *Politics, Philosophy & Economics* 1, no. 1 (February 1, 2002): 5–28.

way to other forms of political organizations. In his article, "Cosmopolitanism and Sovereignty," Pogge advances one version of the anarchist objection.[37] He says that we should replace the prevailing conception of sovereignty with a widely dispersed notion of sovereignty on the vertical dimension, and that we should break up political authority into nested territorial units. The result of this dispersal is that some authority will be delegated upward, to structures above states, and some below, to structures smaller than states such as federative units, counties, cities, towns, and so on, and both centralization and decentralization would accompany this process. Persons should govern themselves through various political units, without any one being dominant, and thus occupying the role of the state.[38]

There is much to value in Pogge's approach, such as his careful rethinking of sovereignty and redrawing the boundaries of our institutional imagination. But I am not sure we should be so quick to dismiss the important role held by traditional states. The lack of information about (1) how the transition to a radically dispersed system of sovereignty will take place, (2) what its costs are, and (3) how various institutional goals, such as the protection of basic human rights will be distributed across institutional levels, makes it difficult to commit to this reform path.

Take the costs of the transition, for instance. In the domestic context, societies rarely, if ever, make institutional choices in a historical and institutional vacuum. They make choices within an existing matrix of laws, institutions, procedures and organizational agents that are subject to being modified, adapted, and changed to bring them more in line with the desired conception of justice. For reasons of stability, citizens must assent to incremental, path-dependent changes that build on existing institutions and laws in order to ensure the compliance of citizens to the institutional system as a whole. This is because peoples' behavior is already converging on the existing set of rules, which are stable due to the fact that people have internalized the expectations and norms associated with them. A wholesale transformation of all institutions and laws will so radically change peoples' expectations and require of them such abrupt modification of their patterns of behavior that it can generate a radical challenge for enforcing and maintaining over time the stability of the new institutional structure.

For example, suppose that Malta decides to revise the nation's traffic laws by switching from driving on the left side of the road (a remnant of British

---

37. Thomas W. Pogge, "Cosmopolitanism and Sovereignty," *Ethics* 103, no. 1 (1992): 48–75.

38. Ibid., 58.

rule) to driving on the right side of the road. However, shifting from driving on one side of the road to another is extremely costly. People have internalized the existing rule and formed driving habits according to it, and it will take a long time for them to adapt their habits to the new rule, for cars to be retrofitted, and for road signs and traffic management to be changed. These high costs may not be decisive reasons against changing driving rules, but they are important considerations, which in conjunction with other factors, such as competing spending goals, can alter the balance of reasons. The downside of these high costs may be that on reflection, driving on the right side, although desirable in some respects, is not a feasible institutional goal in Malta at this time. Facts, and institutional facts in particular, shape the desirability of this goal.[39]

Pogge thinks of cosmopolitan morality just like driving on the right side in Malta, although on a different scale. He rejects states by arguing that from the standpoint of cosmopolitan morality, the concentration of state sovereignty is no longer defensible.[40] However, advocating a wide dispersal of sovereignty may swing too much in the opposite direction. Widely dispersed sovereignty requires a radical and comprehensive revision of the existing political structures and is bound to be accompanied by the unraveling of law and order. Pogge presents an exciting institutional vision but my previous discussion illuminates the ways in which he fails to explain how his vision interacts with the cosmopolitan ideals he favors and what the transition costs in realizing the vision are. If it turns out that the transition costs are low or bearable, and that the realization of cosmopolitan ideals is more likely with the new scheme, then we might be persuaded to get on board with the new vision. The main thing to note is that these features of the new scheme must be part and parcel of the defense that Pogge needs to mount for a radical transformation of the practice of state sovereignty.

For example, it is hard to know what to make of the claim that cosmopolitan morality is not compatible with strong concentrations of sovereignty, by which I take Pogge and other cosmopolitans skeptical of the value of sovereignty to mean that states cannot ensure a uniform protection of individual rights. At the very least, this is a contingent judgment that depends, in part, on how we evaluate the performance of states in respecting their citizens' basic rights, which institutional alternatives to states are available, and how we estimate

---

39. The point is, of course, not that such a change is infeasible in all cases. Countries have in the past successfully switched from driving on the left to driving on the right side of the road. Rather, given the particular constellation of institutional constraints that Malta may face at a particular time, the goal is not feasible as a regulative ideal.

40. Pogge, "Cosmopolitanism and Sovereignty," 58.

the effectiveness of these alternatives compared to states. In short, states are no more anticosmopolitan than a world government or a radically dispersed institutional system, such as Pogge's. Recognizing that some states abuse their citizens or lack the ability to secure their basic rights is no more of a reason to discard states as a mode of social organization than recognizing that some families are inhospitable places to raise children is a reason to abolish the family as a social institution. The state system can be compatible with cosmopolitanism, especially when backed by a system of international institutions whose function is to take over when states fail to fulfill their functions.

The anarchist must compare her account with alternatives that embody less radical departures from the present, such as the one advanced here. Comparatively speaking, we can imagine a system of institutions that provides guarantees for individual rights and does not require a substantial dismantling of state sovereignty, but rather requires the supplementation of state institutions with international ones. Unless the system of states is evidently and fundamentally unjust, causing violence and pain to the majority of people, radical revision of the state system is not warranted. Such revision is bound to cause substantive injustices of its own, by unreasonably pulling the rug out from people who heretofore have relied on the laws, protections, and benefits established by states to order their lives.[41] Therefore, a gradual, incremental approach to institution building that relies on the system of states as its structural beams is a preferable option. Relying on the system of states to impose constraints on the acceptable shape of international institutions and their goals also has the advantage of being politically acceptable here and now. Second, even if the system of states could undergo a radical revision, institutions would still have to figure into the articulation of justice. If the state system fundamentally changed, the new institutional arrangement, whatever its shape and size, would impose its own constraints on regulative ideals for global justice, and those like Pogge who favor radical change must explain the likely effects of such constraints. Pogge could reply that his proposal is not prescriptive in the sense described here, meaning it is not concerned with principles of regulation. But it is difficult to imagine institutional proposals as anything but prescriptive, so the purported explanation that his theory aims at a general moral ideal is not available here.

Using human rights and humanitarian intervention as an example in support of an institutionally dependent conception of justice must face a more

---

41. A. John Simmons, "Ideal and Nonideal Theory," *Philosophy & Public Affairs* 38, no. 1 (2010): 5–36.

fundamental challenge. Some say that the protection of human rights creates important moral requirements, but they stand apart from and are independent of the requirements of justice. Theories of justice are mainly concerned with socioeconomic justice, and questions of justice arise only after some minimal conditions of security, well-being, and stability are met. For instance, Thomas Nagel acknowledges that many people experience severe poverty, human rights abuses, and lack the minimal conditions for security. These facts about the world "are so grim, that justice may be a side issue."[42] We still need to respond to these facts, and humanitarian duties of assistance can provide guidelines in these types of situations, Nagel says. Whatever they are, these are not, in his view, problems of justice. Questions of justice are "morally less urgent but philosophically harder," and kick in after we have solved the problem of starvation and desperate need.[43] He goes on to say that "humanitarian duties hold in virtue of the absolute rather than the relative level of need of the people we are in a position to help. Justice, by contrast, is concerned with the relations between the conditions of different classes of people, and the causes of inequality between them."[44] Consequently, for Nagel, the point of global justice is to respond to social and economic inequality and not to humanitarian emergencies.

Nagel's view effectively rules out the protection of basic human rights as a concern of justice. This, to be sure, is in lockstep with the dominant Rawlsian view of justice. Rawls argues that the problem of social justice can be addressed by assuming that every political society is "self-contained, populated with fully capable adults and exists under favorable natural and historical conditions."[45] He also assumes full compliance with the principles of justice. The consequence of this view is that, while humanitarian intervention requires an institutionally dependent approach, justice does not. This is because justice, properly understood, is not concerned with massive human rights abuses, but with the relative inequality between different classes of people once minimal conditions of well-being and stability have been met.

---

42. Thomas Nagel, "The Problem of Global Justice," *Philosophy & Public Affairs* 33, no. 2 (2005): 118.

43. Ibid.

44. Ibid., 119.

45. Laura Valentini, "On the Apparent Paradox of Ideal Theory," *Journal of Political Philosophy* 17, no. 3 (September 2009): 332; John Rawls, *A Theory of Justice*, (Cambridge: MA: Belknap Press of Harvard University Press, 1999), 4–8.

Even if it is true that this distinction between justice and humanitarian duties holds, a case can still be made that socioeconomic rights also require the specification of the institutional constraints and institutional possibilities for articulating such rights in a way that can offer practical guidance, particularly when projected at the global level. Arras and Fenton's discussion of a human right to healthcare shows this to be the case. Yet what a strange object of contemplation is a theory of global justice that avoids addressing some of the most pressing, recurrent, and troubling injustices around the world! Assuming full compliance in a world in which citizens and political leaders routinely fail to comply with minimal moral demands of respect for others and with existing domestic and international law renders such a theory of justice not just unrealistic, but bereft of practical import as a regulative ideal meant for our world. Less than full compliance creates patterns of violations that a theory of justice should address.[46] Humanitarian intervention as a solution to one such pattern must be an integral part of any theory of global justice.

4. Conclusion

Theories of justice concerned with principles of regulation must be sensitive to institutional facts. For a number of reasons, such principles must be grounded in (shaped by or justified with reference to) formal institutions, legal conventions, and the best available theories about their possible effects on human behavior. First, institutions constrain feasible combinations of moral goals, such as defending the right to life and respecting the sovereignty of a state. The more we intervene in states to protect the rights of their individual members, the more we interfere with autonomous political decision making, and vice versa. These trade-offs cannot be settled in the abstract and are specific to each institutional framework. Second, institutions help to make determinate certain abstract moral commitments. We cannot define the scope, limit, and reach of such commitments absent a specific institutional framework that defines, protects, and circumscribes their exercise.

Theorizing about justice starts with identifying desirable patterns of social cooperation and institutional background conditions. This much is understood in the dominant practice of theory building. But it cannot stop there.

---

46. In fact, David Schmidtz makes an even stronger point. Compliance problems are endogenous to principles of justice. See "Nonideal Theory: What It Is and What It Needs to Be," *Ethics* 121, no. 4 (July 1, 2011): 772–96.

Theorizing must move back and forth between principles of regulation and the institutional scheme to which they apply. Building theories of international justice requires engaging in a dialectic between moral ideals on the one hand and institutional practices on the other. Regulative ideals inform institutional practice and are informed by them in turn.

In conclusion, we need to grant a more central place to institutional theorizing in our political philosophy. It is important to think of institutional models alongside theories of justice and not just consider the first as mere appendages to the latter. This book asks what possible institutional setups are feasible and desirable at the international level given certain modest goals such as the protection of basic human rights. I will argue next that another prominent proposal for a system of global institutions, namely global democracy, is not fact-sensitive in appropriate ways.

5

Romanticizing Institutions

POLITICAL PHILOSOPHERS REFLECTING on global justice are particularly susceptible to ambitious schemes for institution building. The views about what kinds of institutions are necessary at the global level vary. At one end lie modest, issue-specific, or region-specific proposals that seek to correct one major failing of the current international practice or improve the observance of human rights in one area. This solution lies at the core of the institutional pluralist view defended in the next chapter. At the other end lie the proponents of a global democracy, who believe there is a romantic match between a comprehensive institutional scheme modeled after a centralized democratic state and global justice. Proposals for this institutional option belong to a small but vocal chorus of supporters, including David Held, Carol Gould, Peter Singer, Yael Tamir, Raffaele Marchetti, Daniele Archibugi, Amitai Etzioni, Jürgen Habermas, Luis Cabrera, and Gillian Brock.[1]

Human rights abuses, widespread poverty, and international crime continue to frustrate and puzzle us as we move into the twenty-first century. Large

---

1. Peter Singer, *One World: The Ethics of Globalization* (New Haven, CT: Yale University Press, 2002); Jürgen Habermas, *The Inclusion of the Other: Studies in Political Theory* (Cambridge, MA: MIT Press, 2000); Raffaele Marchetti, *Global Democracy: For and Against. Ethical Theory, Institutional Design, and Social Struggles* (Oxford: Routledge, 2008); Luis Cabrera, "The Cosmopolitan Imperative: Global Justice Through Accountable Integration," *Journal of Ethics* 9, no. 1 (March 1, 2005): 171–99; Daniele Archibugi, *The Global Commonwealth of Citizens: Toward Cosmopolitan Democracy* (Princeton, NJ: Princeton University Press, 2008); Yael Tamir, "Who's Afraid of a Global State?," in *Nationalism and Internationalism in the Post-Cold War Era* (New York: Routledge, 2000), 244–67; David Held, *Democracy and the Global Order: From the Modern State to Cosmopolitan Governance* (Stanford, CA: Stanford University Press, 1995); Carol C. Gould, *Globalizing Democracy and Human Rights* (New York: Cambridge University Press, 2004); Amitai Etzioni, *From Empire to Community: A New Approach to International Relations* (New York: Palgrave Macmillan, 2004); Gillian Brock, *Global Justice: A Cosmopolitan Account* (Oxford: Oxford University Press, 2009).

problems require large institutions, or so the thought goes, and we need to build institutions that replicate or surpass the benefits that people in liberal democratic society enjoy, such as stability, the rule of law, equal protection for basic human rights, freedom, and equality. We get these benefits by reproducing the *formal institutional structures* of the liberal-democratic state at the global level.

Comprehensive institutional proposals for international politics focus, just like state-building efforts in failed states, on building large bureaucratic capacities, democratic legislative forums, and global enforcement powers, all of which should work together to provide the conditions of background justice that jointly conspire to make poverty, disease, illiteracy, violence, and war a thing of the past. It is tempting, and to some extent unavoidable, to have big hopes for institutional correctives at the global level. But the bigger the institutional dream, the more likely the disappointment at its results. Accounts of agency slippage, dysfunction, and failure seldom accompany such ambitious proposals, and thus cannot serve, as they should, to temper ambitious plans for institution building. I will argue that institutional reform of this type is accompanied by a high degree of variance, the risk associated with sweeping institutional change is substantial, and the benefits are uncertain. Any institutional proposal, no matter how modest, is likely to face these problems, but the grander the proposal, the more likely that its effects will stray far from the vision of its creators.

I will offer a set of reasons for being skeptical that the institutions that make up any comprehensive scheme for a global democracy can be expected to function satisfactorily and produce the benefits that its proponents assume they will. These reasons will speak in favor of a more measured approach to institutional correctives for global politics. At the very least, the proponents of large institutional schemes will need to make explicit the specific principles of regulation for global politics they defend and offer additional support for the empirical assumptions about institutional performance implicit in defending such principles.

The necessity of this theoretical inquiry is twofold. First, while support for global democracy comes in waves, skeptical attitudes toward it are equally present. But the skepticism is mostly reflexive. The downsides are as obvious to its halfhearted detractors as the benefits are to its passionate supporters. For friends and foes alike, global democracy constitutes a focal point in debates about global institutions as the standard against which alternatives are defined and measured. For this reason, we need to parse out the assumptions and implications of such comprehensive institutional models.

Second, this type of analysis is important beyond evaluating particular proposals for international institutions. Institutions are the point of contact between theory and practice, and proposals for global institutions raise important questions about what normative political philosophy can learn from empirical social science and vice versa. More so than theories of justice concerned with principles of regulation, proposals for institutional reform, or what I call normative institutionalism, must be informed by knowledge about the way institutions actually work in practice, and take into account morally relevant institutional facts.

The first section of this chapter describes some of the main features of the institutional proposals advanced by global democracy enthusiast. Next I focus on one such feature, promoting rule of law. Section 2 details attempts at rule of law reform in Latin America. Based on almost three decades of experience with rule of law reform, the results are uniformly disappointing. Section 3 draws the implications of these results for global democracy proposals. Finally, I review additional dysfunctions and pathologies international institutions are likely to develop given the existing record, and conclude with a skeptical take on global democracy proposals.

Reflecting on the costs and benefits of different proposals is necessary before a full-scale program of global institutional reform is launched. The empirical literature on rule of law reform in Latin America and the literature on organizational behavior invite us to take a hard look at our expectations about the way international institutions will actually function. If existing studies on the sociology of organizations, bureaucratic behavior, and economic analyses of institutions are right, then there is a dark side to political institutions, with implications for a program of institutional reform for international politics. This chapter is about that dark side.

1. *Cosmopolitan Global Democracy*

Cosmopolitan theorists believe that the strengthening of economic transnational ties ushers in a new political era. Previously protected by their borders, societies become ever more vulnerable to the changes visited upon them by transnational flows of goods, resources, people, and regulations. The system of states as we know it is no longer equipped to keep pace with the vast changes their societies face. This transformation requires the extension of liberal democratic institutions at the global level, including representative institutions and the rule of law. States do not have to be abandoned as a mode of social and political organization, but rather must relinquish authority upward to enable people to regulate transnational processes as part of a worldwide community of human beings. Such a transformation entails a substantive reduction in the functions and autonomy of sovereign states, which are supposed to stick to local matters and delegate decision making on issues that cross borders to cosmopolitan institutions. In large measure, the locus of popular sovereignty thus shifts from national governments to the global polis.

Proposals for global governance range from multilevel, dispersed centers of authority to a global democracy model with an executive, a legislature, and world court. What they share is a commitment to an interrelated set of international institutions that transform the relationship among individuals, who must consequently leave behind the idea of thinking of themselves as members of distinct political communities and instead embrace each other as members of one global village.

As a vehicle for justice, global democracy is expected to improve the welfare of the worse-off, to protect against human rights violations, to engage in redistributive justice, and to encourage democratic inclusion by shifting democratic input at the supra-state level. Such a shift is accomplished through the establishment of formal political institutions at the global level that are modeled on Western liberal democratic states. This formal institutional ideal makes a certain implicit assumption about its functioning: that the integrated formal institutions of a global polis would operate effectively to accomplish the goals assigned to them.

This assumption is not unique to cosmopolitan democracy proposals. When political philosophers advance institutional schemes instrumental to justice, they typically consider institutions as black boxes, meaning they are unproblematic social bodies, generally assumed to work efficiently to promote the intended outcomes. They take for granted that the incentives of the agents align with those of their principals or the larger environment such that institutional performance is closely optimal.

Assumptions such as these make their way into some of the more recent defenses of global democracy. David Held was the first to establish with clarity the coordinates of the project of global democracy in his book *Democracy and the Global Order*. He believes that global democracy can bring "global financial flows, the debt burden of developing countries, environmental crises, elements of security and defense, new forms of communication" under better democratic control.[2] Procedurally, reforms involve

---

2. Held, *Democracy and the Global Order*, 268.

the extensive use of referenda across borders on issues that are deeply contested, the creation of a global public sphere, the intense democratization of existing international institutions, the creation of a global legislature, and more powerful enforcement mechanisms that apply to the legal regime created by such a legislature. Of course, not all of these changes could be implemented immediately, and therefore transition steps will be necessary, but the changes requiring the move toward a global democracy will be profound, including the "permanent shift of a growing proportion of a nation-state's coercive capability to regional and global institutions," and the subordination of all politics to the dictates of a global demos.[3]

Carol Gould enters this debate with a particular concern for the important tension between the universality of human rights and the particularity of democratic processes at the national level.[4] She rejects the unitary framework of global cosmopolitans such as Held on the grounds that it does not allow important cultural and other differences to play out in the expression of popular will of different groups. Moreover, global democracy brings about a sort of uniformity that is not desirable from the viewpoint of respecting the political autonomy of existing societies. Shedding much needed light on different ways to conceptualize the global order, Gould distinguishes between international democracy (democracy among states), transnational democracy (democratic associations beyond states), and global democracy (which presupposes a unitary demos).[5]

Gould describes her view as being firmly entrenched in the transnational democracy camp. Democratization beyond the nation-state should be based on the "equal right of individuals to participate in decisions concerning common frameworks of activity defined by shared goals."[6] This "common activity" principle is supplemented by an "all affected" principle. Gould preserves the right of participation for those significantly affected by ecological or economic activities even when these individuals do not normally engage in common political projects. Gould argues that considerations of human rights and universal human needs and interests leave room for global cosmopolitanism as a common framework for regulating the distribution and enforcement of rights. Although she sees herself as a defender of the transnational democracy approach, she has more in common with global democracy

3. Ibid., 276.

4. Gould, *Globalizing Democracy and Human Rights*.

5. Ibid., 173.

6. Ibid., 163, 179.

supporters like David Held than she initially lets on. Indeed, her framework gives priority to the human rights framework over the self-determination of groups.[7] Despite her efforts to gain some distance, Gould comes much closer to the global democracy camp as a defender of a comprehensive framework for international institutions.

Similarly, Jürgen Habermas urges us to reformulate international law in the context of a supra-national institution with greater executive, legislative, and judicial power on the model of the European Union.[8] Habermas uses as a starting point Kant's "Perpetual Peace" in an argument that is both exemplary and instructive for the way it seeks to refashion our institutional future.[9] Kant sought to establish a permanent cosmopolitan order whose main goal was to regulate the conduct of war and create lasting conditions for the peaceful coexistence of nations. Habermas tells us that in a piece published two years before "Perpetual Peace," Kant likened the process of development of cosmopolitan law to the evolution of domestic law from the state of nature and talks about a universal state.[10] However, in "Perpetual Peace," Kant distinguishes between a federation of states (Völkerbund) and "a state of peoples" (Völkerstaat). He opts for the former, a free association of republics, which will act like a "permanent congress of states," as the least intrusive means of realizing the goals of international peace.

Habermas believes that Kant's proposal is flawed because Kant operated with an impoverished institutional imagination, constrained by traditional social contract theory.[11] In Kant's view, individual states are the dominant form of social organization and limitations imposed from the outside undermine the ability of states to provide order domestically. Historically, the problems to which Kant sought to respond were limited to wars between states with local consequences. He did not envision and consequently did not address world wars, ecological imbalances, large-scale terrorism, drug-related criminal activity, and widespread asymmetries in standards of living, which since Kant's time have united the world into "an involuntary community of shared

---

7. Ibid., 181.

8. Jürgen Habermas, "Kant's Idea of Perpetual Peace: At Two Hundred Years' Historical Remove," in *The Inclusion of the Other*, ed. Ciaran Cronin and Pablo de Greiff (Cambridge, MA: MIT Press, 1998), chapter 7, pp. 165–201.

9. Immanuel Kant, *Perpetual Peace, and Other Essays on Politics, History, and Morals* (Indianapolis, IN: Hackett, 1983).

10. Habermas, "Kant's Idea of Perpetual Peace," p. 168.

11. Ibid., 168–70.

risks." [12] Kant's proposals are simply "no longer consonant with our historical experience," as far as Habermas is concerned. [13]

Habermas recommends moving away from Kant's loose federation and closer to a global democracy. The cosmopolitan community should be conceived as a community of individuals, and not a federation of states, as Kant conceived it. This feature of Kant's proposal is inconsistent with his emphasis on the rights of individual human beings "qua human beings" with a right to equal liberties under universal law. Cosmopolitan law should bypass state collectivities and establish the direct, unmediated membership of individuals and subjects of international law. The external character of international relations should thus be transformed into a domestic relationship between the members of a common organization based on a constitution that guarantees individual rights. A UN with its own military force, a monopoly on the use of violence, and greater executive and legislative power could enforce that constitution. The UN legislature would be divided into an upper and lower house, and representation would not be based on state delegations but on directly elected representatives. The World Court would possess greater prosecutorial power, and its jurisdiction would extend from solving conflicts between states to solving disputes between individuals and their governments. [14] These global institutions would also facilitate the development of a global public sphere, which would reflect and constrain the global state. The global sphere would only function on the basis of "permanent communication between geographically distant participants who simultaneously exchange contributions on the same themes with the same relevance." [15]

The dangers of the contemporary world (ecological imbalances, asymmetries in standards of living and economic power, large-scale technologies, arms trade, terrorism, drug-related crime) have already united the world into "an involuntary community of shared risks," so the natural next step is to look for common institutional solutions to these problems. [16] Cosmopolitan law would promote the unmediated membership of individuals in one political community that guaranteed equal rights and liberties. This institutional scheme would come a long way, Habermas hopes, toward replacing the current disarray of

---

12. Ibid., 168, 186

13. Ibid., 166.

14. Ibid., 179–87.

15. Ibid., 177.

16. Habermas, *The Inclusion of the Other*, 186.

human rights protection in separate states, where rights are not only articulated differently from state to state, but where states' capacity or willingness to uphold the rights varies so greatly.

Peter Singer has also supported moving toward stronger, more centralized institutions that are responsible to the people they affect.[17] Since the growing interdependence of people around the world requires global solutions, Singer argues we should support an authority with its own legislature and with a capacity to constrain the different powerful forces that now affect people's lives across borders, akin to the integration model of the European Union, but with an additional concentration of power and enforcement capability. Singer concedes that a world government might become a "bureaucratic behemoth," "a global tyranny" that can grow "unchecked and unchallenged."[18] Nonetheless, he hopes that if progress toward centralized global institutions is gradual, such dangers might be avoided.

Both Singer and Habermas have recently redefined their stance and have become open to alternative ways of conceiving global institutions.[19] But the idea of a global democracy remains a fixed point of reference in debates about our institutional future, and is attracting a growing and enthusiastic train of supporters.[20] Among them is Yael Tamir, who believes that a global state will advance several of the goals of cosmopolitan justice.[21] According to Tamir, the establishment of a global state can "lead to a gain in the enforcement of law and order."[22] In addition, interventions to reduce persecution and suffering will be more likely. Tamir believes that protecting human rights is the most important but not the only moral role of a global state. Other roles include advancing economic justice, preserving peace and security, reducing oppression, and lessening ecological damages.[23] Raffaele Marchetti argues that global

---

17. Singer, *One World*.

18. Ibid., 199.

19. Peter Singer and Andrew Kuper, "Global Responsibilities: How Can Multinational Corporations Deliver on Human Rights?" 2005, http://www.cceia.org/resources/transcripts/5228.html; Jürgen Habermas, *The Divided West* (Cambridge, UK: Polity, 2006).

20. Luis Cabrera, "Review Article: World Government: Renewed Debate, Persistent Challenges," *European Journal of International Relations* 16, no. 3 (September 1, 2010): 511–530; Campbell Craig, "The Resurgent Idea of a World Government," *Ethics and International Affairs* 22, no. 2 (2008).

21. Tamir, "Who's Afraid of a Global State?" 244 ff.

22. Ibid., 262.

23. Ibid., 262–63.

federal institutions can increase democratic inclusion. [24] Allowing individuals to exert democratic control within the confines of states perpetuates illegitimately exclusive schemes. He proposes instead a global democratic forum to enable individuals to reassert control over the powerful forces that govern their lives by shifting democratic control upward to the institutions of a federal government. [25]

This is but a sample of the many recent defenses offered on behalf of global democracy. And although many proponents of global democracy are keen to distinguish themselves from defenders of a world government, there is little functional difference between the two camps.. Therefore, I use the term "global democracy" to refer to a system of institutions made up of a global legislature, centralized enforcement mechanisms, and uniform standards of human rights. Global democracy proposals are comprehensive in two ways: in terms of the range of goals the global institutional system is tasked with realizing, and in terms of the complex and interconnected system of organizations that are entrusted with achieving them. Notwithstanding the aspirational ideals of such proposals, the idea of a cosmopolitan democracy continues to raise red flags in these more recent incarnations, as it did in its pre–World War II versions.[26] Skepticism seems to be the predominant mood among liberal political philosophers.[27] John Rawls in the *Law of Peoples* follows Kant in thinking that a world government "would either be a global despotism or else would rule over a fragile empire torn by frequent civil strife as various regions and peoples tried to gain their political freedom and autonomy."[28] Rawls does not go much further beyond this statement to justify his dark vision of a world government. Still, the theme of tyranny resurfaces in other reactions. Michael Walzer states that it is preferable to have islands

---

24. Marchetti, *Global Democracy*.

25. Raffaele Marchetti, "Interaction-Dependent Justice and the Problem of International Exclusion," *Constellations* 12, no. 4 (2005): 487–501.

26. Catherine Lu, "World Government," in *Stanford Encyclopedia of Philosophy*, 2006, http://plato.stanford.edu/entries/world-government/.

27. Charles R. Beitz, *Political Theory and International Relations*, rev. ed. (Princeton, NJ: Princeton University Press, 1999), 182–83; Kok-Chor Tan, *Justice Without Borders: Cosmopolitanism, Nationalism, and Patriotism* (New York: Cambridge University Press, 2004), 201; Thomas W. Pogge, "Cosmopolitanism and Sovereignty," *Ethics* 103, no. 1 (1992): 48–75; Debra Satz, "Equality of What Among Whom?" in *Global Justice: Nomos XLI* (New York: New York University Press, 1999) 67–85.

28. John Rawls, *The Law of Peoples: With "The Idea of Public Reason Revisited."*. (Cambridge, MA: Harvard University Press, 2001), 36.

of tyranny than a centralized tyranny to end all oppression.[29] Walzer also raises distinct communitarian worries about the centripetal forces of a world government and their capacity to obliterate cultural and social difference. A world order could not accommodate the range of cultural and religious differences, and the richness of distinct historical cultures that surrounds us today.[30] David Copp highlights still another possible weakness. He thinks that a global government would be too prone to corruption and other ills to be an appropriate ideal.[31] Martha Nussbaum also claims that poor accountability and the potential for homogenization of culture, as well as political tyranny, speak against it.[32]

Both confidence and distrust accompany this debate, and so far it is difficult to sort out the conflicting claims advanced by both sides. What reasons do we have to believe that a global democracy will deliver the benefits its proponents aspire to? Are the skeptics justified in their reservations? Pursuing these questions is essential if we want to encourage the development of institutions that aim both to achieve worthwhile moral goals and also, crucially, to do so effectively. Any institutional view requires an understanding of the ways in which the incentives of different actors are structured, how institutions relate to the broader social and legal context, and whether there are institutional or bureaucratic cultures that are more or less conducive to institutions pursuing their goals effectively. My criticism is thus distinctive of any of the ones advanced so far. Global democracy proposals are characterized by an unclear account of political agency as the locus of reform; by a poor specification of the principles of regulation that guide the institutional components of the global order, and the functions each of them serve, by a lack of transparency about the empirical conditions that make such institutions effective, and by a lack of concern for agency slippage and institutional failure. The focus of the remaining sections is to question the assumption of institutional effectiveness that accompanies proposals for cosmopolitan democracy by drawing on social science research and the literature on comparative development of the

---

29. Michael Walzer, "Responses to Kukathas," in *Ethnicity and Group Rights: Nomos XXXIX* (New York: New York University Press, 2000) 105–11.

30. Michael Walzer, *Arguing About War* (New Haven, CT: Yale University Press, 2004), 172–76.

31. David Copp, "International Justice and the Basic Needs Principle," in *The Political Philosophy of Cosmopolitanism*, ed. Gillian Brock and Harry Brighouse (Cambridge, UK: Cambridge University Press, 2005), 39–54.

32. Martha C. Nussbaum, *Frontiers of Justice: Disability, Nationality, Species Membership* (Cambridge, MA: Belknap Press, 2006), 313.

rule of law. I will leave aside equally important, but different questions about the desirability of the aims a global democracy seeks to achieve, such as global distributive justice, or about its likelihood of coming into being in the near future.

2. Rule of Law Experiments

The prototype for a global democracy seems to work well in Western liberal democracies, and gives fodder to its proponents to extol its virtues for global politics. Citizens in these liberal democracies enjoy historically unprecedented social and welfare protections, security for their life and property, due process, economic freedom, freedom of speech, and equality before the law. Comparatively speaking, these people enjoy greater safety, voice, prosperity, and civil and political rights even in areas where Western liberal democracies fall short. Prima facie at least, it seems plausible to want to replicate these institutional features in other countries and ultimately on a world scale through a global democracy. However, efforts to implement formal institutions at the country level have been largely unsuccessful, and this has implications for evaluating the likelihood of such reforms to succeed at the global level. If recent studies on the effects of implementing rule of law reform in developing countries tell us anything, it is that it is exceedingly difficult to set up workable, functioning legal and political institutions from scratch and reproduce the successes these institutions have in some of the more developed countries.

The benefits that citizens of Western liberal democracies enjoy seem to be strongly localized, and to depend on the interaction of a series of social, economic, political, and institutional factors. We simply do not understand very well how all of these factors interact to produce the results they do, and we lack the knowledge of what designing such institutions in different environments entails. What we do know is that most attempts to replicate the successes of political institutions in developing states are failing. And if efforts to institute functioning formal institutions in Latin America and elsewhere have been unsuccessful, the chances of setting up working, effective global formal institutions modeled after Western liberal democracies are small. The risk for institutional pathologies must be weighed against the likelihood of deriving benefits from setting up the institutions of a global democracy. As it turns out, however, the benefits of setting up a global democracy are uncertain at best.

The rule of law is one of the features of functioning democracies that global democracy proponents hope to replicate at the global level. Habermas claims that a global government would embrace added competencies that would improve legal protection for human rights and restore justice. An international court should replace the International Court of Justice, currently the main UN judicial body, which does not have powers of prosecution and is mainly charged with settling disputes among states that are voluntarily submitted to arbitration by the parties in a conflict. Habermas argues instead for a court with expanded prosecutorial functions and one that is empowered to settle cases brought by individuals against states in addition to disputes between states. A constitution would empower the court to protect individual rights and enforce legal equality uniformly.[33]

This sanguine view raises the following question: How would efforts at wide-ranging reform fare in the realm of the rule of law? I argue that we can learn from efforts to institute the rule of law on a much smaller scale, and these past efforts of reform undermine our optimism in the potential for a global democracy. Initiated in the early to mid-1980s by international organizations, NGO's, and developed states, the programs have swept the globe, from Asia, the Middle East, Russia, and the former communist countries, to Latin America and Africa, and are now almost three decades old. "Rule of law" reform programs have targeted developing and postconflict nations to enhance their legal order. It is a project that, not surprisingly, has had enthusiastic supporters in developed and developing countries alike, and across all political persuasions. Indeed, the idea that the rule of law is important to peaceful, prosperous, free societies is not generally challenged. The World Bank alone has supported 330 rule of law projects with $2.9 billion since 1990.[34] Most UN agencies, the United States Agency for International Development (USAID), the Inter-American Development Bank (for Latin America), governments, private foundations, law firms, NGOs, and regional banks have been involved in rule of law programs.

These reform programs seek to render the national legal system more equitable, accessible to the ordinary person, free of corruption, and independent of undue political influences. The main goals of legal reform are "(1) a government bound by law (2) equality before the law (3) law and order (4) predictable and efficient rulings and (5) human rights."[35] Often these goals, proximate to legal

---

33. Habermas, *The Inclusion of the Other*, 179–87.

34. Michael J. Trebilcock and Ronald J. Daniels, *Rule of Law Reform and Development: Charting the Fragile Path of Progress* (Cheltenham, UK: Edward Elgar, 2009), 2.

35. Rachel Kleinfeld Belton, "Competing Definitions of the Rule of Law: Implications for Practitioners," Carnegie Papers, Rule of Law Series, 2005, 27.

justice, are accompanied by more general goals such as democracy promotion, economic prosperity, and enhanced well-being for the populations of the targeted countries. The wide-ranging institutional reforms include extensive judicial and police reforms; retraining of judges, lawyers, and the police forces; rewriting new, clear, and well-publicized laws; and creating a judiciary independent from political influence.

Rule of law reforms target various problems. Corruption and crime, abusive and authoritarian political elites, citizens' low trust in their own governments, those governments' limited ability to dispense justice, and the continued violation of human rights that characterizes emerging democracies are just some of these problems. In addition, strengthening the rule of law is considered essential to economic reform and growth, and to a stable economic environment where the rights and property of investors and the human rights of the employees are protected. Ultimately, rule of law reform aims to enhance the protection of human rights, to guarantee people's access to the legal system, to secure the promulgation of fair and explicit laws, and to ensure that governments are accountable and law-abiding. For these various political, economic, and social reasons, rule of law reform is garnering support and resources from an increasingly large number of groups and organizations within the international community. As Thomas Carothers puts it, "In many countries, people still argue over the appropriateness of various models of democracy or capitalism. But hardly anyone these days will admit being against the rule of law."[36]

With so much good will behind them, how have these programs fared so far? Has writing and rewriting constitutions, writing new law, making the judiciary independent, making the police responsive and accountable, and ensuring that state officials are bound by law succeeded? Here is what we have learned so far. By most accounts, the results are disappointing. With the exception of some small and positive gains in Latin America and Eastern Europe, after almost two decades, the reforms have achieved few long-lasting results. The attempts to help countries obtain Western-style rule of law are not productive because it is not clear how to transplant working legal institutions to countries that do not already have them.

Efforts to set up new institutions and reforming old ones, have met with numerous obstacles, which became most obvious after formal institutions were established. The assumption that once in place, the institutions

---

36. Thomas Carothers, *Promoting the Rule of Law Abroad: In Search of Knowledge* (Washington, DC: Carnegie Endowment for International Peace, 2006), 7.

will work has proven unsustainable. The environment in which these institutions operate and the ways in which they interact with social, political, and cultural norms become crucial. Take judicial independence, for instance. In many countries, reformers have introduced judicial councils, whose role is to appoint high-level judges and to handle ethics complaints. This appointment is concomitant with an extension of the judges' tenure, to make them less liable to being influenced in their judicial decisions by politicians who can reappoint them at will. In countries with highly corrupt judicial systems, such as Egypt, the Philippines, and Indonesia, instead of severing ties with political elites, judicial independence has served to isolate the judiciary from further accountability, perpetuating and exacerbating the problems of corruption.[37] In Latin America, independent judicial councils have been created to ensure that judges' selection leads to more impartial adjudication of cases. But the councils have been co-opted politically, in some cases dissolved or hampered to the point of incapacity by the executive, and in general have been infected ultimately by the underlying maladies of the political culture of favoritism and patronage that they were meant to curb.[38] The reforms have managed to produce little change in the prevalent dynamic of appointing judges who are members of political parties and who continue to be selected "for their ability to reward their political friends and punish political enemies."[39]

Bottlenecks are common and they affect the coordination of the institutional system as a whole. Reforming only one institution can create imbalances, moving the problem from one institution to the next, instead of solving it, as the USAID experience in Haiti has shown.[40] While successful modernization programs were developed in police departments, such measures were not accompanied by programs in the court system, which led police reforms to

37. Frank Upham, "Mythmaking in the Rule of Law Orthodoxy," in *Promoting the Rule of Law Abroad: In Search of Knowledge*, ed. Thomas Caruthers (Washington, DC: Carnegie Endowment for International Peace, 2006), 119–23.

38. Luis Salas, "From Law and Development to Rule of Law: New and Old Issues in Justice Reform in Latin America," in *Rule of Law Reform in Latin America: The International Promotion of Judicial Reform*, ed. Pilar Domingo and Rachel Sieder (London: Institute of Latin American Studies, 2001), 42.

39. Trebilcock and Daniels, *Rule of Law Reform and Development*, 67; Bryant G. Garth, "Building Strong and Independent Judiciaries Through the New Law and Development: Behind the Paradox of Consensus Programs and Perpetually Disappointing Results," *DePaul Law Review* 52 (2002–2003): 383.

40. Margaret Sarles, "USAID's Support of Justice Reform in Latin America," in *Rule of Law Reform in Latin America: The International Promotion of Judicial Reform*, ed. Pilar Domingo and Rachel Sieder (London: Institute of Latin American Studies, 2001), 53.

have few effects on the implementation of justice. In addition, the impact of these reforms on state behavior in many Latin American countries has been limited, as the rule of law reforms have yet to bring the actions of political elites under the effective jurisdiction of the country's laws and courts.

Reforms focused on formal institutions have also missed the important fact that much of the justice-distributing mechanisms in these countries are informal. In some developing countries, customary and traditional legal systems account for up to 80 percent of total cases.[41] This complicates the picture of legal reform, by raising new questions about how much of the informal legal system should be brought under formal legal processes, and whether and to what extent the customary and traditional law should be supported and enhanced, given how big a role it currently plays in giving ordinary people some access to justice, however imperfect. Indeed, in postconflict countries, where formal mechanisms have completely disappeared, informal mechanisms provide the only means to restore some degree of legal order. In addition, informal systems may have distinctive advantages in solving disputes through mediation and arbitration in ways that are sensitive to maintaining social cooperation and promoting harmonious relations in the community. This is an advantage over the adversarial outcomes of a formal court system that may not be as attuned to community dynamics and needs. Paralegal programs such as those in South Africa, neighborhood councils, tribal arbitration forums, and other culturally appropriate dispute resolution mechanisms may partially resolve the problems that undermine the emerging rule of law in developing countries.[42] In supporting such systems, one must be sensitive to the need to reform these informal channels themselves, to overcome biases in favor of men, wealthy individuals, or elites. Still, the preponderance of an informal justice sector, coupled with the lack of trust in public legal institutions, explains the inability of substantive institutional reforms to have wide societal impact.

Likewise, the institutional history of police has significantly hindered the success of reforms. In Latin America, the police were viewed as the arm of the state in combating civil unrest and guerilla movements, which obscured the distinction between police and military functions. Most police work was, in reality, in the service of protecting the political elites against challenges, and tasks such as protecting human rights or upholding the law were neglected. An adversarial relationship developed between the police and citizens over

41. Upham, "Mythmaking in the Rule of Law Orthodoxy," 118; Kristi Samuels, "Rule of Law Reform in Post-Conflict Countries: Operational Initiatives and Lessons Learned," World Bank Social Development Papers, paper no. 37, October 2006), 17–19.

42. Samuels, "Rule of Law Reform in Post-Conflict Countries," 18.

time. The relatively unconstrained mandate of police forces facilitated abuses perpetrated on civilians and further widened the chasm between the police and the people.[43]

The measures for reforming police in Latin America have been numerous: de-politicizing police training, modernizing case management system, and replacing old personnel with new. In order to produce a police force with a new culture, more responsive to citizens needs than politicians' interests, in some countries such as Panama, the reforms have started from scratch with a new civilian police force to replace the military one. Some of the gains made (e.g., in Panama violent crime rates fell in the 1990s) are nonetheless overshadowed by the overall increasing crime rate across Latin America and the fact that the police are often part of the problem, continuing to commit serious human rights violations and colluding with criminals.[44] In places such as Venezuela and Argentina, this picture is complicated by the fact that populations faced with growing criminal activity support a hard-line approach to policing, which ends up reinforcing the power of the police rather than curtailing it.[45]

3. Rule of Law for Global Democracy

In light of good faith and substantive efforts deployed on its behalf, the failures of rule of law reform are puzzling. "No other single political ideal has ever achieved global endorsement. . . . Notwithstanding its quick and remarkable ascendance as a global ideal, however, the rule of law is an exceedingly elusive notion. . . . If it is not already firmly in place, the rule of law appears mysteriously difficult to establish."[46] The rule of law reform program risks running out of steam as did its predecessor, the law and development program initiated in the 1960s, which after a few decades of efforts closed down. This is because relative to the extensive reform effort mounted in Latin America and elsewhere, little has been learned about effective institutional change.[47]

---

43. Trebilcock and Daniels, *Rule of Law Reform and Development*, 108.

44. Ibid., 123.

45. Mark Ungar, *Elusive Reform: Democracy and the Rule of Law in Latin America* (Boulder, CO: Lynne Rienner, 2001), 74–111; Trebilcock and Daniels, *Rule of Law Reform and Development*, 119–21.

46. Brian Z. Tamanaha, *On The Rule of Law: History, Politics, Theory* (]New York: Cambridge University Press, 2004), 134.

47. Carothers, *Promoting the Rule of Law Abroad*, 15–16; Pilar Domingo and Rachel Sieder, eds., *Rule of Law in Latin America: The International Promotion of Judicial Reform* (London: Institute

A realization of these failures has prompted renewed calls to question the assumption behind institutional performance and institutional change in the area of the rule of law. We are only beginning to learn and understand the causes of the failure, and we are far from gaining a good understanding of how social and institutional change must proceed in order to be effective.[48]

Will efforts to promote the rule of law on a world scale by instituting the legal, judicial, and policing agencies of a global democracy fare better than country-level reforms in Latin America and elsewhere? The prospects of such reforms are hard to predict with accuracy. Nonetheless, the parallels are telling. Those who engaged in rule of law reforms in Latin America have assumed that mimicking the institutions of countries with workable legal systems will generate the benefits of these workable legal systems such as human rights protections, governments ruled by law, and a responsive and accountable police force. For instance, even while anticipating problems, Mark Ungar in his book *Elusive Reform* confidently stated that "many reforms stand a good chance of being effective if they become institutionalized."[49] The rule of law reforms have focused primarily on *formal institutional* changes, by reforming existing institutions such as the courts or creating new ones where they were absent.

With the same confidence, proponents of global democracy anticipate significant benefits in the area of rule of law and respect for human rights on the basis of formal institutional reform. The large-scale institutional changes required for realizing those benefits are a world court, a formal constitution, and a coercive enforcement agency to tackle crime, international conflict, and human rights abuses. Given these assumptions, the results of experiments in rule of law reform in Latin America and elsewhere should be sobering news. As more reforms are implemented and assessed, reformers come to the understanding that law is not just an institutional system, but also a cultural system, that relies on the understanding and support of citizens. Values and customs play a substantial role in the legal system. Its health depends on how citizens

---

of Latin American Studies, 2001), 145–46; Samuels, "Rule of Law Reform in Post-Conflict Countries" 15.

48. One serious limitation to learning more appears to be the fact that rule of law programs have devoted far too many resources to formal institutional changes and too little to understanding their impacts on the populations affected by these changes. See Stephen Golub, "The Legal Empowerment Alternative," in *Promoting the Rule of Law Abroad: In Search of Knowledge*, ed. Thomas Carothers (Washington, DC: Carnegie Endowment for International Peace, 2006), 106.

49. Ungar, *Elusive Reform*, 231.

value and use the law. Judges and police forces must embrace a certain ethic and set of beliefs about their role in society in order for their performance to be fair, equitable, and effective.[50] Citizens, too, must understand the laws and support the rationale behind them, and must trust the police and the court system. This knowledge will enable citizens to assert their rights and cooperate with the legal procedures, and trust will ensure the general population's support for the courts and law enforcement system. The culture in support of legal values is not sufficient, but is necessary: "While customs without material institutions can manage to uphold some rule of law ends…institutions without customs are weak and easily circumvented by raw power."[51] Without this ethical and cultural commitment, formal institutions are simply empty vessels that end up reinforcing power inequalities and pathologies rather than producing their intended outcomes.

Still, if we cannot make these institutional reforms have the intended effects on a much smaller, country-level scale, how can we expect these formal institutional reforms to work on a global scale? It seems unlikely that formal institutional reform in global politics will simply generate the institutional effects desired by its proponents. We do not have the knowledge of what it takes to build successful institutions where they do not already exist. This is because we do not understand how institutions interact with the broader social, economic, and cultural conditions to have the effects they do. In the case of rule of law reforms in Latin America, "the chances that large scale transplantations perform the way intended are slim."[52] Basic questions about how effective change happens in legal systems remain open. Even as we are gaining better understanding of the fact that context matters, we realize how daunting it is to affect both the context and the institutions at once. This is even truer at the global level, where the social, economic, and political context is much more fragmented and complex. To be effective, global institutions will need to develop in a culture that understands their mission and is supportive of it. How to change both the institutions and the culture to make them work together is not very clear.

In Latin America, changes in formal structures have had little impact on improving the situation of the disadvantaged. This type of top-down, state-centered approach has failed so far to give attention to legal empowerment, to be attentive to the ways the marginalized and disadvantaged interact with the

---

50. Samuels, "Rule of Law Reform in Post-Conflict Countries," 20.

51. Kleinfeld Belton, "Competing Definitions of the Rule of Law" 22.

52. Upham, "Mythmaking in the Rule of Law Orthodoxy," 100.

law, and to identify the necessary changes to enhance the benefits of the rule of law *for them*.[53] People in Latin America's developing countries do not understand the laws, do not trust that they will receive justice if they resort to courts, and often lack the organization, power, and resources to obtain any access to the legal system at all. This foreshadows a potential problem for global democracy proposals as well. Changing formal structures will have little impact on improving the situation of the disadvantaged, because this type of formal approach will not be attentive to the ways the marginalized and disadvantaged interact with the law and legal institutions; this approach consequently will not be able to enhance the benefits of the rule of law by fine-tuning the institutional response to the concrete and contextual needs of the disadvantaged.

What these experiments in rule of law reform tell us is that refashioning a country's legal system on the basis of Western models accomplishes little. Rewriting a country's laws and establishing a constitution do not have lasting effects, yet these still persist as practices in rule of law reform programs. So, too, persists judicial training, a program component of rule of law reform that according to the existing evidence has had very few tangible benefits.[54] More disquieting is the conclusion that rule of law reform is not possible absent a lack of commitment from local authorities and the public for rule of law values. But how should such a commitment be obtained prior to reform? Institutional change runs into the chicken and egg problem, where success is not possible without a commitment to rule of law values already in place but it is not very clear how to instill those values in a population that does not already endorse them.

Paradoxically, the countries that need reform the most are the least likely to achieve it. While Latin American countries face challenges, their challenges are not as severe as those that face disabling internal conflict and ethnic divisions, such as those in Africa, or economic problems as stark as in some countries in Asia. Even in Latin America, practitioners in the field warn that not all environments are suited to rule of law reform and it should only be tried in countries without rampant corruption and major human rights violations.[55] Harvard Law Professor Phillip B. Heymann, who directed Harvard's

---

53. Golub, "The Legal Empowerment Alternative," 161–87; Wade Channell, "Lessons Not Learned About Legal Reform," in *Promoting the Rule of Law Abroad: In Search of Knowledge*, Thomas Carothers, ed. (Washington, DC: Carnegie Endowment for International Peace, 2006), 141–46.

54. Channell, "Lessons Not Learned About Legal Reform," 145–46.

55. Stephen Golub, "A House Without a Foundation," in *Promoting the Rule of Law Abroad: In Search of Knowledge*, ed. Thomas Carothers (Washington, DC: Carnegie Endowment for International Peace, 2006), 112–13.

Guatemala Criminal Justice project, explained upon terminating the program
due to lack of progress that it

> is not a useful expenditure of United States money to provide train-
> ing or advice to the police, prosecutors or judges of any country whose
> political and military leaders are unwilling to support law enforcement
> efforts against every form of political violence, including that initiated
> by security forces or political/economic groups to which the govern-
> ment leaders may be sympathetic... It will not work, for the people of
> the country... will come to hold the criminal justice system in contempt,
> leaving it deprived of the most valuable resource of any criminal justice
> system, citizen cooperation. And even if it did work, it would create a
> stunted, morally corrupt system of social control, not the rule of law.[56]

The Guatemala case indicates a likely similar problem on a global scale. It
warns that global institutions will have the least effect in places around the
world that struggle the most. Absent a certain threshold of commitment from
local officials, and a preexisting, functioning infrastructure whose goals are
supported by the local communities affected by it, global institutions will fail
to communicate their mission, enforce their mandates, and effect deep social
change.

4. Institutional Assumptions and Bureaucratic Pathologies

We already have good evidence that existing international institutions reproduce some of these failures. Following in the wake of Max Weber, sociologists
and political scientists have pursued the insight that bureaucracies can have
their own behavioral tendencies because they develop peculiar cultures that
can promote both their virtues and their vices.[57] Institutions stray from the
goals we generally assume unreflectively, adopt projects that are contrary to

---

56. Salas, "From Law and Development to Rule of Law," 43.

57. Max Weber, *The Theory of Social and Economic Organization* (New York: Free Press, 1947);
Yingyi Qian and Barry R. Weingast, "Federalism as a Commitment to Preserving Market
Incentives," *The Journal of Economic Perspectives* 11, no. 4 (1997): 83–92; Jonathan Bendor,
Parallel Systems: Redundancy in Government (Berkeley, CA: University of California Press,
1985); Terry M. Moe, "The Politics of Bureaucratic Structure," in *Can the Government Govern?*,
ed. John E. Chubb and Paul E. Peterson (Washington, DC: The Brookings Institution, 1989),
267–329; Terry M. Moe, "The New Economics of Organization," *American Journal of Political*

their mission, ignore contextual differences, and develop organizational cultures that undermine the ways they were anticipated to operate. Examples drawn from the actual experiences of existing international institutions and US domestic bureaucracies pinpoint causal pathways that explain distinct institutional pathologies. They are illustrative and do not exhaust the full range of tendencies for institutional dysfunction and the evidence that could be adduced for them.

First, institutions are likely to have general, vague, and even inconsistent goals. "Keep the peace," "protect human rights," "promote economic development and environmental health" do not offer clear operative guidelines as to what the organization should do.[58] Deep disagreements and conflicting visions of the organizational mission often get exposed in the process of clarifying the goals. In cases where they do not enjoy sufficient autonomy to clarify and define their own mission, bureaucrats deal with goal complexity by substituting goals with rules. Otherwise, they narrow the focus of the organization to develop a coherent organizational mission and end up treating primary goals that come into conflict with the mission as marginal. This is what in the sociological literature gets referred to as "goal displacement."

Take, for instance, the UN's refusal to offer human rights protection during the Rwandan genocide. In 1994, 800,000 Rwandans were killed in approximately three months. The UN Secretariat, which is the main body in the UN entrusted with guarding human rights, had justified its refusal to intervene by labeling the genocide as a civil war instead, claiming that it was a problem internal to Rwanda in which outside intervention was inappropriate and undesirable.[59] The reluctance to intervene can be traced back to the conflicting mission of the UN Secretariat, reflected in its history of peacekeeping. At its inception in the mid-1950s, the peacekeeping mission of the UN was limited to monitoring ceasefire deals between parties in a conflict. The light armed forces that carried the UN mandate were expected to follow the

Science 28, no. 4 (1984): 739–77; Michael N. Barnett and Martha Finnemore, "The Politics, Power, and Pathologies of International Organizations," *International Organization* 53, no. 4 (1999): 699–732; James Wilson, *Bureaucracy: What Government Agencies Do And Why They Do It* (New York: Basic Books, 1991).

58. Moe, "The New Economics of Organization," 760; Wilson, *Bureaucracy*, 26.

59. Michael N. Barnett and Martha Finnemore, *Rules for the World: International Organizations in Global Politics* (Ithaca, NY: Cornell University Press, 2004), 121–55.

rules of impartiality and neutrality, because they were deriving their authority from the consent of those involved in the conflict.

This limited involvement was reassessed after the end of the Cold War, when international pressure forced the Secretariat to expand its mission. It had to intervene in failed states and offer humanitarian assistance. This expansion required a more active role for its military forces. However, humanitarian assistance often required a departure from the rules of impartiality and neutrality. The UN forces had to either become involved in active combat in order to protect civilians in war-torn countries, or retreat to a policy of impartiality and severely curtail their operations in support of humanitarian emergencies. A series of high-profile failures of UN peacekeeping such as Somalia and Bosnia, which were threatening to undermine the organization's moral authority and support base, made the UN Secretariat adopt a culture of nonintervention, even in the face of dramatic human rights violations. The way the UN Secretariat defined its mission led it to refrain from intervention in Rwanda as well. This is an example of goal congestion that created a dilemma which made impossible the simultaneous realization of conflicting values, and ultimately undermined the primary purpose of the UN Secretariat, that of protecting human rights.

The second main feature of every institution is that it breeds a culture, "a persistent, patterned way of thinking about the central tasks and the human relationships" within it.[60] The culture contains internal rules for behavior, explicit or implicit. Among the explicit rules, those for hiring, firing, promotion, reward, and disclosure sanction certain modes of interaction among the employees and discourage others. The "corporate culture" at Google is very different than the culture in the United States Navy.

The outer environment of an organization also influences it culture. Organizations do not exist in a vacuum and their environment often defines, shapes, and constrains how organizations pursue their goals, often in unanticipated or unintended ways. For instance, in the case of the American Civil Service, the Freedom of Information Act has sought to enhance its transparency by making its files available to the public upon demand. This has implicitly encouraged bureaucrats to constrain their internal communication and storage of information.[61]

An organization that has two or more cultures can experience conflict over the proper use of its energy and resources. Tasks that are not part of the central culture become marginal. The culture may over time motivate people to

---

60. Wilson, *Bureaucracy*, 91.

61. Moe, "The New Economics of Organization," 765.

keep the organization in line with its mandate, or it may produce a divergence from it when the collective interests of its agents diverge from the organizational goals. This happened in the US State Department.

The US State Department has for a long time relied on foreign nationals to do much of the work on its embassies abroad. The construction of the new embassy in Moscow, built with the help of mostly local companies, greatly enhanced the collection of intelligence by the Russians, with listening devices strategically placed during the construction phase. The plans were approved in advance by the State Department and successive inspections have failed to report any problems with security. This is not an isolated case.[62] Many other embassies abroad were similarly compromised, and the State Department was not only slow to react when presented with evidence, but even actively opposed measures to enhance security. For instance, it opposed replacing local personnel who acted as chauffeurs, telephone operators, housekeepers, and receptionists with American citizens.

According to James Wilson, this odd behavioral tendency of the State Department to ignore security vulnerabilities can be explained by a culture that values diplomacy above all else. Diplomacy requires communication and communication implies openness. To the Foreign Service official, security undermines openness. It requires keeping foreigners at arm's length, and it creates encumbrances for building trust and inducing cooperation. In such a culture, "security specialists will not win rapid advancements…and security concerns will not win in struggles over scarce resources."[63] The institutional dysfunction of the State Department simply reflected a culture that did not place great value on security.

Third, institutions orchestrate numerous contexts at once. The universal rules they generate are inattentive to contextual and particularistic concerns, and as a consequence, they flatten diversity. In complex organizations, rules develop as a way to make sense of the organizational mission, but also to ensure fairness, equal treatment, integrity, neutrality, and so on. Even when they rise from these legitimate concerns, rules can have an inhibiting effect on the everyday functioning and overall effectiveness of an organization. Rules that ensure equal treatment and neutrality often reduce the ability of organizations to be flexible to special needs and circumstances.[64] One case in point is the International Monetary Fund (IMF). The IMF applied a standardized

---

62. Wilson, *Bureaucracy*, 90–95.

63. Ibid., 94.

64. Not only is it difficult to structure incentives to motivate efficiency in public bureaucracies, but there is no clear way to measure the effectiveness of public bureaucracies, whether

formula in countries affected by the Asian financial crisis, which consisted of budget cuts and rapid currency depreciation as previously instituted in Latin America. But these governments were not profligate spenders, and the result was, by the IMF's admission, to make matters worse.[65]

This brings us to the fourth and perhaps more disquieting feature of public bureaucracies. The IMF, the World Bank, and the UN have accumulated a distinctive record of failures but continue to operate according to the same criteria and reproduce the same failures.[66] Failure has often justified further expansion of the programs and mission of an organization. The main problem is that there is no reliable mechanism to guarantee the optimality of public organizations. Such a mechanism is present in the private sector, for instance. The market weeds out private organizations that are not effective and competitive. Firms that fail to generate profits are not able to refinance and face dissolution or takeover and reorganization. The market process is imperfect, to be sure, but no such mechanism, however imperfect, is available for public agencies.[67]

Paradoxically, some argue that public bureaucracies are ineffective by design, because they are born out of politics and they reflect the interests, strategies, and concession of those who exercise political power. Bureaucracies are, of course, not intended to be ineffective, but the compromises of democratic processes often make them this way. When building up a bureaucracy, political entrepreneurs respond to domestic electoral considerations, satisfy the demands of interest groups, reward partners that align with their policy, take symbolic stands, and claim credit for popular positions and outcomes. All of these considerations have little connection with the effective implementation of the policy for which the bureaucracy was created in the first place.[68]

---

domestic or international. We do not have a nonpolitical, nonarbitrary way to measure organizational performance, especially considering that in addition to their primary mission, public organizations have other goals such as reputation for integrity, confidence of the people, and support of interest groups, or, in the case of international organizations, support of its members and constituencies. There is no objective way to decide how much resources should be devoted to maintaining the honest behavior of the organization itself and its employees, producing a fair allocation of benefits, garnering popular support, and accomplishing its organizational goals. Ibid., 317, 326.

65. Barnett and Finnemore, "The Politics, Power, and Pathologies of International Organizations," 721.

66. For instance, conferences at the UN to collect "lessons learned" from experiences in Somalia were arranged so that no information would come out that might blemish the UN record. Ibid., 723.

67. Moe, "The New Economics of Organization," 762; Wilson, *Bureaucracy*, 315–17, 363.

68. Moe, "The Politics of Bureaucratic Structure," 267, 280.

Patterns of institutional behavior culminate in institutional pathologies. Occasional dysfunctional behavior is inevitable, but when it reflects a persistent pattern, it becomes a serious cause of concern. A UN Commission on Human Rights consistently run by countries with appalling human rights records such as Sudan undermines its ability to accurately evaluate and monitor human rights abuses around the globe.[69]

What follows from these patterns of dysfunction for a program of institutional reform such as creating a global democratic architecture? The pathologies I have just described refer to probabilistic tendencies and not deterministic ones, and it is possible that any one institution might function better than these studies suggests.[70] However, because these problems are embedded in the bureaucratic culture, it is likely that they would appear and persist within intergovernmental bureaucracies, and these pathologies might, in fact, become systematic within one centralized government. A global democracy is not likely to be responsive to plural and conflicting moral demands of people situated in different spaces, because it is prone to developing pathologies that generalize moral priorities in ways that are inattentive to, and do not do justice to, the richness of context and the particular demands of each situation that confronts our deliberations about global problems.

An advocate of global democracy could object to this way of casting the pitfalls of her preferred institutional scheme, that the true lesson from all of these studies of behavioral dysfunction is that we have to learn how to design them better. The fact that some dysfunction is likely does not mean we have to retreat into skepticism about the institutional scheme as a whole, but rather to find ways to avoid the problems described through careful institutional planning. We can learn from past mistakes to improve institutional outcomes in the future.

This conclusion is tempting, but it should be resisted. The fact that we continue to replicate mistakes of institutional design both on large and small scales proves that we do not understand enough about how institutions interact with a wide range of features of their environment to perform well. A long record of institutional dysfunction proves this to be the case. Newly created institutions have potential upsides, but also potential downsides. This means

---

69. The disgraced commission was replaced in 2006 by the UN Human Rights Council in an attempt to remedy some of the obvious deficiencies in the selection of its members and leaders ("The Shame of the United Nations," *New York Times*, February 26, 2006).

70. Barnett and Finnemore, "The Politics, Power, and Pathologies of International Organizations," 719.

that their likely outcomes are characterized by a high degree of variance, which is to say they are riskier. The larger the reach of institutions, the greater the degree of risk.

The claim is not that scaled up institutions are more prone to pathologies than smaller ones. We lack empirical evidence to make predictions about institutional performance based on size alone. Rather, the concern is that as the reach of global democratic institutions extends to larger and larger numbers of people, the negative effects of institutional dysfunction spread as well. More and more people are likely to be governed by institutions that are unresponsive, ineffective, and may act contrary to the interests of the people they are supposed to serve. Institutional dysfunction introduces a kind of arbitrary domination that should be disconcerting from the point of view of justice. We cannot tell precisely at what point the benefits of having a system of institutions such as a global democracy are outweighed by its pathologies, but surely there is a point at which the bureaucratic form is stretched too thin and its advantages begin to evanesce. It is fitting, then, to ask if cosmopolitan democracy spreads its benefits too thin for an area and population as large as the whole world.

5. Conclusion

Assessing the desirability of global democracy on the basis of empirical research is valuable beyond understanding this particular institutional model. Evidence from social science research and empirical studies attunes our peripheral vision to institutional dysfunction that we would otherwise neglect or slight as marginal. Normative political philosophy should cultivate the insights of empirical social science for encouraging vigilance about the range of acceptable institutional models. The data should either constrain the range of acceptable institutional proposals by ruling out institutional arrangements that are ineffective or have deleterious effects, or expand the range of our theoretical models by alerting us to functional institutional arrangements that work in practice but that have not yet been incorporated into the common institutional repertoire available in political philosophy. Theoretical models of international institutions cannot be advanced responsibly without an adequate consideration of the ways institutions actually perform their function. These models should be informed by knowledge of how actual institutions perform, even if empirical social science cannot fully define the acceptable range of such proposals.

This does not mean that the line between normative theorizing and empirical social science should be blurred. Theorizing about the ends of the political life, the good and the right, is bound to produce propositions that are not ultimately testable. One cannot test through social science methods whether individual autonomy is good, or whether justice should require material redistribution.[71] But when such theorizing begins to incorporate testable assumptions, political philosophy can draw on the data provided by empirical studies. Normative theories reflect on both the *ends* of political life as well as the *means*. Institutional analysis is ultimately (but not exclusively) an analysis of means. Discussing the means, that is, the institutions that can best fulfill the desired ends, allows normative theory to learn and benefit from empirical social science.

Making institutional proposals requires an understanding of how those institutions will work in practice, what kinds of practical limitations they face, and whether the practical hurdles are surmountable or end up subverting their goals. The empirical research forces us to reevaluate the ways these patterns of bureaucratic behavior structure the relationship among institutional goals, the incentives to pursue them, and how they affect the normative legitimacy of the international institutional system as a whole.

It may be that the institutions making up a global democracy can achieve at least some of the goals its defenders associate with it. I do not claim that the pathologies I have identified will definitely materialize. I am making a more modest claim. The humble state of our knowledge is such that we cannot be sure that these and other pathologies would not materialize, and they tend to materialize at a fairly high rate, including in the cases I have used as illustrations. This evidence shifts the burden of proof to defenders of global democracy, by inviting them to put forward the evidence that shows that we could dramatically reduce these risks.

Questioning the ideal of a global democracy does not imply endorsing the status quo. The problems its proponents identify are real and pressing enough that passivity in the face of massive injustice is not acceptable. We should, however, explore alternative paths for institutional reform. States are currently the building blocks of the international system, in the sense that they are primarily responsible for the well-being of their populations and also for implementing the terms of international cooperation. There is a wide range of variation in state performance on both fronts, with some states providing acceptable levels of security and prosperity at home and

---

71. Although it could presumably test specific, narrow empirical claims about the effects of individual autonomy on certain measurable individual and social indices, or whether certain kinds of redistribution produce expected social or economic effects.

contributing to common global problem solving, while other states fail to be just and legitimate at home or cooperative abroad.

State failure shows that we do need supplemental layers of authority at the international level to magnify the protection of basic rights. But it does not follow from this that global democracy is the only way to think about fixing the problem. The difficulty of reproducing already existing institutional mechanisms at the international level should encourage more institutional experimentation and innovation. The next chapter will defend an institutional pluralist approach to international institutions, which reduces the risks and damage associated with sweeping and sudden legal changes by generating a process of incremental reform in the legal system. Such a system would diffuse the risk and costs of poor moral judgment in institutional choice and design. Moreover, since change in such a system is incremental and open-ended, it creates the opportunity to revise the moral judgments implicit in the rules and norms with which different legal systems operate. Such moral flexibility is much more difficult to attain where there is a unitary, monolithic deliberating forum, which makes the chances of moral revisability small.

Whatever, in the end, we may think of this or other alternatives to the idea of global democracy, we should challenge and test our assumptions about their purported benefits. In trying to overcome the institutional failures of our current state system, there is a danger in romanticizing the benefits of grand institutional schemes. Empirical evidence of how institutions actually perform alerts us to the downsides and the necessity of expanding the debate about alternative paths to global justice.

6

Institutional Pluralism

IF WE HAVE reason to reject global democracy as a scheme for international institutions, what alternatives do we have left? How should we think about the design of the institutions that make up the supplemental layer of international agency, and the relationships among them? I argue that we should support, on reflection, a system of institutional pluralism based on authority distributed among many nodes, on experimentation with institutional design, and on gradualism in the construction of supra-state authority. This open-ended pluralistic institutional system fosters opportunities for contestation, provides checks against concentrations of power at both the state and international level, and creates incentives for the revisions of institutional procedures that fail to produce substantive benefits in the pursuit of justice.

Pluralism is a feature of the system and not necessarily of the individual issue areas where international institutions might focus their actions. It is possible that in particular issue areas, one agency is best able to provide coordinating functions. Humanitarian intervention might be one such case in which an international body, such as the UN, oversees the entire operation, even though the operation involves many different governmental and nongovernmental agents. What is crucial to institutional pluralism, however, is the absence of a central agency or hierarchy of subordinated agencies that perform all the functions of international cooperation and, in effect, hold a coercive monopoly on power. An institutional scheme without a central authority describes fairly closely the current situation in international law.

Sections 1 and 2 use recent institutional developments in international criminal law to illustrate the potential and limitations of institutional pluralism. Section 3 draws on the theory and practice of institutional design to explain the benefits of certain features of institutional pluralism. Section 4 develops the pluralist account based on complex orders theory. Section 5 takes on a distinctively Hobbesian challenge to institutional pluralism, namely that divided authority leads to conflict.

1. Institutions in International Criminal Law

While support for the idea of institutional pluralism is mounting in debates about global justice, such pluralism is still embryonic in the existing literature. Thomas Pogge, Anne-Marie Slaughter, Matthew Noah Smith, Allen Buchanan, John Rawls, and Simon Caney have proposed various versions of a system of decentralized global governance.[1] For example, in *Justice, Legitimacy and Self-Determination: Moral Foundations for International Law*, Allen Buchanan claims that taking institutional pluralism seriously can enhance the way we conceive the possibilities of a global order: "[O]ne should not assume, that the only options are a unitary approach to international legal reforms in which all progressive change must occur through the UN-based system," he claims.[2] Elsewhere, he insists again that we cannot assume that "the path to moral progress lies exclusively within the confines of the UN-based system or that there is only one path."[3] Progress toward international justice can come through institutional competition, competition of legal norms, and the interaction of systems with "overlapping domains of competence."[4] "It is worthwhile," he says, "to explore the possibility of a more pluralistic conception of the evolution of international law, one in which progress occurs through the development of—and perhaps competition among—different sources of rules and different institutional arrangements for implementing them."[5]

Similarly, in *The Law of Peoples*, Rawls rejects world government in favor of a more decentralized form of institutional authority: "It may turn out that

---

1. Thomas W. Pogge, "Cosmopolitanism and Sovereignty," *Ethics* 103, no. 1 (1992): 48–75; Anne-Marie Slaughter, *A New World Order* (Princeton, NJ: Princeton University Press, 2005); Simon Caney, *Justice Beyond Borders: A Global Political Theory* (New York: Oxford University Press, 2006); Matthew Noah Smith, "Rethinking Sovereignty, Rethinking Revolution," *Philosophy and Public Affairs* 36, no. 4 (Fall 2008): 405–40; Allen Buchanan, *Justice, Legitimacy, and Self-Determination: Moral Foundations for International Law* (New York: Oxford University Press, 2004); John Rawls, *The Law of Peoples: With "The Idea of Public Reason Revisited"*(Cambridge, MA: Harvard University Press, 2001).

2. Allen Buchanan, *Justice, Legitimacy, and Self-Determination: Moral Foundations for International Law* (New York: Oxford University Press, 2007), 455.

3. Ibid., 456.

4. Ibid.

5. Ibid., 455.

there will be many different kinds of organizations subject to the judgment of the law of peoples and charged with regulating cooperation among them and meeting certain recognized duties [emphasis added]."[6] James Bohman extends the idea of institutional pluralism in the language of a plurality of demoi.[7] A system of multiple, overlapping demoi that transcend state boundaries would allow new communities to adapt to new social facts and exercise their normative powers of citizenship at different levels in order to assert and strengthen the human rights of their members. These multiple publics can coordinate and communicate with each other to increase deliberation, inclusiveness, and representation across issues.

But all accounts of institutional pluralism provided so far lack a more fine-grained appreciation of both the comparative benefits and challenges of institutional design at the international level, and of the condition for effective performance in pluralist systems. To get a better grasp of what institutional pluralism means in practice, it is worthwhile to dwell on one example. The last century has witnessed an unprecedented growth of international law. International treaties for solving human rights abuses, economic conflicts, issues of jurisdiction, transnational movements of people, cross border criminal activities, and many other problems have proliferated. As it exists today, international law does not reflect some comprehensive master plan for institutional design but rather institutions that have evolved independently of each other, based on different guiding principles, values, and functional goals. Peace treaties and peace alliances have been the first early steps toward a recognizable system of international norms, while treaties for the protection of the environment or international criminal law are relatively new. Although the process of the development of international law is incomplete, and our interpretation of the results of this process is necessarily tentative, current international law offers a preliminary sketch of a fully grown pluralist institutional order.

If we look at how international law, in particular, international criminal law, is legislated, adjudicated, and enforced in the real world, there are good reasons to celebrate the recent developments. Until well into the mid-twentieth century, there was no international law that held states responsible for violating citizens' basic human rights. Violations went unrecognized

6. John Rawls, *The Law of Peoples: With "The Idea of Public Reason Revisited"* (Cambridge, MA: Harvard University Press, 2001), 36.

7. James Bohman, *Democracy across Borders: From Dêmos to Dêmoi* (Cambridge, MA: MIT Press, 2007).

and uncorrected by international bodies. The Nuremberg Trials generated momentum for changing this practice. They led to the creation of legal norms and mechanisms to ensure criminal liability for at least some abusing states. As international efforts have spawned international treaties and supranational criminal courts, states are no longer the last resort for human rights violations. However, individual states still play an important role in protecting such rights. They do so by, first, ensuring that their citizens enjoy humane treatment under state policies, and second, by providing outlets for prosecutions of human rights abuses that have occurred elsewhere.

The "Universal Jurisdiction" principle, as it has been labeled by its supporters, enables states to claim criminal jurisdiction for crimes committed outside of their borders, even if no relationship can be traced between the alleged criminals or the victims and the prosecuting country. Universal jurisdiction holds the promise of casting national courts as a wide net to catch alleged criminals and to buttress a global system of accountability.[8] This practice enjoys growing support. In 1993 Belgium adopted a law of universal jurisdiction, which allowed Belgian authorities to seek criminal convictions for individuals involved in the Rwandan genocides. Universal jurisdiction over crimes against humanity, genocide, torture, forced disappearances, and other crimes was asserted at various times by Canada, Australia, France, the United Kingdom, Israel, Spain, and Malaysia.

There are limitations to universal jurisdiction. States do not meet the emergent legitimacy principle and, thus, the question of how they acquire authority to prosecute crimes committed elsewhere arises. In this respect, universal jurisdiction resembles vigilante justice in the Wild West. Yet even vigilante justice can meet the functional justification and play an important institutional role in a system in which enforcement of minimal limits on the most harmful behavior is sorely undersupplied. Related to this concern is the fact that many observers are wary of politically charged prosecutions, and are apprehensive about the procedural fairness of trials arising out of universal jurisdiction.[9] And sure, this is always a danger, but in the end, the legitimacy of such a concern will depend on the institutional history of the country that asserts universal jurisdiction. Countries with reliable due process procedures

---

8. Stephen Macedo, ed., *Universal Jurisdiction: National Courts and the Prosecution of Serious Crimes Under International Law* (Philadelphia: University of Pennsylvania Press, 2006).

9. Henry Kissinger, "The Pitfalls of Universal Jusridiction," *Foreign Affairs*, July/August 2001, 86–96.

will suffer large internal and external reputation costs and undermine public trust if they engage in politically motivated prosecutions. The loss of trust will endanger their ability in the long term to provide redress for injustice.

It appears that some of the states asserting universal jurisdiction have been overwhelmed by the strain placed on their justice system by the sheer number of prosecutions. Belgium later reduced the scope of its law in order to better handle the large proliferation of suits. These problems and imperfections notwithstanding, universal jurisdiction is an improvement over the previous system because it increases prosecutorial and judicial capacities in an area of international law in which they are in short supply.

Universal jurisdiction operates in concert with other mechanisms designed to prosecute human rights violations. The UN has been successfully involved in the creation of a number of ad hoc war tribunals for the former Yugoslavia and Rwanda. Other regional or global forums also have jurisdiction in matters of international criminal law. The European Court for Human Rights has had marked success in this area.[10] The success of the European Court has spurred attempts at emulation in other parts of the world, with considerable progress in some regions and slow progress in others.[11] More salutary is the development of the ICC, a permanent international court that operates like a "court of last resort." The role of the ICC, as defined by its statute, is to intervene when national courts are not willing or able to investigate crimes against humanity, leaving the national courts to exercise primary responsibility. The ICC is a young organization, and the jury is still out on how well it can pursue its mission, especially since it lacks a dedicated mechanism to enforce its arrest warrants. But because of its broad-based support, it has more legitimate authority than countries operating under the principle of universal jurisdiction. In contrast to universal jurisdiction, where the range of cases covered depends on the content of domestic law, the ICC has a well-defined mandate covering a wider range of cases involving egregious violations of human rights.

In addition to multiple forums for prosecution and adjudication, the current international legal system relies increasingly on sophisticated mechanisms

---

10. Laurence R. Helfer, "Consensus, Coherence and the European Convention on Human Rights," *Cornell International Law Journal* 133, no. 26 (1993).

11. The American Convention on Human Rights of 1978 led to the formation of the Inter-American Commission and Court of Human Rights. There are similar efforts to develop a regional forum for the African continent. The African Commission on Human and People's Rights has been mostly ineffective so far due to the persistence of tyrannical and corrupt political cultures, the lack of funds, and the many social, economic, and political troubles. See Conor Gearty and Costas Douzinas, *The Cambridge Companion to Human Rights Law* (New York: Cambridge University Press, 2012).

to monitor human rights norms across the globe. Human rights conventions, intergovernmental and nongovernmental agencies that evaluate and monitor human rights violations, and international and regional judicial bodies that review cases and interpret international human rights law are all changing the ways human rights are interpreted and protected for the better. The evolution of legal norms and institutions in international criminal law is far from complete, and the intractable political headaches in different parts of the world in the last decade alone make us acutely aware of the inability of the present system to deal comprehensively with human rights violations. Nonetheless, we should acknowledge that the process of evolution has produced the development of institutions that are complementary and overlapping, each filling a serious gap in global governance. Their regional and specialized character grants them knowledge of the local circumstances and makes them more sensitive to different cultural and legal traditions. The institutions of international criminal law are not only complementary, but also competitive to some extent. The greater the number of forums, the more channels there are for individuals whose rights have been violated to seek justice. Institutional competition here can work to increase reliance on "good" mechanisms or organizations and phase out the use of "bad" or less effective ones. If, for instance, the ICC becomes over time both reliable in addressing different kinds of human rights violations and efficient in doing so, then the international community might rely less on universal jurisdiction and ad hoc tribunals. What emerges is a pluralist system, in which no single international agency defines, interprets, and enforces the rules of international criminal law.

2. Fragmentation and Conflict

The fragmented nature of international criminal law and international law more generally has triggered new concerns about the ability of a pluralist system to induce rule-governed behavior, and to ensure peace, stability, and the observance of human rights. Some of these concerns have been highlighted by the authors of the United Nations' commissioned report *Fragmentation of International Law: Difficulties Arising from the Diversification and Expansion of International Law*.[12] International law has evolved through "the emergence of specialized and (relatively) autonomous rules or rule-complexes, legal institutions and spheres

---

12. Study Group of the International Law Commission, *Fragmentation of International Law: Difficulties Arising from the Diversification and Expansion of International Law*, 2006, http://www.un.org/ga/search/view_doc.asp?symbol=A/CN.4/L.682.

of legal practice."[13] In particular, the large and increasing number of treaties with little historical, functional, and geographic continuity creates the possibility of conflicting legal norms. There is trade law, environmental law, human rights law, law dealing with diplomacy, communications, medicine, crime prevention, energy production, security, indigenous cooperation, and so on. The treaties codifying these laws have different goals and sometimes recommend distinct, even incompatible courses of action. There is no clear hierarchy of legal norms in international law and no hierarchy of institutional authority either. The "conflicts between rules or rule-systems, deviating institutional practices and, possibly, the loss of an overall perspective on the law" should cause concern.[14] Some practitioners believe that the fragmentation of international law leads to "the erosion of general international law, emergence of conflicting jurisprudence, forum-shopping and loss of legal security."[15]

Extrapolating from international law, we can group these concerns under three types of interrelated challenges to a pluralist institutional order: (1) A pluralist system will *lack consistency*, and it will fail to apply rules uniformly across a variety of cases and situations; (2) a pluralist system will *lack coherence*, the ability to systematically organize the relationship between different authorities and rules and to provide a clear hierarchy of decision making; (3) the existence of multiple agents in addition to states will generate overlapping areas of competence and authority and, as a result, will breed confusion about who is in charge and will lead to *jurisdictional conflict*. I will confront each of these challenges in order.

The first challenge to institutional pluralism is that the very fragmentation of international institutions leads to the uneven application of rules. In international law, the diversification of bodies of law in different fields creates disparate and even conflicting recommendations for the same subject of international law, or for different subjects in different places. For instance, commitments to liberalize trade barriers under World Trade Organization (WTO) agreements clash with trade restrictions justified under environmental treaties.[16] States that belong to both legal regimes often face conflicting recommendations about the proper course of action. Consistency is desirable for a number of reasons, and chief among them is that consistency leads

---

13. Ibid., para. 8.

14. Ibid.

15. Ibid., para. 9.

16. Joost Pauwelyn, *Conflict of Norms in Public International Law: How WTO Law Relates to Other Rules of International Law* (New York: Cambridge University Press, 2003).

to predictability, legal security, and a sense of fairness and equality in the application of rules.

This concern for consistency is underscored by two assumptions about (1) the goal of law and legal institutions and (2) the cause of inconsistency in international law. The first assumption holds that we should presume equality before the law: Like cases should be treated alike. A strong presumption of equality in international law leads to an insistence on uniformity across the board. But this insistence fails to note the conditions of social complexity that give rise to international legal arrangements. The purposes of signatories to international treaties, whether these are states, private actors, or nongovernmental organizations, often reflect differences in factual and circumstantial evidence that an abstract insistence on uniformity conceals. Human rights violations differ in the Middle East from those in Africa or Southeast Asia, and the regional or international treaties that seek to prevent them will differ in focus and the solutions they offer. Lack of consistency reflects the fact that the conditions are different, and consequently, the remedies embedded in the legal rules are also different. Rather than insisting that "like cases should be treated alike," one must acknowledge that some of the time, the complementary principle of justice "unlike cases should be treated unalike" should prevail. The apparent lack of consistency can be simply a response to the plurality of problems international agents seek to address and the institutional responses created to address them.

So, as the report on "fragmentation" itself acknowledges, deviations in international law should not be understood as legal-technical mistakes or simply instances of inconsistent rulemaking driven by states' self-interested behavior. This is the second assumption that punctuates a concern for consistency. Deviations reflect the situation of social complexity in which international law operates. But fragmentation also reflects the varied interests and preferences that actors in a pluralistic (global) society have. WTO arrangements seek to reduce barriers to trade and create open and equal access to global markets, while environmental treaties emphasize the value of natural resources and promote responsible use. Sometimes the two goals conflict, and there is no unique trade-off to guide a consistent resolution of all conflicts. Insisting too much on uniformity and consistency might actually be counterproductive if it brushes over legitimate differences between the values relevant in particular problem areas.[17] Consistency in this case, far from being required by justice, ultimately constitutes a failure of justice.

---

17. Study Group of the International Law Commission, *Fragmentation of International Law*, para. 16.

This is not to say that we should encourage the perspective of self-contained international institutions, insulated from other institutions and international law. Signatories to international treaties can and should consider how one value or principle that they promote (e.g., preserve international peace) interacts with others (e.g., intervene with military force to prevent genocide). These signatories should be aware that conflicts will likely arise between different legal norms and regimes, and must make good faith efforts to address the conflicts either in the treaties and charters of international organizations or by considering specific legal rules in the context of general international law. This would ensure that with respect to the same set of facts and actors, the law is the same regardless of the identity of the authority arbitrating the dispute.

Coherence is a different but related idea. Coherence in international law means that the different rules and institutions of international law fit well together, that there is a clear hierarchy of both the principles of international law and also of the institutional authorities that define, promote, and enforce those principles. Coherence in legal systems presupposes clear decision procedures for adjudicating conflict. For instance, the US domestic legal system is hierarchical in both its laws and institutions. The US Constitution is the document whose principles underlie all the laws and statutes passed by the Congress and by individual states and to which ultimately these laws and statutes must conform. The United States also relies on an order of judicial review and oversight, with the Supreme Court being the final interpreter of the law and legal arbiter in cases of disagreement. Likewise, international law would seem to require a clear set of underlying principles to which all treaties must conform, and a system of uniform guidelines and institutions for adjudicating disputes that arise from conflicting interpretations of those principles. The fact that no such hierarchy exists is believed to threaten the coherence of the international legal system.

Clearly, the international legal system is less coherent than many domestic legal systems. However, stated this way, the objection to existing international law as a system of institutional pluralism both underestimates the extent to which coherence is present in international law, and overestimates the extent to which coherence is a desirable feature of any institutional architecture. Although there are no formally recognized hierarchies, informal hierarchies do exist in international law. They can help to generate coherence, by serving as a primitive basis of a future formal hierarchy of international law norms. These informal hierarchies rely precisely on the distinction between values that protect fundamental, nonnegotiable human interests, and values that are important but can be trumped. Jus cogens represent the category of norms invested with protecting fundamental human interests. These norms are formalized in the Vienna Convention on the Law of Treaties (VCLT), Articles 53 and 64, as norms from which no derogation is acceptable. These norms include genocide, including systematic rape, forceful displacement, inflicting other conditions calculated to bring about the destruction of a group, crimes against humanity such as slavery and apartheid, war crimes, and the crime of aggression.

Primary rules are those that lay down rights and obligations for the subjects of international law, and they presuppose secondary rules, which are rules that stipulate how primary rules can be enacted, modified, and terminated. The VCLT, which is a document drafted by the UN's International Law Commission, represents one very important group of secondary rules in international law. It lays out the rules under which treaties among states may be created, ratified, and modified. The VCLT defines, for instance, what counts as a treaty, the requirements for formal consent, the procedures for determining when breaches of treaties have occurred, and the role and nature of jus cogens norms.

The role of jus cogens in international law is significant, and it is part of a larger toolbox of rules—primary and secondary—used by legal practitioners to bring conflicts under familiar patterns of legal reasoning. Norms of jus cogens have priority in two possible types of legal conflicts: those regarding treaties and those involving customary law. In these cases, the treaty or customary norm that comes into conflict with a jus cogens norm is simply invalidated. There is no automatic resolution in a third type of case, in which two norms of jus cogens clash. According to VCLT, disputes that involve clashes of this sort must be submitted to the International Court of Justice (ICJ) or to common arbitration.[18]

One example offered by the debate over the immunity of Augusto Pinochet illustrates just how jus cogens norms can work. Pinochet, the former head of state of Chile, was alleged to have tortured and killed thousands of citizens of Chile and of other nations, including Spain and the United States, as part of an operation to eliminate political opponents while in office.[19] Pinochet was living in Great Britain when Spain asked the British courts to extradite him to be tried under the universal jurisdiction principle.[20] Traditionally, heads of state were granted immunity under international law for acts committed

---

18. Ibid., para. 368.

19. Ibid., para. 370.

20. Ibid.

while in office.²¹ The British high court, however, denied Pinochet immunity on the grounds that that jus cogens in the prohibition of torture overrides immunity for heads of state.²²

Jus cogens acts as a minimal moral standard that establishes an order of importance for values that are too fundamental to human interests to be overridden. So what of the other moral values in international law and the possibility of conflict between them? Normative hierarchies can be helpful to a certain extent, but are undesirable as a comprehensive methodology for dealing with legal conflict. Beyond a rudimentary but weighty moral baseline, conflicts cannot be settled a priori, and the necessity to deal with them in legal practice will remain. That means that for most values that fall outside the scope of the minimal standard, the possibility of legal conflict is both real and enduring. If the moral world is fractured, as ethical pluralists would have us believe, then it is inadvisable to establish hierarchical relationships within the law that rely on precarious orders of precedence.²³ For example, to establish the principle that sovereign independence takes precedence over human rights violations or vice versa, so that every case involving a conflict between the two is settled in favor of the one true value, would be a mistake. This move would fail to take into account the fact that protecting sovereign autonomy and defending people against violations of their basic rights each involves its own morally important interests. A legal order that would permanently subordinate one interest to the other would rob us of the opportunity to try to distinguish how different interests interact in various contexts and of the moral clarity necessary to give each interest its due.

In addition, procedural norms and principles can also help to settle legal conflicts. Anticipating legal conflict among various norms in international law, the signatories of treaties often articulate procedures according to which conflicts can be settled in international courts and tribunals. For example, the procedures specify who may file a complaint for an alleged breach of treaty, the rules of evidence, whether amicus briefs may be submitted on behalf of

---

21. Ibid., para. 371.

22. Ibid., para. 370. In the end, although he lost his immunity, Pinochet was deemed unfit to stand trial in Spain for health reasons. He was set free by Britain and returned to Chile. In Chile, he managed to avoid being tried for human rights violations for the rest of his life. Jonathan Kandell, "Augusto Pinochet, Dictator Who Ruled by Terror in Chile, Dies at 91," *The New York Times*, December 11, 2006, sec. International/Americas, http://www.nytimes.com/2006/12/11/world/americas/11pinochet.html.

23. Carmen E. Pavel, "Normative Conflict in International Law," *San Diego Law Review* 46, no. 4 (2009): 883–908.

either party, and terms and deadlines according to which all conflicts will be settled.

International law practitioners have developed procedural principles that allow them to respond in flexible ways to substantive problems of legal conflict, many of them borrowed from domestic legal practices. International law contains interpretative maxims and conflict resolution techniques such as *lex specialis, lex posterior*, and Article 103 of the UN Charter. Treaties are considered special law—*lex specialis*—with respect to general law, and there is an established principle in international law that says *lex specialis derogat lege generali*—special law takes priority over general law. This means that if general law does not have the status of jus cogens, from which no derogation is permitted, then treaties supersede general law. Thus, for instance, the ICJ decided that both human rights law, which is general international law, and the laws of armed conflict apply in times of war, but what counts as arbitrary deprivation of life in times of war is derived from the law of armed conflict.[24] The principle of *lex specialis* establishes an informal hierarchy in international law. *Lex posterior* helps to establish temporal relations between treaties. *Lex posterior derogate legi priori* means that more recent law prevails over earlier law. Similarly, Article 103 of the UN Charter, signed by and binding on all UN members, also establishes orders of priority. It states that in a case of conflict between members' obligations under the Charter and their obligations under any other international agreements, the Charter obligations shall prevail.[25]

To conclude, institutional and norm pluralism in international law does not cripple the proper functioning of international law. There is good reason to believe that the lack of formal legal hierarchies, the multiplication of treaties, and the general fragmentation of international law do not undermine legal coherence, predictability, or the equality of legal subjects. This is also the optimistic conclusion of the International Law Commission's fragmentation study.[26] Pluralism in international law is acceptable because coherence can be created by establishing a priori hierarchies among norms that protect fundamental human interests and other norms of international law. Moreover, when such hierarchies are not available, the legal principles and interpretive maxims developed by international law practitioners to deal with conflict

---

24. Study Group of the International Law Commission, *Fragmentation of International Law*, para. 96.

25. Ibid., para. 329.

26. Ibid., para. 492.

allow for a flexible, contextual, and balanced procedural approach to recurring normative conflicts. As such, institutional and norm pluralism has positive features that we should try to preserve and enhance.

International institutions more generally can function well together if they rely on international law as the normative basis that both informs their mission and constrains the acceptable ways in which they can pursue their goals. International law itself need not be uniform in order to generate uniformity among international agents. It suffices if all agents submit to the same set of laws, such as human rights laws. Still, coherence is valuable only to the extent that it integrates and makes possible the workable, just, and legitimate procedures of international law. Coherence is no virtue if it merely replicates and amplifies the injustices already present in the system. This does not mean that coherence is not valuable at all. The desirability of coherence must be assessed in conjunction with the justness and legitimacy of the laws themselves.

Coherence and consistency are desirable to the extent they allow a legal system to handle jurisdictional conflict. This brings us to the third challenge of international law as an institutional pluralist system. Jurisdictional conflicts ensue when, absent a hierarchically structured institutional system, two or more agents claim jurisdiction over a problem that spans international borders. A few general points must be made before addressing this concern. Conflicts are more likely to occur under a system of institutional pluralism than under a hierarchical system, and so the necessity of finding acceptable solutions to them is more pressing. Still, those who worry about the potentially disruptive effects of conflict often fail to note the productive effects conflicts can have. Conflicts conjure up clashes of interests and the lack of a common ground that leads to bitter feuds, but conflicts often produce a search for common ground, opportunities for the contestation of settled norms and procedures, and the creation of new institutional forms designed to resolve recurrent problems. Anne-Marie Slaughter talks about the positive power of conflicts as an engine to increase trust and, ultimately, cooperation.[27] In domestic politics, she argues, conflict through competition and contestation can lead to a greater understanding of different viewpoints. New information about the constraints under which different agents operate emerges in this process, as do a greater appreciation of the alternatives and a desire to work together to produce lasting solutions to recurring conflicts. So, too, can conflict in international politics have positive effects, Slaughter claims. For instance, it can lead to the generation of "procedures and substantive principles…developed over the

---

27. Slaughter, *A New World Order*, 208.

course of repeated conflicts among the same or successive actors," that "take on prudential weight, both through learning processes and the pragmatic necessity of building from experience."[28] It is through managing conflicts that we build institutions that are both reliable and responsive to the actual conditions that generate the conflicts in the first place.

Nonetheless, the fact that conflict has positive value does not mean we should not attempt to minimize its likelihood. General norms, procedures, and decision-making rules about which agent possesses authority over what issue, or divisions of authority that are settled between particular agents, are effective ways of dissolving conflicts of authority. Therefore, the substantive reply to those who worry about jurisdictional issues is to argue that there is no ground for requiring that problems of jurisdictional conflict be solved by appealing to a rigid institutional hierarchy on the model of a centralized state.[29]

Jurisdictional conflicts are a contingent feature of an institutional system, in the sense that they materialize when and to the extent to which there are no clear rules outlining the extent of an institution's authority. Due to the young age of the existing international system, jurisdictional conflicts are addressed on an ad hoc basis between contending authorities, as illustrated by the Pinochet case. However, patterns are slowly emerging that may encourage a more systematic approach to the problem of conflicting jurisdictions. Extradition treaties are one way to deal with this type of conflict. So, too, are the agreements that seek to specify more precisely the issues over which international agents have jurisdiction and the proper division of labor both among them and between them and individual states. One can avoid the problem of conflicting jurisdictions by giving precedence to one agent over another in a case of conflict. For instance, the ICC statute affirms that the ICC should be considered as a court of last resort and assigns states the primary authority to deal with criminal matters. Another example is Article 2005 of the North American Free Trade Agreement (NAFTA), which states that NAFTA dispute settlement courts are preferred over the General Agreement on Tariffs and Trade (GATT), the treaty preceding the WTO, on standards-related issues, such as sanitary and phytosanitary measures or the environment.[30]

---

28. Ibid., 211–12. Slaughter draws on Robert Cover's work on "jurisgenerative process" in "The Supreme Court, 1982 Term-Forward: Nomos and Narrative," *Harvard Law Review* 97 (1983): 4.

29. Smith, "Rethinking Sovereignty, Rethinking Revolution," 428.

30. North American Free Trade Agreement, U.S.-Can.-Mex., art. 2005, December 17, 1992, 32 I.L.M. 289 (1993). John H. Barton et al., *The Evolution of the Trade Regime: Politics, Law,*

It obliges a complainant state to withdraw from a WTO dispute if the defending NAFTA state prefers to settle the dispute under NAFTA.[31] Existing conflicts could be resolved or brought into more familiar patterns through international agreements that clearly delineate jurisdictional authority.

Jurisdictional conflicts can prove instrumental in keeping concentrations of power in check in international politics. The move from a world fragmented into sovereign states to a world fragmented into specialized "regimes" places limits on absolute state sovereignty and provides layers of governance that can both constrain the unacceptable impulses of existing states and be constrained in turn. Checks and balances are a side benefit of overlapping jurisdiction. In conclusion, there are problems in a pluralist system of international law, but the problems can be addressed through existing techniques and procedures. Pursuing the unity of international law at the expense of diversity of values and contextual variation is not attractive. Thus, the features I emphasized at the beginning of the chapter, such as contextual solutions to problems by specific problem areas (WTO) or regional treaties and compliance mechanisms (NAFTA), experimentation with institutional design, and redundancy among its various courts and tribunals, are strengths, rather than weaknesses of the system of international law.

3. The Benefits of a Pluralist System

In order to better appreciate the benefits and challenges of a pluralist institutional system, we must turn to institutionalist theory and empirical social science. The features of the current institutional order highlighted below characterize both coercive and noncoercive institutions. What distinguishes such institutions is whether they have been authorized to use force or the threat of force against noncompliers. Three features stand out: the importance of contextual solutions; the value of experimentation; redundancy as a source of reliability for institutional performance. These features are of broader relevance for future international institutions, whether coercive or not.

The value of experimentation under these conditions is clear. We have limited knowledge of the solutions needed to address different problems and of the solutions needed to address the same problem in different environments. We also know that institutions misfire, are prone to dysfunctional behavior, and often fail to reach the outcomes for which they were designed.

and Economics of the GATT and the WTO (Princeton, NJ: Princeton University Press, 2008); Pauwelyn, *Conflict of Norms in Public International Law*, 114–15.

31. Pauwelyn, *Conflict of Norms in Public International Law*, 115.

International institutions are no exception. The distinct potential of international institutions to reach vast numbers of people forces us to pay particular attention to the forms the dysfunctions may take and the remedies needed to address them.

One strategy for reducing institutional failure is to encourage institutional experimentation. Experimentation allows multiple problem-solving approaches. As such, it animates a competitive process of institutional design (how best to deliver services), a more careful selection of ends (what goals are we best positioned to achieve), and parallel efforts to attract funding. A pluralist, competitive order can capture more adequately the incentives to direct the process of institutional learning and can encourage trials, experiments, and innovations that will generate more effective approaches to global problem solving. Under this system, new institutional arrangements can be developed in response to past failures, and may be able, on the basis of accumulated knowledge, to reduce organizational errors. Thus, an institutional pluralist system can engender a process of "creative destruction" in which institutional efficiency increases over time.[32]

Experimentation leads to duplication of institutional effort as a strategy for increasing reliability. This may seem counterintuitive, and it goes against fundamental principles of public administration. After all, the goal with public and private bureaucracies alike is to minimize redundancy, reduce expenses, and streamline organization. Doing more than is strictly necessary is considered excessive and wasteful. Nonetheless, as Jonathan Bendor argues, not all duplication is wasteful. In *Parallel Systems,* Bendor says that if we want things to be not just inexpensive, but also effective, we may need more than one public agency to operate in a given policy area.[33] Due to the inevitable blunders that accompany complex organization missions, reliability requires organizational redundancy.[34] Drawing on the work of political scientist Martin Landau and economist William Niskanen, Bendor argues that redundancy "can provide a measure of reliability in the face of uncertainty. Where one agency fails, a second may succeed."[35] Consider the following example:

> Suppose an automobile had dual breaking circuits: each circuit can stop the car, *and* the circuits operate independently of one another so that

32. The term "creative destruction" was coined by Joseph A. Schumpeter in *Capitalism, Socialism, and Democracy,* 3rd ed. (New York: Harper Perennial, 1962), 82–85.

33. Jonathan Bendor, *Parallel Systems: Redundancy in Government* (Berkeley: University of California Press, 1985).

34. Ibid., 1–3.

35. Ibid., 2.

if one malfunctions it does not impair the other. If the probability of either failing is 1/10, the probability of both failing simultaneously is $(1/10)2$, or $1/100$. Add a third independent circuit and the probability of the catastrophic failure and no brakes at all drops to $(1/10)3$, or $1/1000$.[36]

The point of the example is to explain that the reliability of a system can be enhanced over the reliability of its individual components *when those components operate independently*. Burton Klein makes the same point with respect to weapons development.[37] Klein observes that design choices made early in the development of a weapons project rarely meet performance specifications. He recommends that the same design tasks be assigned to competing teams. The teams would provide different proposals for the same problem, increasing the chance of a satisfactory design. A program conceived this way avoids committing the entire project's resources to faulty design in the early stage of planning. Though these examples are taken from domestic politics, the point applies more broadly. When the stakes are high, the chances of failure are significant, and uncertainty abounds concerning the best course of action, institutional competition provides a better chance of discovering effective solutions to problems. When public agencies compete for jurisdiction and resources, this rivalry stimulates greater efficiency on their part, more public oversight, and reduced rates of spending compared to a monopolistic agency.[38] Contrary to popular opinion, redundancy can induce a more effective use of resources.

Bendor examined public transportation systems in three different US metropolitan areas, two of which display redundancy and one that is monopolistic. The first, the San Francisco Bay area, has two redundant transit agencies: Bay Area Rapid Transit (BART) and Alameda-Contra Costa Transit District (AC). The second, the Washington Metropolitan Area Transit Authority (METRO), runs a monopolistic, integrated bus and rail service. For the third, Bendor chose the competitive planning of a transit system in Minnesota rather than its operation. The diversity of the cases was intended to provide structural variety in order to better assess bureaucratic competition at both the planning and operation stage, and test the hypotheses that competitive

---

36. Ibid., 26.

37. Burton Klein, "The Decision Making Problem in Development," in *The Rate and Direction of Inventive Activity: Economic and Social Factors*, ed. Harold M. Groves (Cambridge, MA: National Bureau of Economic Research, 1962), 477–508.

38. Bendor, *Parallel Systems*, 2–3.

planning produces reliable information and redundant operations provide reliable service.[39] The conclusion of the study supported these hypotheses. Among other things, the Minnesota example demonstrated that competitive planning is more reliable than monopolistic planning in alerting superiors to questionable factual premises. It also showed that competition in planning is more likely to reduce the probability of errors. Similarly, the BART-METRO comparison revealed that redundancy creates increased reliability and is more likely to increase a system's ability to absorb errors and reduce their costs.[40]

There is a clear lesson here for the design of a system of international institutions. Relying on multiple, discrete, independent institutional channels can increase the reliability of the system as a whole. Duplication of institutional effort is not necessary across the entire range of institutional goals, but is essential when the chances of failure are high and when failure is costly in terms of human lives. Diversity, modularity, and decentralization help to localize damage and to prevent shocks from percolating throughout the systems. Competition enables experimentation with institutional design and encourages the discovery and imitation of successful procedures. New institutionalist theorists have internalized this lesson. Elinor Ostrom has studied how institutional diversity allows communities to cope with various common resource problems.[41] Douglass North has shown that institutions that compete tend to display more adaptive, flexible behavior and perform better.[42] He also says that

> "conformity can be costly in a world of uncertainty. In the long run it produces stagnation and decay as humans confront ever new challenges in a non-ergodic world that requires innovative institutional creation because no one can know the right path to survival. Therefore, institutional diversity that allows for a range of choices is a superior survival trait, as Hayek has reminded us."[43]

---

39. Ibid., 227. Bendor also says: "Organizations can rarely be evaluated by absolute yardsticks; the social comparison of how similar organizations are faring is often the best one can do. Consequently, monopolies are in a comfortable position: clients, lacking comparative yardsticks, have difficulty evaluating a monopoly's performance. But redundant organizations, whether public or private, must live with the anxiety that they can be weighed and found wanting" (p. 241).

40. Ibid., 249–53.

41. Elinor Ostrom, *Governing the Commons: The Evolution of Institutions for Collective Action* (New York: Cambridge University Press, 1990).

42. Bendor, *Parallel Systems*, 227; Douglass C. North, *Institutions, Institutional Change and Economic Performance* (New York: Cambridge University Press, 1990), 16, 25, 81, 99.

43. Douglass C. North, *Understanding the Process of Economic Change* (Princeton, NJ: Princeton University Press, 2010), 42.

One might worry that competition will erode the disposition of different international institutions to cooperate with one another in addressing multidimensional problems that require a concerted effort from many quarters. But competition does not preclude cooperation. Indeed, if it did, one would expect to see the least amount of cooperation among private firms competing in international markets. However, private firms cooperate across borders even though their cooperation has been little acknowledged or formalized. Competition among firms for market share is often paralleled by cooperation pacts to solve problems that arise from operating in different environments, especially where risk and uncertainty are pervasive. Firms cooperate for a variety of purposes: to exchange information and learn from each other's experiences (business associations); to create rules so that they enhance the stability of the environment and they act according to predictable patterns (financial clearing houses, international stock exchanges, arbitral courts); to develop standards for products; and to create mechanisms for assessing the reliability of economic or political partners (bond rating agencies).[44]

These cooperation pacts are part of complex orders that create rule-governed behavior at the international level. We have good evidence from a variety of social sciences and even biological sciences that socially complex systems can evolve without a central planner or central enforcement mechanism and still operate well in the aggregate, meaning that they provide relatively stable behavioral patterns and opportunities for peaceful and productive interactions among members. Emergent orders develop over time in a path-dependent fashion, so they are determined by the point of departure. But the pathways in which the nodes develop channels of communication are indeterminate and, thus, unpredictable. Economists often talk about unplanned, spontaneous orders in this way, and Hayek is one of the foremost theorists of complex orders. We turn to him for insight into how complex orders emerge and function.

4. *Complex Social Orders*

Complexity creates problems for theorists and practitioners of institutional design. Complex orders are difficult to understand and predict, but institutional design requires the ability to predict how an institution will fare in a

---

given environment and how different design choices will change its actions and results.[45] Complex orders exhibit patterns of regularities, but such patterns are consistent with the irregular and unpredictable behavior of agents at the micro level. Complexity theorists emphasize the randomness of the connections between various individual elements, the indeterminacy of each element's behavior, and continuous evolution and change that create new patterns. Complexity lies between complete, predictable order and randomness, and it cannot be easily described, evolved, engineered, or predicted.[46]

The fact that the social world we inhabit and the space in which we need to design institutions are complex is increasingly vivid as connections among people and places around the world multiply. While complex orders raise challenges for pluralists, they also do not make things any easier for the proponent of a virtual monopoly of power at the global level. On the contrary, complexity highlights the hubris of engaging in large-scale institutional design because the components of a system can be tightly linked, and the opportunities to misunderstand these connections, as well as the possibility of institutions misfiring and producing unintended consequences, are considerable.

Most economists understand this well, and F. A. Hayek understood and explained the challenges of complex orders better than most.[47] Hayek is well known for deriving the idea of complex orders from market processes. In a centralized economy, one authority, the state, dictates how to allocate resources toward different ends—what to produce, how much to produce, and at what price.[48] By contrast, in a market, prices provide information to different producers about how to allocate resources, and help over time to reallocate those resources where there is the most demand for them. The market creates incentives for individuals to use their unique abilities, resources, and knowledge for productive uses, and this brings about an overall order.[49] Hayek argues that a discovery procedure takes place through competition that produces a system in

45. Scott E. Page, "A Complexity Perspective on Institutional Design," *Politics, Philosophy & Economics* 11, no. 1 (February 1, 2012): 6.

46. Ibid.

47. He won the Nobel Prize in Economics in 1974 for his contribution to the theory of business cycles. Hayek is mostly known as an economist, but he also made important contributions to social and institutional theory, as well as the philosophy of law. See also Edward Feser, ed., *The Cambridge Companion to Hayek* (New York: Cambridge University Press, 2006).

48. F. A. Hayek, "The Use of Knowledge in Society," *The American Economic Review* 35, no. 4 (September 1945): 519–30.

49. Friedrich Hayek, *New Studies in Philosophy, Politics, Economics and the History of Ideas* (Chicago: University of of Chicago Press, 1985), 91–92.

which all that is produced is produced at the lowest possible cost. The economic "order" is thus defined by regular patterns of production, allocation, and exchange that allow supply and demand to effectively communicate and respond to each other. Prices that fluctuate freely with the market, property rights, and the rule of law are the preconditions of making economies work.

In one of his most important contributions to social theory, *Law, Legislation and Liberty,* Hayek develops the key insight that not all order resulting from *human action* is the result of *human design.*[50] Knowledge in society is dispersed, and the institutions that are best able to cope with incomplete, dispersed knowledge are those that evolve over time in response to local problems. Such institutions harness local knowledge for various ends pursued by diverse participants in a market. In a complex order, the patterns of regular behavior are not the result of conscious design. In a market, for instance, given some exogenous basic rules, like well-defined property rights, the order of the system is produced endogenously. Dispersed information is accessible only because of forces that produce order without centralized guidance and control.[51]

In complex systems, large numbers of variable elements interact to produce patterns "which have properties that are not reducible to the particular properties of each element."[52] The shape of complex orders depends on the makeup of and connection between the initial components and thus is path dependent. It is also made up of modules that are tightly connected, so that change in one ripples through others. This does not mean that we have no ability to comprehend and predict complex orders, but that our predictions cannot be about specific states, only about ranges of outcomes, or what Scott E. Page calls "social choice correspondence," which is a set of idealized outcomes given the environment.[53]

Thus, institutional design must be context dependent, that is, take as its starting point the existing social and institutional order, and reactive, which means accounting for the range of behavioral responses from other elements in the system that will affect its outcomes. Complexity theory suggests,

---

50. F. A. Hayek, *Law, Legislation and Liberty,* Vol. 1: *Rules and Order* (Chicago: University of Chicago Press, 1978), 37.

51. David Schmidtz, "Friedrich Hayek," in *The Stanford Encyclopedia of Philosophy,* ed. Edward N. Zalta, ed., Fall 2012, http://plato.stanford.edu/archives/fall2012/entries/friedrich-hayek/.

52. Gerald Gaus, "Social Complexity and Evolved Moral Principles," in *Liberalism, Conservatism, and Hayek's Idea of Spontaneous Order,* ed. Peter McNamara and Louis Hunt (New York: Palgrave Macmillan, 2007), 152.

53. Page, "A Complexity Perspective on Institutional Design," 6; Gaus, "Social Complexity and Evolved Moral Principles," 153.

therefore, that because "behaviors may depend significantly on the entire collection of institutions facing an agent," thinking of institutional mechanism design in isolation of the actual circumstances in which the institution will operate is a substantial error.[54]

There are, however, important differences between institutional and market orders that are not adequately captured by focusing on Hayek's description of markets. First, markets require institutional norms such as property rights and the rule of law to be able to develop at all. While norms and rules can be created endogenously in a market, for example by building on the precedents of arbitral courts to create rules for enforcing contracts, most economists, including Hayek, assume that the rule of law predates the emergence of markets and is a precondition for it.

The question we face in international politics is how to create the rule of law from scratch. At any one point, different agents follow rules and behavioral patterns that may be implicit. The task of institutional design is to render those patterns of behavior acceptable relative to a moral standard. This requires changing rules or making existing rules more effective, but the likelihood of that happening depends on how the different parts of the system—individuals, states, international institutions, economies, social groups—interact and adapt their behavior to institutional change. Therefore, while pluralist institutional orders belong to the class of complex orders much like market orders, pluralist institutional orders have different aims, different metrics for the success of individual elements and the system in the aggregate, and produce different patterns of regularities than markets. Instead of efficient allocation of resources for competing ends, institutional orders aim to produce rule-governed behavior; instead of profits and the productive employment of resources to desired ends, institutional orders are measured by how well they protect individual rights, generate social peace, and foster cooperative behavior; instead of production and exchange patterns, institutional orders seek to render individual behavior compliant with general rules. In a pluralist system, institutions act independently and there is no one authority telling each which goals to pursue and how to pursue them, just as in a market system. But institutions are not firms producing consumer goods. Profit is not an adequate metric to analyze institutional performance as it would be for firms in a market. Moreover, the price system cannot perform the function of directing the allocation of resources to multiple and sometimes incommensurable ends, as it does in a market.

---

54. Page, "A Complexity Perspective on Institutional Design," 19.

Yet Hayek provides important insights for the design of international institutions. Rule-governed behavior need not be the result of large-scale planned orders. It can result from the interaction of individuals and organizations that coordinate in different domains of social interaction. We can plan and design particular institutional agents with specific mandates at the international level. Such institutions must respond to real problems, harness specialized knowledge, and take into account existing patterns of interaction in a given area. But to enhance the observance of human rights across the globe, we need not have a "global" institutional plan. Such a plan would not take due note of the limits of human knowledge in understanding and organizing complex systems, would not be able to exploit local knowledge to solve problems, and would lack an appreciation of how different institutional components interact with each other.

Thus, it may come as a surprise that Hayek himself recommends a world federative state for international politics. He believes a world state would be the best equipped to ensure minimal guarantees for individuals at the international level. A full-fledged, cosmopolitan world government, entrusted with the realization of a multitude of purposes, is undesirable in his view because such a government would be too coercive and interfere with too many areas of individual people's lives. But a minimal world state, one that maintains the existing political divisions as federative units, constrained to the provision of minimal guarantees for individual rights, Hayek argues, could best realize order among states.

To be both an advocate of market orders and a world state might strike some as inconsistent. But Hayek believes we can distinguish between the spontaneity of an order and the "spontaneous origin of the regularities in the behavior of elements determining it."[55] According to Hayek, order can rest on rules and regularities that are imposed. So, for instance, at the international level, the best approach is one that secures order in the system through a supra-national authority whose strictly limited role is to enforce the rule of law. He envisions this authority as a supra-national federative body that respects national sovereignty, limiting it only insofar as it leads to harm for others. Such a federation would have only a negative kind of authority, meaning that it would not interfere with economic policies or other internal matters of states. It would keep its own planning minimal while being a barrier to undesirable political and economic planning at the global level.[56]

---

55. Hayek, *New Studies in Philosophy, Politics, Economics and the History of Ideas*, 74–75.

56. F. A. Hayek, *The Road to Serfdom: Text and Documents—The Definitive Edition (The Collected Works of F. A. Hayek)* (Chicago: University of Chicago Press, 2007).

The relevance of articulating his view for a global order here, however, is to highlight that his proposal for a world state is ostensibly contradictory to his emphasis on spontaneous order *only* if one takes the view, which Hayek did not, that there is no distinction between markets and economic order on the one hand and political order on the other.

Hayek's proposal is not wrong to distinguish market and institutional orders. His proposal for a minimalist world government does, however, clash with his emphasis on modesty about institutional design in complex systems. The knowledge-based component of Hayek's view stresses the limits of accurate planning of institutional agents. Hence, institutional pluralism with its emphasis on small, narrowly focused institutions and incremental change is more Hayekian in spirit than Hayek's own plan for the global order. We have both limited moral knowledge—knowledge about moral goals and their required trade-offs—as well as limited institutional knowledge—knowledge about the best means to achieve those moral goals. Moreover, we also know with a fair degree of certainty that institutional dysfunctions are likely to materialize, leading to failures in reaching institutional goals. To make institutional structures large is to ensure that the mistakes are large.[57] This limitation should moderate institutional design ambitions. This moderation follows Hayek's lead in insisting that providing order is inseparable from questions of knowledge more widely construed—economic, technical, and scientific. In the international realm, where the scale of moral problems can be quite daunting (as in the case of genocide, for instance), it is important to allocate resources efficiently, and to have access to the best technical and scientific knowledge. In such situations, we need to act fast, and rely on flexible and specialized expertise to improve the conditions of many thousands or possibly millions of human beings. The need for specialized knowledge and mobility in the face of urgent crises calls for international institutions that are specialized, a kind of division of labor that ensures that not all tasks are performed by, or entrusted to, a single body.

5. A Hobbesian Challenge

With multiple bodies with coercive authority, the problem of conflict remains. Jurisdictional conflict is not merely a problem in need of a technical solution, such as coordination and a clear division of authority. Hobbes worried that

---

57. I thank David Schmidtz for this point.

fragmentation leads to violence. He was emphatic that sovereign authority not be divided: "For that were to erect two sovereigns, and every man to have his person represented by two actors that by opposing one another must needs divide that power which (if men will leave in peace) is indivisible, and thereby reduce the multitude into a condition of war, contrary to the end toward which all sovereignty is instituted."[58] Multiple centers of authority, especially when those centers have coercive powers, can engage in destructive conflict.

Those who push the Hobbesian worry would say that perhaps the different courts and compliance mechanisms that evolved in international law function precisely because most of them lack coercive capacity. What happens, though, if we have two security councils or two organizations tasked with humanitarian intervention, and they disagree about what the best course of action is in a given situation? Does institutional pluralism have the fatal flaw of generating a new kind of international war—war between independent and powerful international institutions?

I believe it does not. To see why, it helps to distinguish between a strong and a weak reading of the Hobbesian worry. On the strong reading, divided authority inevitably leads to conflict. On the weak reading, divided authority may lead to conflict, but not necessarily. Probabilistically speaking, war is likely in both scenarios, but it is all but certain on the strong reading compared to the weak one. While we lack the counterfactual evidence to affirm with certainty that institutional pluralism would do better than a unitary democratic state on that account, we live in a world where authority is divided on multiple levels and we can draw some tentative conclusions about the viability of institutional pluralism.

We have good evidence that the strong thesis is not defensible. In Western democracies, power is divided among multiple branches of government, and war does not seem more likely because of it. In fact, constitutional division of power has probably led to a decrease in conflict by making predatory government action less attractive. The situation also looks promising at the international level. A survey of the international politics scene reveals the existence of power centers with coercive capabilities that include both states and international institutions. The UN Security Council, NATO, ECOWAS (The Economic Community of West African States), the United States, and Russia are all major players in international politics with military capability. Theoretically, their disagreements can lead to conflict. What makes the

---

58. Thomas Hobbes, *Leviathan: With Selected Variants from the Latin Edition of 1668*, ed. Edwin Curley (Indianapolis, IN: Hackett, 1994), 119.

system work relatively peacefully is that the participants to international politics, both states and international institutions, have internalized a series of norms about appropriate behavior and have developed, however haphazardly and incompletely, forums where their disagreements are arbitrated by neutral third parties. The United States and Russia can air their disagreements in the Security Council and the UN and come to a mutually acceptable compromise before resorting to war.

Not all states have internalized such norms, and nondemocratic states in particular lack the internal accountability mechanisms that prevent their political leaders from engaging in risky and violence-inducing foreign policy. A further point is that not all violence is made equal. A system of international institutions may, in the short run, increase justified violence (in order to prevent genocide, e.g.), while decreasing it in the long run. Or, violence may increase overall even if such institutions would be reducing occasions for outlaw states to engage in unjustified violence.

We have further reasons to believe that increased fragmentation of authority at the international level will not increase unjustified violence compared to a system without fragmentation. Given the limited powers of international organizations and the fact that they will depend heavily on democratic states, an increase in unjustified violence does not seem more likely. The limited powers will reduce opportunities for international institutions to engage in power plays that can trigger conflict. In addition, citizens in democratic states can exert control to temper the bellicose tendencies of secondary agents, just as they do for their primary agents. If the democratic peace hypothesis is to be believed, a democratic public will constrain the reasons for which their secondary agents can go to war and the means to fight such wars.[59]

The key to an institutionally pluralist system working without major disruptions while peacefully integrating different agents into a complex organizational whole is that its components are themselves beholden to shared norms of right conduct. When pluralist systems lack common norms and decision procedures that are inclusive, the risk that disagreements will deteriorate into armed conflicts is greater. However, when states and other international actors

---

59. Michael W. Doyle, "Liberalism and World Politics," *American Political Science Review* 80, no. 4 (2012): 1151–69; Bruce Russett et al., "The Democratic Peace," *International Security* 19, no. 4 (1995): 164–84; Bruce Russett, *Grasping the Democratic Peace* (Princeton, NJ: Princeton University Press, 1995); James Lee Ray, "Wars between Democracies: Rare, or Nonexistent?," *International Interactions* 18, no. 3 (1993): 251–76. For a critique of the democratic peace hypothesis, see Leif Wenar and Branko Milanovic, "Are Liberal Peoples Peaceful?," *Journal of Political Philosophy* 17, no. 4 (2009): 462–86.

are subject to norms about appropriate behavior and accept as legitimate the existence of third-party arbiters, the possibility of conflict diminishes.

The risk of war is not zero, but no potential institution alternative comes close to zero probability in this regard. This is why the second, weak reading of the Hobbesian thesis is true but trivial. The alternative, a monopoly of force, does not guarantee a community free of conflict. It merely converts potential conflicts from external into internal ones. If the history of our post-Westphalian state system is any guide, this is quite a common problem in many states for which moving to one central authority did not eliminate conflict. In fact, it might have exacerbated it.

Faith in global democracy as a more peaceful solution compared to institutional pluralism is based on the mistaken Hobbesian prediction that a monopoly of force leads to peace, all else being equal, and that a pluralist system cannot develop the tools to deal with disagreements and nonviolent conflicts over the most favored policy, law, or course of action. The lesson of economic and institutionalist theory is that complex, unplanned orders with multiple centers of authority can create relatively harmonious patterns among the units composing them such that over time they devise both mechanisms for resolving conflicts peacefully and for integrating new nodes of authority, without creating large disturbances.

The Hobbesian solution to war, a monopoly of coercive power, leads to a different problem, which I identified in Chapter 1 as the "infinite regress problem." The second mutual assurance problem arising in a state is whether the political authority will fulfill its function reliably. This assurance problem is left unresolved by the state model. Anthony de Jasay has observed that in order to ensure adequate performance by an executive, we need an external enforcer, and then an additional enforcer to oversee the external enforcer, and so on. This leads to an infinite regress of contracts for enforcement and adjudication of previous contracts.[60]

A monopoly of power at the global level illustrates precisely the problem de Jasay identifies. There is no outsider enforcing the supposed contract between the global government and the people as a whole, or the world government and the people living in various states in the case of a federalist arrangement. The problem of regress is simply moved one level up without being solved.

---

60. Anthony De Jasay, *Against Politics on Government, Anarchy, and Order* (London; New York: Routledge, 1997), 19, 22–23, 197, 204; Anthony De Jasay, *Justice and Its Surroundings* (Indianapolis, IN: Amagi/Liberty Fund, 2002), 49–53.

Institutional pluralism is the only arrangement able to solve the problem of infinite regress. International institutions constrain states and can be constrained by states, in turn, in a complicated but feasible reciprocal enforcement relationship. Here is how. The infinite regress problem arises because in the case of a single state, whoever has control of the state's political power can, alone or in collusion with a segment of the population, subdue the rest of the population with no chance for the latter to withdraw authorization from those abusing political power. An extreme case of this is North Korea today. An international institution could step in and ensure that the authority of North Korean leaders stays within acceptable limits, by holding current leaders accountable for their crimes, and requesting that future leaders respect minimal guarantees for basic rights as a condition of their staying in power. But what about the possibility of collusion between the North Korean government and the international institution?

First, the number of international institutions ensuring the minimal morality of the exercise of political power in North Korea would be several, not one. The greater the number of international organizations, the lesser the possibility of collusion between the North Korean government and all of these organizations. If North Korea colludes with a China-led Asian human rights organization, for example, the ICC and NATO could step in to enforce minimal standards for human rights. Second, other states will have an interest in preventing any international institutions from colluding with any one state, and will seek to block unsavory alliances that will be detrimental to their interests as well. Even a China-led Asian human rights organization can expect to encounter resistance from South Korea, India, or Indonesia in its attempts to support the North Korean leader. An international system characterized by horizontal and vertical division of authority creates reciprocal accountability mechanisms. This upshot of institutional pluralism does not only alleviate concerns about infinite regress problems with international authority, but can also dismantle, in part, the anarchist objection on which de Jasay relies to reject the state. If the reason to reject the state as a mode of social organization is that there is no higher power to enforce a contract between citizens and their political leaders, the creation of international institutions as secondary agents makes that reason moot.

6. Conclusion

A bird's-eye view of the international scene reveals vast challenges for making states compliant with minimal human rights standards. At the start of the twenty-first century, we are in a relatively fortuitous position of working with an emerging consensus of what the minimal standards are thanks to jus cogens norms. With the goal of making citizens less vulnerable to the abuses of their states, the main question becomes what kind of international order can deliver results. This chapter establishes some of the benefits of a dispersed, pluralist institutional model. A pluralist order consists of multiple nodes of authority such as states and international institutions, none of which has final authority in all domains. Its features are contextualism, experimentation, and redundancy. The conditions for the success of pluralist orders are that its various agents internalize over time the central norms that guide the order and build rules of priority to deal with jurisdictional conflict.

If one takes a comparative perspective to include other possible alternatives for a system of international institutions such as a global democracy, more must be said in order to settle the relative desirability of each alternative. One could argue, for example, that all of the three challenges I have identified in this chapter (inconsistency, incoherence, and jurisdictional conflict) would be better handled by a more unitary institutional order, one that offers a more hierarchical and uniform application of rules and procedures. A vertically integrated institutional order is preferable over a system of institutional pluralism. This is precisely the basis on which recent advocates of global democracy have argued their case. One way in which they could react to institutional pluralism is to argue that the incremental, trial-and-error process of building up an institutional system is too slow-paced and uncertain. After all, the pace at which problems are created as a result of state abuse or failure is fast and the severity of these problems is extreme. Violent conflict, human rights abuses, and poverty are still rampant in many parts of the world, and the international community is either unwilling or unable to get involved. Slow institutional buildup of agents devoted to specific problems leaves a lot unresolved.

However, if one takes a long-term view of the evolution of international institutions, a view that aims to build up effective, responsive international agents and that allows for the revision for institutional solutions that prove to be inappropriate, incrementalism is the appropriate path. There is no necessary inconsistency between incremental progress and the idea of a better society and better world. Importantly, however, slowness is not a limit specific to institutional pluralism alone. A more centralized, institutional, monist system is likely to face the same kinds of difficulties. The sheer scale and geographical reach of global problems make it difficult to solve them in a short period of time by any imaginable institutional setup.

This chapter maintains that global democracy simply may not be necessary because a system of institutional pluralism can achieve a more acceptable, legitimate institutional order, one in which respect for human rights is high. But an approach that defends the desirability of international institutions must face a final and more formidable challenge, that mounted by realists who claim that such institutions have no significant effects on state behavior, and that, moreover, states are better off not abiding by international rules constraining their actions. Realists deny the very possibility of a normative order at the international level. The next chapter takes on this realist challenge.

7

The Possibility of Rule-Governed Behavior in International Politics

CAN INTERNATIONAL INSTITUTIONS be effective tools for constraining the pathological behavior of states? Prominent international relations theorists claim that they cannot. After all, international institutions are the powerless puppets of great military and economic powers, with no real effect on the ways states behave toward each other and toward their own citizens, realists say. According to realists, it is naive to expect international institutions to constrain state behavior or to hold political leaders accountable.

Like most scholars of international relations, realists regard international relations as a positive discipline engaged in explanatory social science. Thus, they claim not to take any view on the normative status—that is, the rightness or wrongness—of particular courses of action, rules, or institutions. Tracing their intellectual ancestry back to Thucydides, Machiavelli, and Hobbes, realists describe a world without a global sovereign as a world of permanent conflict, in which each state is exclusively preoccupied with its own survival. The fight for survival leads to competition and conflict. In this environment, cooperation is dangerous because it exposes states to the predatory behavior of other states and makes them vulnerable in the battle for survival.[1]

---

1. Classic realist texts include Kenneth Waltz, *Theory of International Politics* (New York: McGraw-Hill, 1979); Kenneth N. Waltz, *Man, the State, and War* (New York: Columbia University Press, 2001); Joseph M. Grieco, "Anarchy and the Limits of Cooperation: A Realist Critique of the Newest Liberal Institutionalism," *International Organization* 42, no. 3 (Summer 1988): 485–507; John J. Mearsheimer, "Back to the Future: Instability in Europe after the Cold War," *International Security* 15, no. 1 (Summer 1990): 5–56; John J. Mearsheimer, "The False Promise of International Institutions," *International Security* 19, no. 3 (Winter 1994–1995): 5–49.

Despite their professed intention to stay within the realm of explanatory social science, realists often mesh together two different claims about international politics. On the one hand, they make a *descriptive/predictive empirical* claim about the permanence of war as the normal state of affairs in an anarchic system. As long as states remain permanent pillars of the international system, the creation of international institutions will not affect the dynamic of state interaction in conditions of anarchy, and will not effectively constrain state action, they say. On the other hand, they make an implicit *normative* claim about the appropriateness of moral guidelines for the conduct of states' foreign policy. Morality, at best, is superfluous and, at worst, exacerbates conflict by making those who follow rules vulnerable to the ruthless behavior of those who disavow any moral constraints on their actions. States who cooperate with other states or who submit themselves to international law lose out in the battle for survival.[2] The second claim challenges not so much the effectiveness of international institutions, but the desirability of a normative order considered from the perspective of states interested in maximizing their self-interest. On realist grounds, effective international institutions are, thus, neither likely, nor desirable.

The present chapter replies to the realist challenge raised against the view defended in this book. First, to defuse the worry that relying on international institutions to cement the protection of individual rights is hopeless and confused, I review the evidence offered by liberal institutionalists and constructivists, who show that international institutions can have independent effects on state behavior and can effectively constrain them. Second, I challenge the self-conception of at least a part of international relations literature as value-free social science. While international relations scholars have added to the repertoire of explanatory social science, I will show that some of the rational choice models that international relations scholars use for their explanatory theories rely on questionable normative assumptions about state agency, preferences, and goals. Finally, I defend the possibility of an international normative order that makes it desirable and prudent for state behavior and the behavior of all other actors in international politics to be guided by shared principles and norms.

---

2. Few realists would admit to making normative claims or being motivated by normative concerns rather than purely descriptive, causal explanatory accounts of the way things are. But normative assumptions are inevitably packed into the theoretical machinery of realism. And occasionally, such assumptions are made explicit. See, for example, Waltz, *Man, the State, and War*, 37.

1. *Cooperation Under Anarchy*

Anarchy is a powerful explanatory variable for the realist worldview. Anarchy describes a condition of coexistence among states without a centralized, hierarchical rule-maker and enforcer. This condition determines state preferences, behavior, and likelihood of cooperation. As Joseph Grieco explains, realists argue that anarchy "fosters competition and conflict among states and inhibits their willingness to cooperate even when they share common interests." Furthermore, "international institutions are unable to mitigate anarchy's constraining effects on inter-state cooperation."[3] The realist worldview can be summed up in five assumptions. (1) States are dominant in international politics. (2) Anarchy is the main determinant of states' preferences and actions. (3) States in anarchy are preoccupied with material power and security, and are predisposed toward conflict and competition. (4) Cooperation creates vulnerabilities and severe penalties for states, which are cost sensitive and behave like unitary, rational actors. Thus, it is in states' interest to shun cooperation. (5) International institutions have marginal effects on states' behavior.[4]

While realists are right to warn against indulging in a rosy picture of international institutions, their claim about the futility of international institutions has been successfully challenged. Liberal institutionalists and constructivists have questioned the realist understanding of the structure and dynamic of international politics. According to them, the empirical record shows that cooperation is possible and likely in a world of independent states, and it is bound to have positive effects on how states behave toward each other. International institutions generate significant patterns of order by creating rules for state behavior, and states comply with them even if compliance runs counter to their short-term interests.[5] Institutions solve collective action problems, reduce transaction costs, make commitments credible, provide information, facilitate the choice of stable cooperative equilibria, and encourage reciprocity among parties. Cooperation in one area engenders cooperation in other areas, and patterns of order can spread and multiply.

Cooperation in world politics is not inevitable, always effective, or guaranteed to be permanent once it happens. But the fact that distinctive patterns of

---

3. Grieco, "Anarchy and the Limits of Cooperation," 485.

4. This is Grieco's list. Ibid., 488; For a different list see Mearsheimer, "The False Promise of International Institutions," 10.

5. Peter M. Haas, "Do Regimes Matter? Epistemic Communities and Mediterranean Pollution Control," *International Organization* 43, no. 3 (July 1, 1989): 379.

cooperation among states have become more pervasive in the last half century does not fit well with the realist worldview. Liberal institutionalists such as Robert Keohane and Joseph Nye have established the importance of international institutions relying on realist assumptions about state behavior under conditions of anarchy. They also treat states "as rational egoists operating in a world in which agreements cannot be hierarchically enforced," and argue that interstate cooperation occurs only if states share common interests.[6]

But liberal institutionalists challenge the conclusion that states must compete in order to survive.[7] When realists say that the structure of international politics conditions states' strategies, and states concerned with survival will choose not to cooperate, they mean that states will find themselves in a repeated prisoner's dilemma scenario and the rational strategy will be for them to defect. However, as liberal institutionalists predict, a repeated prisoner's dilemma allows players under a sufficient shadow of the future to build trust and expect to receive benefits in the future in exchange for present cooperation. Indeed, it is more rational for them to seek to achieve their ends by interacting in cooperative ways than to do so by fighting. Repeated interactions can generate stable cooperative equilibria because they change the incentives of states to cheat, reduce transaction costs, provide focal points of cooperation, and link issues, which makes it harder for states to defect in one area of cooperation if they have interests in other areas.[8]

Realists counter that this scenario is likely *only if* states rest content with gaining absolute advantage compared to the precooperation status quo, that is, if they gain more than they had before, irrespective of how much other states gain. But states are rarely content with absolute advantage. They are actually preoccupied with relative advantage. Relatively better material capabilities enable states to better preempt or defeat attacks. If states believe cooperation offers strategic advantages to their partners by allowing them to gain relatively more from cooperation, they will choose not to cooperate. But realists again

---

6. Robert O. Keohane and Lisa L. Martin, "The Promise of Institutionalist Theory," *International Security* 20, no. 1 (Summer 1995): 39.

7. Robert O. Keohane, *After Hegemony: Cooperation and Discord in the World Political Economy* (Princeton, NJ: Princeton University Press, 1984); Kenneth A. Oye, *Cooperation under Anarchy* (Princeton, NJ: Princeton University Press, 1986); Robert O. Keohane, "International Institutions: Two Approaches," *International Studies Quarterly* 32, no. 4 (December 1988): 379–96; Joseph S. Nye, "Review: Neorealism and Neoliberalism," *World Politics* 40, no. 2 (January 1988): 235–51; Kenneth W. Abbott and Duncan Snidal, "Why States Act through Formal International Organizations," *Journal of Conflict Resolution* 42, no. 1 (February 1, 1998): 3–32.

8. Keohane and Martin, "The Promise of Institutionalist Theory," 45, 49.

have this dynamic wrong. Rather than precluding cooperation altogether, a concern with relative gains makes cooperation impossible only if no mutually acceptable equilibrium over distributional outcomes is available.[9] A concern with relative gains does not prevent cooperation, it just changes the nature of the cooperation problem to be solved.

Certainly, those who hum to the realists' tune that international treaties are nothing more than declarations of good intentions with no real effect on state behavior have plenty of reasons to roll their eyes. The proliferation of human rights treaties is a case in point. Despite the hundreds, or perhaps thousands of human rights treaties over the last half-century, human rights violations remain large and persistent today.[10] But we would be mistaken to dismiss all of these treaties as insignificant. Although not all treaties have had an impact, some have changed states' human rights practices, and the evidence detailing their effects is solid and mounting.

Beth Simmons documents the mechanisms that induce compliance with human rights treaties and the effectiveness of these treaties in improving the problems they were meant to address.[11] Certainly, they do not solve every social or political problem, but even absent an external enforcer, human rights law has improved the condition of many people around the world. She argues that as states enter human rights treaties, multiple audiences are empowered to hold them responsible, and the pressure to comply increases after they commit. According to her analysis, there are several mechanisms that play a vital role. At the international level, treaties help make governments accountable to each other, to international organizations, and to international civil society (e.g., transnational NGOs).[12] But she claims that the major salutary effect is to provide tools for the citizens of signatory states to make effective rights claims against their own governments. Treaties are crucial resources because they empower local agents to articulate and authenticate requests with respect for rights.[13] This is especially true in transitioning or unstable regimes.

---

9. Robert Powell, "Anarchy in International Relations Theory: The Neorealist-Neoliberal Debate," *International Organization* 48, no. 2 (April 1, 1994): 340; Keohane and Martin, "The Promise of Institutionalist Theory," 45.

10. Barbara Koremenos estimates that there are 50,000 international treaties registered with the UN in "If Only Half of International Agreements Have Dispute Resolution Provisions, Which Half Needs Explaining?," *The Journal of Legal Studies* 36, no. 1 (January 2007): 190.

11. Beth A. Simmons, *Mobilizing for Human Rights: International Law in Domestic Politics* (New York: Cambridge University Press, 2009).

12. Ibid., 27–36.

13. Ibid., 130–35, 150–54.

Simmons's research underscores the important role that nonstate actors play in international politics. Her findings are consistent with the growing awareness of nongovernmental advocacy networks as significant actors in international politics, in addition to states and international organizations. Margaret Keck and Kathryn Sikkink have earlier argued that NGOs and their networks multiply the channels of access for individuals to international organizations, make resources available to citizens in domestic political and legal struggles, and help hold politicians accountable to their citizens and international institutions.[14] Hence, NGOs amplify the effects international institutions have on states by changing the relationship states have with their own citizens and with the international community.

Institutions have significant effects on states, but these effects are neither uniform nor automatic, and whether they have any effect depends on the nature of their rules and enforcement procedures.[15] Ronald Mitchell shows that in the case of oil pollution, compliance with a treaty depends on the design of the treaty's enforcement mechanism.[16] Design choices make a big difference in whether treaties induce behavioral changes for states or not. In the 1970s, two different subregimes targeted the problem of ships discharging waste oil into maritime waters after they delivered their cargoes. One established limits on how much oil tankers could release, and the other required tankers to install equipment that would reduce pollution.[17] Compliance with the first treaty involved adopting a relatively affordable and economically sound technology that ensured less pollution by introducing a more efficient separation of water from oil in the cargo and less waste.[18] This technique was both environmentally friendly and economically advantageous. Compliance with the second treaty required retrofitting tankers with expensive equipment that was costly and reduced cargo-carrying capacity.[19] Despite the stronger rationale for adopting the discharge standard, discharge violations have

---

14. Darren Hawkins, "Protecting Democracy in Europe and the Americas," *International Organization* 62, no. 3 (2008): 373–403; Margaret E. Keck and Kathryn Sikkink, *Activists Beyond Borders: Advocacy Networks in International Politics* (Ithaca, NY: Cornell University Press, 1998).

15. Barbara Koremenos, "Contracting around International Uncertainty," *American Political Science Review* 99, no. 4 (2005): 549–65.

16. Ronald B. Mitchell, "Regime Design Matters: Intentional Oil Pollution and Treaty Compliance," *International Organization* 48, no. 3 (Summer 1994): 425–58.

17. Ibid., 427.

18. Ibid., 432.

19. Ibid., 434.

continued to be the norm rather than the exception, while the equipment standard has had a 98 percent compliance rate.[20]

The difference in observed compliance was due to differences in the two treaties concerning monitoring and enforcement. The discharge treaty rules made it hard to detect, identify, prosecute, and penalize violators, and as a result left their incentives largely unchanged.[21] It was unlikely for violations to be attributable to a specific ship, for that ship to be successfully prosecuted, and for it to receive a stiff penalty after prosecution. In fact, most violations were not prosecuted.[22] By contrast, the equipment treaty relied on information provided by builders, classification societies, and insurance companies to establish compliance. Such information was relatively easy to gather. The treaty further induced greater sanctions for noncompliance, allowing governments to detain tankers in case violations were detected. Detention imposed significant reputational and economic costs, which made tankers more motivated to comply. The staggering difference in effectiveness between the two treaties can be attributed to different provisions for implementation and compliance. This case shows that a regime's effectiveness is, in part, a function of institutional design.

Cooperation is not just a product of a few powerful states seeking to subdue smaller and weaker states. If it were, systemwide patterns of cooperation, where both weak and small states engage in cooperative behavior and mutually beneficial agreements with each other, could not be explained. Furthermore, large states, which should regard each other as potential enemies according to the realist picture, in fact, still commit to common goals. Liberal institutionalists are not naive about the overall effects of institutions. International institutions can be superfluous, even detrimental to certain common goals (when based, for instance, on misguided economic theories). But liberal institutionalists argue that cooperation unfolds as part of a process in which complex learning takes place, learning that affects both how states behave and how they conceive of the structure of international politics.

Constructivists refine the insights of liberal institutionalists by relaxing some of the rigid assumptions that characterize the debates between realists and liberals in international relations.[23] They argue that processes of interaction

---

20. Ibid., 435–37.

21. Ibid., 439.

22. Ibid., 449.

23. Alexander Wendt, "Anarchy Is What States Make of It: The Social Construction of Power Politics," *International Organization* 46, no. 2 (Spring 1992): 391–425.

in international politics not only transform the nature of anarchy, but also fundamentally affect how states view themselves in relationship to other states. Common norms that build trust and prepare the terrain for further cooperation result from repeated interactions in which states redefine their identities and interests in response to each other's actions. For instance, the norm of sovereignty changes the dynamic of raw power. In a strictly Hobbesian state of nature, state security has its only basis in material capability and not in shared understanding of a state's entitlements to its territory or citizens. Alexander Wendt argues that once states establish and internalize the norm of state sovereignty, state security has a basis in "mutual recognition of one another's right to exercise exclusive political authority within territorial limits."[24] This shows that state behavior can be guided by shared norms even in the absence of an external enforcer.

The dynamic character of international politics enables institutions to change the nature of state interests. Significantly, the interests of states do not remain static over time. States define their interests in the process of responding to various situations and circumstances. The nature of state interaction—cooperative or conflictual—depends on how states view each other. Thus, according to Wendt, conflict among states is not essential to anarchy, but is a contingent feature of an anarchic system. Consequently, states are part of a dynamic process in which they "construct" norms, and those norms, in turn, constitute the identities of the units of the international system.

Furthermore, in contradiction to realists' expectations, norms develop in certain areas even absent or prior to the establishment of international institutions. For instance, Nina Tannenwald shows that the most important phenomenon of the nuclear age is the *nonuse* of nuclear weapons.[25] The prohibition on nuclear use is not a fully robust norm yet, but it has stigmatized nuclear weapons as unacceptable weapons of mass destruction for states. The empirical record shows that nuclear weapons have not been used even in cases where there was no fear of nuclear retaliation, such as military conflicts between a state with nuclear capabilities and one without.[26] This was the case in the US war in Vietnam and in the Persian Gulf War. In addition, even though nuclear weapons are considered a veritable vehicle of deterrence, they have not prevented nonnuclear states from attacking nuclear ones: China

---

24. Ibid., 412.

25. Nina Tannenwald, "The Nuclear Taboo: The United States and the Normative Basis of Nuclear Non-Use," *International Organization* 53, no. 3 (1999): 433–68.

26. Ibid., 432.

attacked the United States in Vietnam, Argentina attacked Great Britain in the Falklands, and Iraq attacked the United States and Israel during the Gulf War.[27] The nonuse of nuclear weapons is an example of a shared norm that affects the behavior of states. Such shared norms allow partners in international cooperation to build social trust, develop reputation, and reciprocate cooperative behavior.

That fact that international institutions have real, substantive effects on state behavior is documented by the many empirical studies that explain when and how such effects manifest themselves. Martha Finnemore shows convincingly that many states have developed new bureaucracies in charge of scientific research as a result of UNESCO's (the United Nations Educational, Scientific, and Cultural Organization's) efforts to impress on states the importance of scientific research for economic development and security.[28] In the early 1950s, UNESCO undertook a teaching mission to promote science policy and innovation among member states.[29] In the beginning, UNESCO did not see promoting state research capabilities for its member states as part of its mission.[30] This changed in 1960, when a UN report portrayed scientific policy as "one of the most important preoccupations of governments."[31] The report claimed that scientific research was necessary and desirable, and a domestic research bureaucracy was the means to achieve it. The report thus redefined the role of states with regard to science.[32] Following this change, teaching and spreading ideas about how to build a research bureaucracy became part of the central mission of UNESCO, and the organization would even provide on-site consulting about establishing such programs.[33] The majority (79 percent) of state science organizations were created between 1955 and 1975.[34] The article did not explore whether such an effect on state behavior is desirable or not. But the case does show that international institutions have real effects on states. Constructivism has consequently contributed to the

---

27. Ibid., 433.

28. Martha Finnemore, "International Organizations as Teachers of Norms: The United Nations Educational, Scientific, and Cutural Organization and Science Policy," *International Organization* 47, no. 4 (Autumn 1993): 565–97.

29. Ibid., 576.

30. Ibid., 578.

31. Ibid., 582.

32. Ibid., 583.

33. Ibid., 585–86.

34. Ibid., 576.

insight that disorder is a function of a certain stage of development within a process of transformation, and not a function of the structure of the international system itself, as realists argue.

Moreover, constructivists provide empirical evidence to show that international institutions socialize states by making their members' interests more alike over time. Institutions promote the transformation of state interests and their convergence.[35] Thus, they effectively falsify the assumption of rationalist international scholars that states have stable preferences and that those preferences are given exogenously by the structure of international anarchy. Constructivist findings are not incompatible with rationalists' causal explanations when those explanations investigate how institutions affect state behavior when interests are held constant.[36] But their findings do refute the stronger and less defensible claim that state preferences and behavior never change as a result of international anarchy.

Given their assumptions about states as rational, self-interested, power maximizing entities, realists have difficulty explaining the propensity of states to form and join international organizations, particularly when joining them is costly and when such organizations have the capacity to be binding. Environmental protection is one such area that is at once costly and has the potential to tie the hands of state leaders in ways detrimental to advancing material interests. The 1973 Convention on International Trade in Endangered Species, the same year's Convention for the Prevention of Pollution from Ships, the 1979 Convention on Long-Range Transboundary Air Pollution, and the 1985 Convention for the Protection of the Ozone Layer are anomalies if one assumes a realist worldview. But as John W. Mayer et al. show, the rise of a world environmental regime is evidence of collective action in a world that clearly lacks a strong central actor such as a world state.[37] NGO activity, rising scientific agreement about common environmental problems, and the existence of already established international institutional structures with open-ended agendas, facilitated the development of environmental treaties.[38] Most of these treaties took hold under the umbrella of the UNEP (United Nations Environment Program), a special body of the UN secretariat

35. David H. Bearce and Stacy Bondanella, "Intergovernmental Organizations, Socialization, and Member-State Interest Convergence," *International Organization* 61, no. 4 (2007): 703–33.

36. Ibid., 730.

37. John W. Meyer et al., "The Structuring of a World Environmental Regime, 1870–1990," *International Organization* 51, no. 4 (1997): 623–51.

38. Ibid., 623.

established by a resolution of the UN General Assembly in 1972.[39] The realist can grant that such institutions arise but would argue that they merely reflect the interests of powerful Western nations, who only participate in these arrangements to control resource flows and tip the scales of environmental security in their favor. However, the empirical record shows that with regard to environmental treaties, the opposite is true. Western nations have not only been reluctant to lead in the creation of the regime in order to ensure control of the agenda and favorable terms, but have been reluctant to participate and ratify as well.[40]

Perhaps most surprising, states have joined an international institution, the ICC, that makes unprecedented demands on their sovereign prerogative, especially their jurisdictional authority to provide justice within their territory. Even the institutions-friendly rational choice approach of the liberal institutionalists has difficulty accounting for the creation of this institution. The ICC is obviously not in any government's interests since a member government exposes its ranks to investigation, prosecution, and punishment, or at the very least to costly demands to provide evidence and expertise, and to apprehend and turn over alleged criminals to the organization.

In Beth Simmons and Allison Danner's view, what explains the propensity of states to form and join the ICC is a credible commitment strategy that allows unaccountable autocracies with a recent history of internal conflicts "to tie their hands as they make tentative steps toward conflict resolution."[41] Simmons and Danner note that the pattern of joining the organization is consistent with credible commitment theory, and that of the more than one hundred states that have joined so far, the governments of states such as Afghanistan, Peru, and the Democratic Republic of Congo enter a self-binding commitment in which they attempt to persuade political opponents, their constituencies, or other states that they abandon the option of engaging in violence. For advanced democracies that are neither in danger of being subject to the court's prosecutions nor require credible commitments to reduce internal conflict, the authors posit that their reasons are external, mainly to enhance peace and stability in the international realm and to create avenues for the protection of other peoples' rights.

---

39. Ibid., 624.

40. Ibid., 627.

41. Beth A. Simmons and Allison Danner, "Credible Commitments and the International Criminal Court," *International Organization* 64, no. 2 (2010): 227.

The formation of the ICC is surprising because it cannot be explained in terms of either the realist or the liberal institutionalist framework. The realists argue that powerful states use international institutions as cover to pursue their own goals, even at the expense of other states. Given the express aim of the ICC to prosecute mass atrocities, it is not plausible to see the ICC as advancing the interests of powerful states, especially since they incur significant costs by joining. Liberal institutionalists believe that international institutions can be mutually advantageous for all states that join, but the act of joining can be explained solely by self-interested reasons. This does not appear to be the case with the ICC. Perhaps the more likely explanation is a constructivist one, in which states have changed their interests in the process of negotiation due to the presence of persuasion from others by achieving a shared understanding of common goals with other states that were part of the negotiation process.[42]

The process of negotiation reveals an endogenous transformation of states' attitudes. From a starting point of mistrust, a dissonant representation of the organization's objectives, and a varied ranking of states' preferences concerning the protection of human life in the face of massive threats versus the preservation of sovereignty and the immunity of heads of state, the group of negotiating states shifted over a number of years in repeated consultations and conferences to a common set of priorities and an agreement about how those priorities would be entrenched in institutional structures.[43]

The significance of this entire empirical record of institutional cooperation in international politics is that realists are wrong to be skeptical about the possibility of international institutions to effectively constrain state behavior and to do so in a way that enhances, rather than undermines, the protection of their citizens' rights. There are both theoretical and empirical reasons to believe that states will choose to cooperate in a variety of situations, and that they will choose to do so even when they contemplate serious restrictions on their sovereign autonomy to make decisions within their own territory. Realists can add valuable insights to the understanding of conditions that prompt states to engage in cooperative versus competitive behavior. Such an understanding is important for knowing how most effectively to build desirable international institutions that achieve worthwhile moral goals. However, the focus in this chapter so far has been to deflect the worry

---

42. Nicole Deitelhoff, "The Discursive Process of Legalization: Charting Islands of Persuasion in the ICC Case," *International Organization* 63, no. 1 (2009): 33–65.

43. Ibid., 55–59.

that cooperation will not happen, and that if it happens, it is not likely to be effective. Displacing the worry that cooperation is undesirable is a different task. It requires first exposing the hidden normative agenda embedded in international relations theories.

2. Assumptions and Implications of International Relations Theorizing

Both realists and liberal institutionalists eschew normative theories, that is, theories about what the state should do, in favor of explanatory theories about what causes states to behave the way they do. Their explanatory theories aim to produce social-scientific testable hypotheses about state behavior and rely on quantitative models and qualitative analyses to test them against alternative explanations. Borrowing from the assumptions of rational choice theories, international relations scholars assume that states are rational, strategic actors who pursue self-interested goals, and whose behavior is influenced by the special conditions of anarchy in a world without a global leviathan.[44]

Rational choice international relations theories contain assumptions and lead to implications that are problematic from a moral standpoint. Three dimensions of rational choice analysis of states raise questions. (1) Realists assume that state preferences and goals are given exogenously by the international system. This cannot be true. State preferences might be informed by the environment in which they operate, but states make choices about what goals to pursue, and how to allocate resources to satisfy competing goals. In the process of choosing an order or priorities, states can make moral or immoral choices. (2) Although states exhibit "preferences," these preferences are not always synonymous with the preferences of their citizens. States are made up of a collection of individuals and to say that states have preferences is to some extent incoherent. (3) The incoherence is revealed when we discuss self-preservation as a state interest.

International relations theorists are aware that they are working with theoretical constructs that may not reflect the real behavior and motivations of states in international politics. Keohane in *After Hegemony* points out the many limitations of classical assumptions of rationality.[45] For one, decision

---

44. The extent to which realists are fully committed to the rational choice framework is less clear. See Miles Kahler, "Rationality in International Relations," *International Organization* 52, no. 4 (October 1, 1998): 924.

45. Keohane, *After Hegemony*, chapters 5–7.

makers at the state level suffer limitations in their cognitive abilities, information, attention, effort, the number of alternatives they are able take into account when making decisions, time horizon, and so on. Their rationality is "bounded" by such constraints, which is why political leaders don't always maximize but rather "satisfice," that is, they economize on effort and information by "searching only until they find a course of action that falls above a satisfactory level."[46] This limitation speaks in favor of international institutions that help decision makers satisfice by giving them rules of thumb to follow. Yet at least for realists, the awareness of relying on idealized constructs that may be far from reality does not inspire humility about the implications of their theories.

For instance, theories that posit agents with a structure of preferences cannot be merely explanatory.[47] As critiques of instrumental rationality show, a hierarchy of preferences implies a more or less coherent ordering that reflects that agent's good. The agent makes choices about how to rank preferences based on what she determines her own good to be. The preference ranking depends on chosen moral and nonmoral ends that together make up a conception of the good. Therefore, stipulating a certain preference ordering for states means, in effect, stipulating a specific conception of the morally desirable ends states must pursue.

Charles Beitz emphasizes this point about the choices of states in his book *Political Theory and International Relations*.[48] He argues that questions such as "what should I do?" or "what should states do?" come about because moral agents typically confront multiple courses of action. When an agent chooses a certain course of action, she makes an implicit or explicit determination of her goals and her means for achieving them. Choices regarding the ends and means of political action, as well as the rules and institutions that govern behavior, depend on the agent's understanding of the appropriate moral principles. This is as true of the international realm as of the domestic one.[49]

This is "why instrumental reasoning isn't instrumental," as Jean Hampton explains in her book *The Authority of Reason*.[50] Or, to put it more carefully,

---

46. Ibid., 112, 111–15.

47. An "agent" here means any person or group (or organization) with the ability to make decisions and act on them. This sense of agency is different from (but consistent with) the one used in the rest of the book.

48. Charles R. Beitz, *Political Theory and International Relations*, rev. ed. (Princeton, NJ: Princeton University Press, 1999).

49. Ibid., 5.

50. Jean E. Hampton, *The Authority of Reason* (New York: Cambridge University Press, 1998).

instrumental reason is not solely instrumental. An agent who has more than one end must sort out how to allocate resources to pursue her different ends. To make that determination, the agent cannot simply rely on instrumental reasoning, that is, reasoning about what is the best means to achieve an end. She must also determine the structure of her ends in a manner consistent with the agent's good or identity. She must decide, for instance, if certain ends are incompatible, what trade-offs are acceptable, or which short-term and long-term preferences are worth investing in. These are all moral choices. "They define certain aspects of the content of the agent's good by setting out the sort of preferences that can or cannot be included in the agent's good-defining preference set," Hampton says.[51] Thus, agents can never be simply "instrumentally" rational. In the process of asking themselves what means can achieve their ends, they also engage in reasoning about the rationality of ends themselves, and when they do so, they make moral choices.

States also make such choices. They do not act like deterministic cogs in a preprogrammed machine, and questions about what they should or should not do arise all of the time in states' deliberations about how they must act. The assumption that states only act instrumentally in the pursuit of *given ends* may be useful in some theoretical contexts, but it is not an accurate representation of the behavior of states as acting, choosing agents. Pretending that this assumption is a social-scientific fact serves to rationalize and reinforce problematic state actions that promote the interests of state elites or that only advance citizens' self-interest narrowly construed.

The second assumption concerns whether we can consider states to have preferences. States take positions with respect to a variety of policies with international effects or implications. In this sense, it is plausible to say that they have "preferences." The conception of states as unified agents with a straightforward set of limited preferences is methodologically parsimonious for the rational choice analytical framework, but it distorts reality in significant ways.

The principal–agent model can highlight the inadequacy of this picture. First, we cannot assume that states have one unique and coherent set of preferences because it is difficult to aggregate individual choices to establish the preferences of a group. A state is made up of parts that may have divergent or conflicting preferences over particular policy areas. The citizens and political leaders may have divergent preferences, and different groups of citizens may diverge from each other. Producers of agricultural products may prefer

---

51. Ibid., 168.

protectionist policies, while consumers may prefer free trade. Leaders may prefer not to be subject to the judgment of international institutions with respect to their human rights records, while citizens may well think that this external scrutiny is essential to ensuring the protection of their interests. Ronald Rogowski illustrates this well by explaining how a state's trade policy "preference" emerges from the competition of three groups: landowners, capital, and labor. As the balance of power among these different constituencies changes, so does the state's preference with respect to trade.[52]

Jon Elster calls the regular practice of treating states as unitary actors with stable and coherent preferences "treacherous and misleading," and somewhat puzzling in light of the fact that other social sciences have abandoned treating collective agents that way.[53] Governments often pursue contradictory goals when they respond to different constituencies, and the alternation of different groups in power makes state preferences inconsistent and even cyclical over time.[54] It is puzzling then to hold onto the assumption that states "seek to maximize value across a set of consistently ordered objectives," when the more realistic assumptions about cyclical behavior undermine some of the darker predictions of the realist project.[55]

Even when the choice is binary, and the population explicitly affirms a preference for one of the two options, the extent to which the leaders will accurately reflect the majority position depends on how representative these leaders are. The variance across states in terms of how accurately political leaders represent their citizens is large, and in many cases, "state preferences" will simply mean the preferences of state leaders. This is not a problem in instances where the citizens' interests converge with those of their leaders, and the latter can accurately represent their constituents' interests. But there are clearly cases in which this assumption makes trouble. We cannot, for example, assume that Sudan's refusal to accede to the ICC, as the preference of that state, is anything more than the preference of its leader, Omar al-Bashir, not to be subjected to international scrutiny for his actions. It is not implausible

52. Ronald Rogowski, *Commerce and Coalitions: How Trade Affects Domestic Political Alignments* (Princeton, NJ: Princeton University Press, 1990).

53. Jon Elster, *Nuts and Bolts for the Social Sciences* (New York: Cambridge University Press, 1989), 177.

54. Robert Jervis, "Rational Deterrence: Theory and Evidence," *World Politics* 41, no. 2 (1989): 203–05.

55. Keohane, *After Hegemony*, 66. This description of state rationality comes from Glenn H. Snyder and Paul Diesing, *Conflict among Nations: Bargaining, Decision Making, and System Structure in International Crises* (Princeton, NJ: Princeton University Press, 1977), 81.

to imagine that the majority of Sudanese citizens would refuse to join the ICC, yet we cannot infer their preference *either way* from the official state position on the issue. Sudan is an autocratic, one-party state that is neither representative of nor responsive to its citizens in any significant measure.

Note that this skepticism of the value of state preferences does not apply only to instances of refusal to join and abide by international treaties. Liberal institutionalists claim that states operate on the basis of means-ends rationality and that the international arrangements that states help create and maintain are justified as a means to further their goals.[56] Thus, international arrangements (treaties, organizations, regimes) are an efficient way for states to pursue their goals. But whose goals are they pursuing? If we abandon the idea of states as unitary agents, the possibility that international arrangements may be pursuing goals that are in the interests of state leaders but are detrimental to the citizens' well-being becomes vivid. The fact that they do so efficiently is even more worrisome. For example, informal and formal agreements into which political leaders enter to prop each other up when their authority is challenged by legitimate and widespread internal dissension are at the very least troubling. The more effective such agreements are, the more troubling they are. As Alexander Wendt puts it, if the effects of "rational" institutions are immoral, we may do better by doing the moral rather than the rational thing.[57]

The idea that rational institutions can pursue immoral ends is in a way a surprising conclusion. But it is the result of an impoverished conception of rationality. States are considered rational "when they choose strategies that they believe will have the optimal consequences given their interests."[58] Yet given a very narrow picture of what constitutes state interests, and the assumption that states engage solely in instrumental rationality, this conclusion is not surprising. A revised, thicker conception of rationality that incorporates the idea that states are capable of selecting their goals, and are able to take into account moral and other constraints on the nature of the goals they pursue, would avoid the more implausible conclusion that rationality and morality conflict.

Realists say that in a world such as ours states have no choice but to act self-interestedly. Positing states as self-interested is as close as international

56. Lisa L. Martin and Beth A. Simmons, "Theories and Empirical Studies of International Institutions," *International Organization* 52, no. 4 (1998): 738.

57. Alexander Wendt, "Driving with the Rearview Mirror: On the Rational Science of Institutional Design," *International Organization* 55, no. 4 (October 1, 2001): 1022.

58. Ibid., 1023.

relations theory comes to a natural law of international politics, in the same sense that gravity is a natural law of physics. To take this metaphor too far would be to do a disservice to international politics as a discipline. International relations theory that takes narrow self-interested preferences as given, unchanging, and dominant creates the false impression that they are fixed and part of the natural fabric of the universe, which means neither subject to change nor to scrutiny. Yet states' preferences are not fixed by some kind of deterministic law of social interaction in international politics. They are both subject to change, as the constructivists have aptly showed, and open to criticism. Just as any other acting organizations or individuals, states can question both what kind of preferences are worth acting upon and the structure of those preferences. They have the ability to reflect on, discard, and revise their preferences. To the extent that states provide reasons for preferring some courses of action over others as better, they engage in a form of normative justification. States can consider how their actions affect other persons or states, and can modify their behavior accordingly, so that the pursuit of their self-interest does not occur at others' expense.

Realists and liberal institutionalists differ in the range of possible preferences they attribute to states. Liberal institutionalists tend to be more flexible in describing state motives and goals, and their vision of the range of preferences that states can have makes it more plausible that states will have overlapping interests in a variety of policy areas that can lead to convergence and cooperation. States have preferences with respect to trade, the pollution of territorial waters and open seas, and policing international crimes, all of which can, but do not automatically lead to, opportunities for institutionalized cooperation. Still, all of their preferences are cast in terms of self-interest. As Stephen Krasner noted, "[T]he prevailing explanation for the existence of international regimes is egoistic self-interest."[59] The most prevalent interpretation of self-interest is self-preservation or survival.

3. Self-Preservation as the Dominant State Preference

The third problematic assumption in the realist arsenal is reducing the vast array of state self-interested preferences to a dominant one: self-preservation or survival. John Mearsheimer describes survival as "the most basic motive

---

59. Stephen D. Krasner, *International Regimes* (Ithaca, NY: Cornell University Press, 1983), 11.

driving states."[60] Kenneth Walz assumes that "states seek to ensure their survival," and deploys this and other assumptions about the role of the environment in which they act as a basis to predict state behavior.[61] Realists often derive this assumption about self-preservation from other assumptions, such as the assumption that anarchy is here to stay, and that states can never be certain about the intentions of other states.[62] But observed state behavior does not support the plausibility of the dominance of the survival motive. Repeated interactions give states information about the behavior and intentions of other states. As states discover trustworthy partners, they can shift their focus from survival to other, more advanced, long-term cooperative goals. Even if they start with incomplete information about each other's preferences, states can use repeated interactions to gain information, to change their beliefs about each other, and, ultimately, to change their order of preferences.[63]

The language of self-preservation suggests that the state acts to "preserve" the interests of its citizens. But state preservation may be in serious tension with, and be pursued in violation of, the interests of entire groups that are under the rule of the state. State self-preservation can have at least two different meanings: (1) territorial integrity and (2) the preservation of the government in power. States' territorial integrity can be challenged from the inside, as when a part of the population wishes to secede, or from the outside, when states are attacked in a territorial dispute or other territorial demands are placed on them by other states. The acceptability of the regime in power could also be challenged from the inside or the outside.

Given this multidimensional picture, state self-preservation is not always a legitimate goal, especially when it involves massive violations of the rights of some or all of its citizens. Minorities who may have a legitimate claim to secede can be silenced or "persuaded" via violent means to give up their claims for the sake of preserving state territorial integrity. Ethnic dissension is sometimes violently repressed for the sake of preserving the unity of the state, even when more peaceful alternatives that involve devolving political autonomy to different groups or dividing up the territory may be available. In addition, when state preservation is equated with the preservation of the regime in power, any internal challenge to the regime can be mercilessly crushed to preserve

---

60. Mearsheimer, "The False Promise of International Institutions," 10–11.

61. Waltz, *Theory of International Politics*, 91.

62. Mearsheimer, "The False Promise of International Institutions," 10.

63. Powell, "Anarchy in International Relations Theory," 319.

the political positions and status of the existing leadership. While it may be seen as acceptable from the outside, and indeed unproblematic, in all of these instances (but not in all instances), state preservation is deeply antithetical to respecting the rights of the individual citizens within those states and should not be considered a legitimate pursuit of state interests either domestically or internationally.

Realists have great affinity for the Hobbesian framework, and indeed import many of its features uncritically. They view international politics as a state of anarchy in which states are constantly threatened with war by one another, and in this self-help system states are primarily concerned with defense and survival. There is an important sense in which this realist picture is true. Given a world of sovereign states the possibility exists of rogue and outlaw states with predatory interests to create instability in the system and a need for every state to look out for itself. However, this picture does not reflect a dynamic process in which states create alliances, seize opportunities to realize Pareto improvements, create linkages among issue areas to strengthen reciprocal trust, use past interactions and institutional cooperation to redefine their future interests, and build institutions that engender generalized trust over time. This dynamic interaction reduces the possibility of conflict and the need to focus on self-preservation even in an anarchic system. While the Hobbesian framework has some explanatory power, at least for the early stages in the development of the Westphalian system and with respect to pockets of anarchy still remaining among different states today, as states adopt more rule-governed behavior, the framework becomes less and less salient to the actual world we live in. States are not Hobbesian individuals, they are complex agents with constituencies and hierarchal relationships, and state leaders are bound to and must serve their citizens' interests. This means that there are substantive moral constraints on how states define their preferences and on how they pursue them. International relations theory "normalizes" its assumptions by claiming not only that they are realistic behavioral assumptions about states, but also that they are carved in stone. To the extent that it does so, it perpetuates a view of states as self-serving entities, thereby justifying immoral state action.

Therefore, international relations theory, or a hybrid of international relations and international political theory, should ask not only why states build the institutions they do, but also what kind of goals states should pursue. What kinds of institutions should states build? What kinds of values, principles, and goals should those institutions advance and through what means? And what kind of state behavior should international institutions proscribe, permit, or require? The insights produced by the positivistic, social science approach to international institutions and state behavior can help us incorporate lessons learned into future institutional design and understand the realistic set of possible alternatives, but they do not determine their legitimate range or the possible functions such institutions can serve.

4. The Possibility of a Rule-Governed Order

What are the lessons from this analysis of rational choice approaches to international politics? Insofar as such theories of international relations provide explanations of processes and dynamics in the international realm that determine and constrain possible outcomes, such as whether and to what extent states will support the creation of international institutions, we should have reservations about their predictions and the normative weight we accord them.

Realists say that cooperation is not only unlikely, it is also detrimental to the preservation of states. Let us focus on the empirical claim that cooperation is unlikely first. States do not act on ends that are given from the outside; they are able to reflect on and choose their ends. This means that states can choose to act on cooperative ends and to develop rules of behavior in concert with other states—and the empirical record clearly shows that they have done so. Liberal institutionalists have argued that even when we assume that states act in their self-interest narrowly construed, we can still explain the penchant of states to cooperate with one another and accept effective constraints on their behavior. But the assumption that states act from narrow self-interest alone is false. Any state has a wide range of interests, some of which are other-regarding, and mutually advantageous bargains are possible when states' interests converge.

What about the normative implication of realist arguments? When international relations scholars describe state action in terms of state interests, their language suggests that if states refuse to join international organizations, then it must be because joining is not in the interests of that state. The language of rational, strategic action and self-interest suggests that state choices are welfare enhancing across the board, and should be accepted at face value. I have shown that such a claim equivocates between at least two meanings of state interest: One is the interest of state leaders, and another is the interest of its citizens broadly construed. Often submission to international institutions is in the interests of the citizens in most states for many reasons, not the least of which is that they can protect themselves against abusive state power. The refusal of some states to submit themselves to international institutions does not reflect decisions that protect the interests of the people living in those states, but rather decisions that reinforce and magnify certain pathologies inherent in the domestic power dynamic.[64]

Therefore, the motivations that result in states joining or not joining international organizations should be subject to critical assessment from the point of view of the interests of the citizens of that state. If one can plausibly represent political leaders as the agents of the people with specific and limited functions, then the question one should ask is not the general one of whether it is in states' interests to follow international rules, but whether it is in their citizens' interests for states to do so. While the answer to the first type of question may not be straightforward, the answer to the second is clearly yes. When the variety of agency problems at the state level are taken into account, citizens can benefit from their states following international rules that seek to diminish these problems.

Realists and liberal institutionalists alike talk as if states can choose between acting for purely instrumental reasons and acting for moral reasons. Realists go one step further and advocate the former choice as preferable. But this is a false dichotomy. Prioritizing self-interest (or self-preservation) amounts to making a morally significant choice because it means according self-interest a dominant position in the structure of a state's preference ranking. States make choices when they act, and when they prioritize self-interest, they prioritize a certain preference ranking over another. Thus, moral choices are unavoidable in international politics, despite what the language of international relations scholarship sometimes implies.

The realist view says that states need to follow self-interest and avoid becoming preoccupied with questions of morality, lest they lose out in the battle for political survival. Even if it is the case that self-interest *does* drive state behavior in interactions with other states, it is not obvious why it *should be* the only or primary motive for state action. As I have argued above, the pursuit of state interests sometimes produces morally unacceptable outcomes. For instance, state preservation does not always imply a concern for the preservation of its citizens. Indeed, the preservation of state integrity or political power might sometimes require that the rights of a part of the population be sacrificed, as is sometimes the case with groups that have a legitimate right to self-determination but are prevented from seceding out of consideration for territorial integrity or political stability. In addition, in the course of pursuing the interests of its citizens, states may harm or take advantage of the citizens of other states.

---

64. Kahler, "Rationality in International Relations," 931–32.

Thus, standards of moral evaluation can and should apply to the actions of states, just as they apply to the actions of individuals pursuing their self-interest. We consider it acceptable to bind the pursuit of individual self-interest so as to protect others from harm; so, too, we should bind the pursuit of national interests by norms regulating state interaction vis-à-vis other states or individuals. Debates about the structure of the international order, the appropriate goals of international cooperation, the appropriate ways to reach those goals, and the acceptable conduct of different agents operating internationally require that we articulate and defend principles based on reasons that are acceptable from a moral point of view. Moral norms should help distinguish between situations in which it is appropriate for states to act based on self-interest, and situations in which it is not. The difference might, for instance, require a limitation of state sovereignty, rather than an enhancement, when states act in ways that are detrimental to their own citizens.

Charles Beitz emphasizes the liberal institutionalist finding that following moral rules may have beneficial side-effects for the pursuit of state interests, although this need not be the primary justification for states acting morally. States that act on established moral principles may be seen as more reliable, predictable partners in international negotiations, and this perception can enhance the terms of cooperation in their favor. Morality and self-interest need not be at odds, although any normative theory concerned with international morality would have to specify the way in which the two can accommodate each other.

One can argue that moral reasoning is both possible and necessary at the international level by questioning the other realist assumption: Although states may find it desirable to act according to moral principles, without an agency ensuring that states are bound *in foro externo*, there is no widespread compliance with those principles.[65] Even if states recognize binding principles *in foro interno* that could serve to regulate international actions, states will not follow through with their commitments unless conditions to ensure the successful implementation of those principles are established.

In order to rebut this assumption, one would need to show that, absent a global sovereign, states can coordinate to select the principles and institutions necessary to achieve common goals, a point that international relations scholars have plainly demonstrated.[66] It is true that principles that apply to

---

65. Beitz, *Political Theory and International Relations*, 27–34. Beitz refers here to the Hobbesian dilemma in the state of nature at the international level.

66. Beitz also claims that there is an additional requirement, namely that states agree on a list of normative principles that should bind them. Beitz is optimistic about such an agreement,

states would not be effective if states were the only actors in international relations and no higher authority existed. But contemporary international relations display, in addition to states, a thick and growing network of supra-national arrangements that articulate and impose norms, many of which have moral content. While some existing alliances do create problems for the stability and peacefulness of the international order, many others promote worthwhile goals. Existing cooperative arrangements also assist the different actors in international politics to find and build common interests on the basis of which further cooperation can be extended and maintained. International human rights law, conflict settlement treaties, economic and financial institutions, and jurisdictional arrangements are just some examples of cooperative practice. The established, stable international arrangements challenge the claim that international relations are similar to a Hobbesian state of nature.[67]

Morality is inseparable from international politics, and this point is clear even if we have not established what the content of that morality is, that is, what kind of principles should govern state actions. And this is true, even if the principles that guide choice in the international realm are different than in the domestic realm, as I have argued in Chapter 4. The main point of the debate about order and morality in international politics is that institutional pluralism does not imply disorder. Indeed, international institutions can overcome the logic of anarchy that realists posit as inescapable.

The rational choice approach to the study of international politics has yielded big leaps in our understanding of the nature of interactions among states and between states and other nonstate actors. One of the main insights generated by international relations scholars concerns the conditions under which cooperation among states is possible and the forms that cooperation can take. The strength of this insight is that states will tend to repeatedly face generic types of cooperation problems. Many situations of cooperation give rise to opportunities for cheating and reneging on agreements and conflicts over the distribution of benefits.[68] Understanding the dynamics that create these recurring problems is valuable for institutional design efforts. But international relations theorists ignore the normative dimension of their theorizing

---

but the claim seems too strong. States only need agree on specific areas of international cooperation and create effective enforcement mechanisms to uphold their agreements. This can take place absent more general agreement on fundamental moral principles and norms.

67. Beitz, *Political Theory and International Relations*, 37.

68. Martin and Simmons, "Theories and Empirical Studies of International Institutions," 743.

at their own peril.[69] Completely value-free social science is both impossible and undesirable.

If we understand the development of order in general and moral order in particular in the international system as a function of process, then we can expect the international system to encourage more orderly behavior and the pursuit of a broader array of moral goals over time. Surely, progress cannot be expected to be linear. Stagnation, redundancy, and even regress can occur at times. But as states transform the nature of their relationships by engaging in institution building in one area, they will be able to build on and strengthen their cooperation, or at least see each other as potential allies, in other areas as well.

---

69. Richard Price, "Moral Limit and Possibility in World Politics," *International Organization* 62, no. 2 (2008): 191–220.

Conclusion

STATES ARE IMPERFECT, incomplete political forms. They presuppose a monopoly of coercive power and final jurisdictional authority over their territory. These twin elements of sovereignty and authority can be used by state leaders and political representatives in ways that stray significantly from the interests of citizens. In the most extreme cases, when citizens become inconvenient obstacles in the pursuit of the self-serving ambitions of their leaders, state power turns against them. Genocide, torture, displacement, and rape are often the means of choice by which the inconvenient are made to suffer or vanish.

The potential for abuse is latent in the very structure of power that enables state authorities to perform their functions. The concentration of power in the hands of state leaders allows them to act as the effective protectors of their citizens' safety and well-being from internal and external threats, but it also enables them to turn against their citizens. Individuals are not nearly as vulnerable to abuse in advanced democracies as they are in authoritarian regimes, but they should be equally watchful of the potential for their political agents to be abusive both openly and in secret. Indeed, the abuses perpetrated by these democracies against their own people well into the second half of the twentieth century are stark reminders of how new and fragile the advances in the protection of basic rights are. Think of the Japanese American internments in the United States, or the forced sterilization of gypsies and other "inferior" minorities, a practice that has continued throughout Europe long after World War II.[1] State abuses are not merely the result of unfortunate historical circumstances, but of the incompleteness of the state model, which does not offer adequate mechanisms to fully remove the considerable perils inherent in state power.

---

1. Jeffrey White, "Report: Czechs, Others Sterilize Gypsies," *The Christian Science Monitor*, September 6, 2006; "Sweden Plans to Pay Sterilization Victims," *The New York Times*, January 27, 1999.

What are we to make of this incompleteness of the state model? Since Hobbes, state sovereignty without external constraints has been defended on the grounds that it best protects citizens' interests. But how can this be the case, unless the citizens' interests and those of the sovereign always converge? Virtually no one defends unconstrained sovereignty today, yet few have pursued the question of how to justify a system of international institutions that can plausibly limit state authority. A world in which states remain indefinitely the sole authority entrusted with the protection of their citizens and the enforcement of criminal responsibility is a world in which the potential for abuse of citizens remains an especially acute problem.

It is a world in which individuals and groups have no institutional escape valve when they are subjected to human rights violations. For those such as Alex Bizimungu, coming out of the Rwandan genocide alive, and for countless others, survival depends on brute luck alone, and the chance to redress the injustice they suffer is slim to none. Until recently, apart from the occasional ad hoc military tribunal, no permanent international agency has been designated with intervening, preventing, or prosecuting cases of severe human rights violations. The UN's Security Council has been tasked with preserving international peace and security, and it does occasionally justify humanitarian interventions on this ground. However, many state abuses do not cross borders and do not therefore affect international peace and security. What is required is an institutional insurance scheme that has the authority to intervene coercively when states are unwilling or unable to perform their most basic functions, regardless of whether international peace is affected or not.

International institutions may not offer better human rights protection than the most advanced democracies, such as Sweden or the United States. But they need not do so. The metaphor of the insurance scheme is meant to suggest that coercive international institutions should act as secondary agents of justice that intervene only when states as primary agents have failed dramatically. When they do so, these institutions need not provide maximal protections for human rights, but minimal ones that prevent standard and grave threats to individual security.

A right to collective self-determination enables states to enjoy substantive autonomy over internal matters, and it limits the scope and reach of the authority of international organizations. I have not defended such a right. I have rather relied on the assumption that many of our practices, including effective delegation of power from individuals to state institutions, decolonization, and the norms of noninterference in the affairs of states present in international law, do not make sense without it. Interference with sovereign autonomy is justified for a set of norms regarded as nonderogable by the international community, namely jus cogens norms. In cases of human rights violations such as crimes against humanity, war crimes, genocide and the crime of aggression, state sovereignty must give way to the authority of international institutions specifically designated to act as the secondary agents of their citizens, such as the International Criminal Court.

Ideally, the ICC is the beginning of an international regime whose purpose is to compensate for grave failures of state agency. Primarily tasked with upholding criminal responsibility, the ICC must be complemented with other institutions that prevent and intervene in situations of grave human rights violations. Of course, existing international institutions such as the UN, its Security Council, and powerful Western states already take turns performing some of these functions. Yet, their actions are more akin to keeping the order in the Wild West: sporadic, capricious and arbitrary, and at times counterproductive. When no single international agency is designated for protecting jus cogens norms, or is beholden to ex facto and ex post facto accountability mechanisms, a troubling authority vacuum remains. If everyone is responsible, in the end no one is. It is easy for any substitute to shirk responsibility, or to assert the authority to intervene on illegitimate grounds.

But what should the structure of our common institutional future look like? To answer this question, we must give free reign to our imagination while tempering its excesses. Forward-thinking engineers are envisioning the city of the future as a hyper-skyscraper. This "sky city," with its peak in the clouds but firmly planted on the ground, consists of horizontal modules of houses, shopping malls, parks, entertainment areas, and office spaces vertically layered on top of each other, with triple-decker elevators running between levels and trains going around each level. This multifunctional building is meant to give thousands of people a place to live, work, and play, in a self-sufficient, vertical world.

It is tempting to think about our global institutional future in similar terms. Proposals for the vertical integration of institutional functions in a global democratic structure parallel the actual physical integration of the "sky city." The layering of political authority in this institutional scheme seeks to ensure widespread inclusion of individuals' voices in the process of governance and the equal protection of their fundamental needs and interests. The system of global democracy seeks to guarantee that the world can become a safe place for everyone to live, work, and play.

I have argued that it is not useful to think of international institutions as a vertically integrated system, but rather as a collection of diverse and dispersed agents, authorized by people living in separate states to keep the latter in check and fill in governance gaps when states fail to fulfill their fundamental sovereign responsibilities. We are better off proceeding with a pluralist, competitive institutional order, especially in areas of international politics where the outcomes are uncertain, the chances of failures are high, and the costs devastating in terms of human lives.

What is to keep coercive international institutions from arbitrarily interfering with the affairs of states? International institutions with coercive powers can conceivably pursue politically motivated prosecutions and interventions, they can themselves be subject to capture by self-serving interests, and can become stifled by institutional pathologies and dysfunctions similar to those that mar domestic institutions. After all, the latently benign power of international institutions is laced with malignant potential as much as domestic ones. This book takes this concern seriously and has a couple of responses in turn.

While people living in separate states would do well to stay vigilant about the additional dangers that another layer of institutions invites, we would go too far in denying the legitimacy of a system of international institutions altogether based on these worries. Such institutions are required to supplement and constrain the authority of states over their citizens and to enforce jus cogens norms. Leaving individuals alone to fend off against state power is not an acceptable default. Just as the possibility of corrupt cops or judges does not delegitimize the idea of a police force or a court of justice, so too, the possibility of a corrupt ICC does not delegitimize the idea of an ICC-like authority for the purpose of enforcing international criminal responsibility.

Consequently, the solution lies not in the outright rejection of a system of international institutions to stop and prevent human rights violations, but in designing the system in such a way as to render its abuse, capture, and dysfunction less likely. One way to enhance such design features is to impose structural constraints on the power of international institutions. I have argued that a system of institutional pluralism, in which no single institution has final authority over all others, and in which power is carefully apportioned to each institutional node, whose mandates are straightforward and well defined, and whose capacities match their mission, imposes such constraints. International institutions could check each other and could, in turn, be checked by states, to limit the extent of arbitrary domination any one of them could inflict.

Despite worries to the contrary, such institutional fragmentation need not lead to jurisdictional conflict, inconsistency, and forum shopping, as long as the decisions and actions of all international institutions are made against the background of a common system of laws that both sets the limits of acceptable behavior on how international agents act and enables coordination for reaching shared goals. Conflicts of jurisdiction can be avoided by clearly outlining the boundaries of jurisdictional authority between states and international institutions and among international institutions, and by renegotiating those boundaries when necessary. For example, the ICC exercises criminal jurisdiction only when states renege on their responsibility to exercise it within their territory; so there is a clear hierarchy of jurisdictional authority in place starting with states. Moreover, inconsistency and forum shopping can be discouraged if international institutions rely on the entire body of international law, as opposed to isolated treaties or legal regimes, to make determinations about what the law requires. This will ensure that the pronouncements of different legal forums on the same legal matter will converge, so no matter what the choice of forum is, the decisions should be the same.

Confidence in how well such a system, or any system of international institutions, will perform should be tempered by a dose of humility with respect to the state of existing knowledge about institutional design. Because we do not understand fully how certain institutions that have a track record of working well in advanced democracies interact with their social, economic, and cultural environment to produce the effects they do, efforts at institution building in different parts of the world as well as at the international level have shown that we are failing to replicate those effects in environments very different from the original ones. We possess very limited knowledge to erect working, successful institutions from scratch.

Several implications follow from this. First, institutional success requires experimentation with different institutional forms and a degree of redundancy. Especially where the risk of failure is high in term of human lives lost, competition among institutional forms should encourage innovations to reduce organizational errors and enhance the ability of the system as a whole to find solutions to global problems. The second implication is that the scope of authority for coercive international institutions should be modest. We should resist agglomerating international institutions with an endless list of mandates that would result in conflicting organizational missions and would unnecessarily encroach on the sovereign autonomy of states. Third, understanding the limits of existing knowledge on institutional design should make one suspicious of proposals for grand institutional schemes, such as a global democracy, understood as a comprehensive system of international institutions structured hierarchically that act as the functional equivalent of the state at the global level.

At the core of this book's argument is the idea that philosophical inquiry about the goals of justice should be profoundly committed to institutional thinking. That is, it should be committed to understanding how the range of institutional possibilities both limit and organize the array of moral and non-moral goals we can achieve at the local and global level. More fundamentally, the book provides a way to think about the interaction between principles of justice and institutional analysis that departs from the dominant mood in political philosophy.

I have articulated a general worry about theories of global justice as limited in their ability to guide solutions to practical problems. Political philosophers typically grant priority to abstract theorizing about the principles of justice over understanding the institutional context and possibilities in which those principles are to be realized. Institutional analysis is marginal to determining what justice requires. I have claimed that this way of seeing the relationship between moral theory and institutional analysis is counterproductive. By generating a view of justice that is devoid of institutional context, existing philosophical practice foists upon us a conception of moral goals bereft of practical guidance in concrete institutional settings. In opposition to this view, I have argued that institutions are not just instrumental to justice, but constitutive of determining what justice requires. The careful characterization of the institutional context and the moral implications that follow from it should play a substantive role in refining our understanding of the demands of justice.

One implication of this theoretical shift in the way we connect moral theory and institutional analysis is that what justice requires in the international context will be different than the domestic context, due to the fact that the existing system of states imposes requirements and constraints of its own on what moral goals are possible and desirable in international politics. Sovereign states have rights and obligations that any conception of global justice would do well to take seriously. International institutions derive their legitimacy, in part, by safeguarding state autonomy and by enforcing fundamental sovereign responsibilities. In addition, respecting the sovereign prerogative will be consequential for the scope of human rights protection by international agents.

For example, as an element of a theory of international justice, a theory of humanitarian intervention requires sensitivity to the institutional constraints—the existence of states and their sovereign prerogatives—that restrict when and how interventions are appropriate. In addition, whether interventions are appropriate depends on which international agents have standing to intervene, how they acquire their authority, and what the expectations related to their effectiveness are. I do not provide an in-depth look at the moral and practical constraints humanitarian intervention imposes, or at the institutional apparatus necessary to make it work within acceptable bounds. Nor do I engage in the much more ambitious task of specifying the full range of concerns for global justice and the detailed account of the institutional pathways required for their pursuit. *Divided Sovereignty* proceeds with a much more modest ambition of offering a general justification for coercive international institutions that protect jus cogens norms and of providing broad guidelines for translating such norms into institutional proposals. The consequences of the view developed here for massive failures of state agency in relation to its citizens in areas such as criminal liability, humanitarian intervention, military coups, and stateless persons still need to be worked out into specific institutional recommendations. This book remains agnostic on what the best such recommendations for institutional design are.

The larger point is that a well-developed conception of justice should therefore explain and defend the connection between its moral ideals and the institutional setup required for their implementation. The book aims to motivate political philosophers to rethink the mental maps that connect their views about justice with specific institutional models. If it impresses the necessity to make that connection more explicit and defensible, it will have fulfilled its ambition.

One important assumption throughout the book has been the functionalist, instrumental view of institutions that says institutions are desirable if and to the extent that they achieve certain functions. Institutions are the means by which individuals make concrete the abstract goals of social cooperation. The idea of regarding state institutions as agents of their citizens is predicated on such a functionalist view. *Divided Sovereignty* builds on the functionalist view to argue that under certain specific conditions, national institutions can be trumped by international ones if states fail to fulfill their sovereign functions. Consequently, the argument does not address and incorporate the concerns of those who regard state institutions as possessing intrinsic worth. On the "intrinsic worth" view, it makes sense to separate the value of an institution from the pragmatic measures of the extent to which it achieves certain goals. For such a view, a different account of the justification of the authority of international institutions and their relationship with state authority than the one offered here is necessary.

The vast literature in international relations scholarship has focused mainly on why states, if they do so at all, enter international treaties and join international institutions that end up tying their hands with respect to their domestic or foreign policy. This question is important for assessing how and why change happens in international politics, but from a normative standpoint, it is not the most important question. Another question to ask is whether binding international institutions are a desirable, morally appropriate goal from the perspective of individuals living in different states all over the globe. I have claimed that potentially massive failures of agency in the relationships individuals have with their own governments justify such international institutions. The answer to these two questions may be different because what makes sense for the protection of individual interests may not make sense for the protection of state interests, understood as a collection of institutions and individuals in a position of power that can develop distinct interests in self-preservation. However, the chasm cannot be too big. International institutions depend on state consent for their authorization, and to the extent that they are contrary to state preservation, they may never get off the ground. And yet, to the extent that citizens in liberal democratic societies exercise some control over their political leaders, they can pressure the leaders to redefine their state's interests and sign on to international institutions as a way of binding current and future governments to respect citizens' interests. Against realist skepticism, there is good evidence that this is already happening.[2] This development gives us reason to believe that institutional reform aimed at curbing the most serious of state abuses is not a distant utopian dream but an promising attainable, if challenging, possibility.

---

2. Andrew Moravcsik, "The Origins of Human Rights Regimes: Democratic Delegation in Postwar Europe," *International Organization* 54, no. 2 (2000): 217–52.

Index

CPSIA information can be obtained
at www.ICGtesting.com
Printed in the USA
BVHW04s0023050518
515302BV00002B/2/P